Reliability
Simplified

Other McGraw-Hill Books by H. James Harrington

- *The Improvement Process: How America's Leading Companies Improve Quality* (1987)
- *Business Process Improvement: The Breakthrough Strategy for Total Quality, Productivity, and Competitiveness* (1991)
- *Total Improvement Management: The Next Generation in Performance Improvement,* written with James S. Harrington (1995)
- *High Performance Benchmarking: 20 Steps to Success,* written with James S. Harrington (1996)
- *The Complete Benchmarking Implementation Guide—Total Benchmarking Management* (1996)
- *ISO 9000 and Beyond—From Compliance to Performance Improvement* (1997)
- *Business Process Improvement Workbook,* written with Erik K. C. Esseling and Harm van Nimwegen (1997)
- *The Creativity Toolkit—Provoking Creativity in Individuals and Organizations,* written with Glen D. Hoffherr and Robert P. Reid, Jr. (1998)
- *Statistical Analysis Simplified—The Easy-to-Understand Guide to SPC and Data Analysis,* written with Glen D. Hoffherr and Robert P. Reid, Jr. (1998)
- *Area Activity Analysis—Aligning Work Activities and Measurements to Enhance Business Performance,* written with Glen D. Hoffherr and Robert P. Reid, Jr. (1998)

Reliability Simplified

Going beyond Quality to Keep Customers for Life

H. James Harrington
International Quality Advisor
Ernst & Young LLP

Leslie C. Anderson
President of Les Anderson & Assoc.

McGraw-Hill

New York   San Francisco   Washington, D.C.   Auckland   Bogotá
Caracas   Lisbon   London   Madrid   Mexico City   Milan
Montreal   New Delhi   San Juan   Singapore
Sydney   Tokyo   Toronto

McGraw-Hill

*A Division of The **McGraw·Hill** Companies*

1 2 3 4 5 6 7 8 9 0 DOC/DOC 9 0 1 0 9 8 7 6

P/N: 134705-4
PART OF
ISBN: 0-07-027051-1

Library of Congress Cataloging-in-Publication Data

Anderson, Leslie.
   Reliability simplified : going beyond quality to keep customers
for life / Leslie C. Anderson, H. James Harrington.
     p. cm.—(Harrington's performance improvement series)
   Includes index.
   ISBN 0-07-027051-1
   1. Reliability (Engineering)   I. Harrington, H. J. (H. James)
II. Title. III. Series.
TS173.A53 1998
620′.00452—dc21   98-30824
                                            CIP

The sponsoring editor for this book was Roger Marsh. The editing supervisor was John M. Morriss and the production supervisor was Suzanne W. B. Rapcavage. Production was managed by John Woods, CWL Publishing Enterprises, Madison, WI. It was designed and composed at Impressions Book and Journal Services, Inc., Madison, WI.

McGraw-Hill books are available at special quantity discounts to use as premiums and sales promotions, or for use in corporate training programs. For more information, please write to the Director of Special Sales, McGraw-Hill, 11 West 19th Street, New York, NY 10011. Or contact your local bookstore.

Contents

About the Series

Reliability Simplified is one title in McGraw-Hill's *Harrington's Performance Improvement Series*. Each of the products in this series is a complete communication system that includes a book and a support CD-ROM. The series is designed to meet an organization's need to understand the most useful approaches now available to bring about improvements in organizational performance as measured by

- ▶ Return on assets
- ▶ Value-added per employee
- ▶ Customer satisfaction

Each title in the series is easy to read, view, and listen to. It has a user-friendly style designed to reach employees at all levels of an organization. Our goal is to present complex methodologies in a way that is simple but not simplistic. The following are other subjects covered in the communication systems in this series:

- ▶ Statistical process controls
- ▶ Process redesign
- ▶ Process reengineering
- ▶ Establishing a balanced scorecard
- ▶ Twenty-first Century Management Profile
- ▶ Fostering teamwork
- ▶ Simulation modeling
- ▶ Rewards and recognition
- ▶ Managing the change process

Communication systems already released are

- ▶ The Creativity Toolkit—Provoking Creativity in Individuals and Organizations

▶ Statistical Analysis Simplified—The Easy-to-Understand Guide to SPC and Data Analysis

▶ Area Activity Analysis—Aligning Work Activities to Enhance Business Performance

We believe that the products in this series will provide an effective way to learn about these practices as well as a training tool for use in any type of organization. The series design features a set of icons that are placed in the margins that call your attention to different points. Use these icons to guide your reading and study

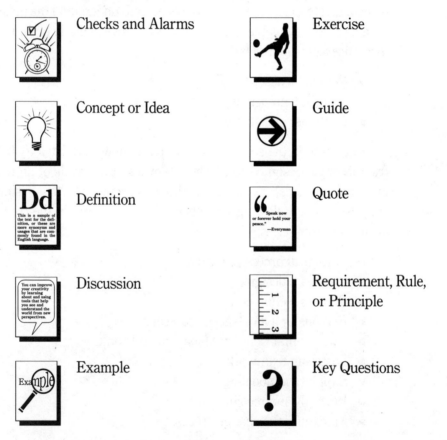

Checks and Alarms

Exercise

Concept or Idea

Guide

Dd Definition

Quote

Discussion

Requirement, Rule, or Principle

Example

Key Questions

It is our hope that you will find this series of Performance Improvement Management books enjoyable and useful.

H. James Harrington
Principal, Ernst & Young LLP
International Quality Advisor
(408) 947-6587

About the Authors

Dr. H. James Harrington is one of the world's performance improvement gurus with more than 45 years of experience. He has been involved in developing improvement management systems in Europe, South America, North America, and Asia. He currently serves as a principal with Ernst & Young LLP and is their international quality advisor. He is also chairman of Emergence Technology Ltd., a high-tech software and hardware manufacturer and developer.

Before joining Ernst & Young LLP, he was president of the consulting firm Harrington, Hurd, and Rieker. He was a senior engineer and project manager for IBM, and for almost 40 years, he worked in quality function. He was chairman and president of the prestigious International Academy for Quality and the American Society for Quality Control. He has released a series of videos and CD ROM programs that cover ISO 9000 and QS-9000. He has also authored a computer program on benchmarking, plus members' video tapes on performance improvement. He has written 13 books on performance improvement and hundreds of technical reports.

The Harrington/Ishikawa Medal was named after him in recognition of his support to developing nations in implementing quality systems. The Harrington/Neron Medal was also named after him to recognize his contribution to the quality movement in Canada. China named him their Honorary Quality Advisor, and he was elected into the Singapore Productivity Hall of Fame. He has been elected honorary member of seven quality professional societies and has received numerous awards and medals for his work.

Dr. Les Anderson was born and grew up in Minnesota. He presently resides in San Jose, California. He and his wife, Patricia, have been married for 35 years. The Andersons have five adult children and three grandchildren. Les' hobbies include woodworking and automotive restoration. His present backlog of work projects is estimated to be 10 years.

Dr. Anderson received his B.S. degree in Chemistry from Marist College and a Ph.D. in Physical Chemistry from Syracuse University. His doctorate study was the small-angle x-ray scattering from protein molecules.

After serving a 5-year military obligation, Dr. Anderson worked for IBM for 33 years. His early career was spent as an engineer in the area of materials science of semiconductor devices and electronic packaging. Dr. Anderson has a prolific invention record with 32 patents and disclosures. Dr. Anderson later spent a considerable amount of his IBM career as a corporate executive. He was the IBM Corporate Director of Chemical Engineering and the IBM Corporate Director of Product Safety. The latter part of his career was devoted to resolution of IBM issues across all products. Product reliability was part of those assignments.

Since leaving IBM in 1993, Dr. Anderson has taught many courses at the college or continuing education level. The central focus is product reliability, design of experiments, and manufacturing processes. Dr. Anderson is an Adjunct Professor at Santa Clara University. He has also worked and taught as a consultant at several places such as Seagate, Western Digital, and Johnson & Johnson. He has been busier than ever.

His motivation for writing this book with his long-time friend, Jim Harrington, is simple. An appropriate text for explaining product reliability to management and engineers wasn't available; so a text has been written for use in the classroom and for a more effective use by business. It is a step forward in addressing the almost abstract national priority, reliability.

Dedication

This book is dedicated to Pat. She not only sacrificed her time and personal goals but encouraged me to achieve the best in all efforts. What we have done together has been the center of my life.

Les Anderson

Preface

Customers buy the first time based upon quality. They come back to buy again based upon reliability.

Although everyone is talking about quality today, it isn't quality that gets your customers to come back: it's reliability. Quality is what makes the first sale, but reliability keeps the customers. Reliability is the most important thing to customers of both products and services. Customers expect that their new car will start when they pick it up at the dealer, but it is even more important that it starts every time they get into it to drive to the airport for a flight that they are already late for (reliability).

We are amazed at the way reliability is being overlooked. In fact, it's hard to find a book on quality management that directly addresses reliability. In 20 books on quality that we pulled at random from our bookshelf, only two had reliability even listed in their index: Joe Juran's old, faithful *Quality Control Handbook*[1] and Val Feigenbaum's classic *Total Quality Control*.[2]

Unfortunately, management has been trained to understand quality but has little understanding about the methodologies that result in improved reliability; as a result, they do not ask the right questions of their engineers and supporting managers. This results in misguided focus all the way through the organization. There are two rules that must be followed to remedy this situation: **Rule 1:** To get quality, everyone must understand what quality is. **Rule 2:** To get reliability, everyone needs to understand what reliability is.

Maximum reliability is determined by product design. The production process can only detract from the reliability limit set by the original design. Once the product goes into production, the inherent reliability can be degraded further as a result of variations in supplier-supplied components, the manufacturing process design, and poor workmanship. But the possibility of reduced product reliability doesn't end there. Once a product is turned over to the customer, field service support activities may further degrade the inherent reliability of the product as support personnel try to maintain and repair it. This is the source of IBM's field engineering unofficial saying, "If it isn't broken, don't fix it." It's easy to see, therefore, that reliability impacts anyone who comes in contact with the design concepts and the physical product. As a result, all participants in this cycle need to have a thorough understanding of their impact upon the inherent reliability of the product. With this in mind, we begin each chapter with a description of

▶ what management needs to know about the subject covered in the chapter, and

▶ what engineers need to know about the subject covered in the chapter.

Quality today takes precedence in most organizations over reliability. Let me relate a recent personal experience. I bought a new $30,000 convertible from one of the big three U.S. auto manufacturers. The car did not come with side moldings to protect the car from other car doors in parking lots. These moldings were listed as a feature. When I tried to order them, I was told that moldings were a feature for fleet cars only. I escalated my request to the owner of the dealership, the manufacturer's complaint department, and all the way up to the vice president of Quality and Process Leadership at the automanufacturer. Each person I talked to agreed that it was a problem and that they would add it to the customer suggestion list for consideration during the next new design. One person I talked with explained that the more features that a car has, the more quality problems it has, so eliminating these features would improve the quality of the car. The assistant to the vice president of quality confided in me that he had the same problem, and as a result, he parked way out in the parking lot away from other cars. He also explained that they asked customers if they liked the appearance of the cars better with or without the side moldings, and the customers liked the appearance better without the side moldings. He explained that this was the reason that this normally standard feature was dropped from this particular car. I asked him if the customers were shown newly painted cars or cars that had completed the reliability tests for dings, and he did not know. It's safe to assume, however, that they were shown only newly painted cars, not cars that looked like the ones in our parking lot. In fact, the new car does look better without the side moldings, and it would also look better without its bumpers and license plate holder. Protecting the car's body is more important than an appearance consideration. In this case, the designers designed in a major long-term reliability problem because of aesthetics. It is a good example of an organization that was unable to design an aesthetically pleasing car with proper reliability considerations designed in.

Our thinking about reliability needs to go far beyond will the car start to considering things like: How long before the chrome platings start to peel off? Will the coating on the rear mirror flake off? Will the view screen on my PC scratch? And so on. I have all of these problems and more on the car that I drive to work. Is it any wonder that when I bought a new car, I bought a different kind? Management and engineering must think about all of a product's deteriorating effects that aggravate and alienate customers. That's the purpose of this book: to assist you in establishing a reliability program that will result in products that meet and exceed customer expectations, products that will delight your customers and keep them coming back to buy more while optimizing the organization's profitability.

Overview of the Book

This book will enable professional engineers and managers to understand

- ▶ the basic concepts of reliability
- ▶ the importance of having a reliability program
- ▶ the implementation of a reliability program

Our objective in writing this book was to take the complex subject of reliability and demystify it so that it could be easily understood. The book provides a comprehensive review of reliability and will serve as a useful reference for making sure you design reliability into your products and the processes by which they are delivered. It specifically addresses those topics that are often unfamiliar to individuals who are not reliability professionals. Here is a brief overview of what you'll find in this book:

Chapter 1, Shared Product Reliability Experience, explains four major characteristics of today's product reliability programs: (1) applications of reliability principles vary widely within the business world, (2) implementation of reliability principles in the workplace appears to be extraordinarily frustrating, (3) management of unreliable products often connotes questionable business practices, and (4) the positive aspects of reliability for the business. Chapter 1 provides the foundation for the rest of the book.

Chapter 2, The Reliability Cycle, presents an overview of the reliability process. It describes the eight phases of reliability that an organization must implement to provide competitive, reliable items or services.

Chapter 3, Product Reliability Economics, addresses the economics of product reliability. It develops in detail the method of optimizing product reliability designs and processes. Creating reliability economically is a key ingredient in business survival and growth.

Chapter 4, Interpreting Product Failure Data, is directed at the importance of understanding product failures. It clarifies the common misunderstandings of product failures that exist within our business decision structure. This is a very important subject that you need to understand to make the best business decisions.

Chapter 5, Product Reliability Mathematics, explains the three major applications of product reliability mathematics. The fundamentals of probability and statistics are not presented in this book because they are presented in other books in this series. However, what you'll find are three key requirements for understanding product reliability: (1) the mathematical distributions of failures that represent and model your product; (2) the application of the exponential distribution, which represents the ideal case of mathematically expressing your product; and (3) the effective use of the Mean Time Before Failure (MTBF) concept.

Chapter 6, Reliability Design Development, presents the major tasks to achieve optimum reliability in product design. There are three components here: (1) to specify and predict the reliability of the product; (2) to apply physical techniques in a disciplined manner to achieve the optimum reliability at optimum cost; and (3) to design in system redundancy, which is used when high levels of reliability are required.

Chapter 7, Manufacturing a Reliable Product, describes two methods for achieving product reliability management and control in manufacturing. First, we present methods for controlling product reliability through a statistically based incoming inspection. (These methods are based on the Poisson distribution.) Second, we explain statistical process control (SPC). SPC is the common method of manufacturing control based on the normal distribution.

Chapter 8, New Product Reliability Qualification, presents the details of product reliability qualification. You cannot use product failures during customer use as data for management measurement and control. It would be too late for responsible corrective actions and could result in a high level of customer dissatisfaction. You have to predict (or qualify) product reliability before shipments are ever made to customers. Qualification reduces catastrophic business risk for both the producer and the consumer. This chapter explains how to implement qualification techniques.

Chapter 9, Environmental Stress Screening (ESS) to Improve Product Reliability, addresses the technique of ongoing product reliability control through ESS. The major thrust of Chapter 9 is to furnish background on the methods and cost factors that possibly apply to your specific ESS application.

Chapter 10, Product Failure Database and Field Failure Analysis, explains methods of obtaining product failure information for each specific business and structure of appropriate communication and cause-of-failure validation system. Understanding product failures is the single most important reliability factor.

Chapter 11, The Customer/Consumer, addresses the needs of customers in terms of product reliability. Chapter 11 includes three major topics for dealing effectively with customers: communications, catastrophic response, and partnership. It also reviews the importance of a reliability strategy, a key to customer retention and business growth.

Chapter 12, Product Reliability Management Structure, is directed at the aspects of management unique to product reliability. If your product reliability is not managed, the value of *Reliability Simplified* is substantially reduced. Reliability management helps you understand how to execute the principles presented in Chapters 1 through 11.

Chapter 13, Product Reliability Management Problems, addresses the problems frequently encountered in managing product reliability. The problem examples included provide helpful information in anticipating and effectively eliminating generic product reliability management problems.

After a long period of providing lip service to the notion of product reliability, it is finally coalescing into a complete science. This book is designed to help you understand the basics of this science.

References

1. J. M. Juran, Frank M. Gryna Jr., and R. S. Bingham Jr., *Quality Control Handbook,* 3rd ed. (New York: McGraw-Hill, 1974).
2. Armand V. Feigenbaum, *Total Quality Control,* 3rd ed. (New York: McGraw-Hill, 1983).

Acknowledgments

I would like to acknowledge the excellent work and effort put in by Pamela Simeon and Teu Feagai, who converted and edited endless hours of dictation into this final product, Aimee Tham, who prepared the storyboard, and Dale Mann, who prepared the excellent art work. John Woods and Bob Magnan of CWL Publishing Enterprises have worked closely with me in giving the manuscript one final review and managing the production, turning it into the book you now hold. I would also like to acknowledge the effort put forth by the personnel at SystemCorp in preparing the CD ROM. Richard Rosenbloom, who brought the storyboard to life, and Ari Kugler, who provided the resources to create the CD ROM free of charge. And last, but not least, Jaime Benchimol, who managed and followed the process that created the CD ROM.

I would be remiss if, as always, I did not acknowledge the excellent contribution my wife, Marguerite, made to the book by challenging my thinking.

—H. James Harrington

1

Shared Product Reliability Experience

Since reliability is one of the more important "qualities" of the product, it cannot be operationally or systematically separated from other product-quality considerations.

—ARMAND V. FEIGENBAUM, LEADING QUALITY EXPERT[1]

Introduction

Managers should read Chapter 1 to understand the present environment of product reliability. This book develops your skill and knowledge to achieve the best product reliability for your business. Chapter 1 presents shared experiences and best business practices common throughout the business world.

Engineers should read Chapter 1 to understand the business realities that surround their reliability efforts. Engineers cope with reliability perplexities by default. How many times have you heard "If management only knew how important this is"? In order to communicate product reliability issues credibly, you need to understand the general concepts presented here.

Chapter 1 covers the significant, general aspects of the present product reliability activity. Because the readers of this book experience many unique situations, it is logical to first discuss common elements that most have experienced. This shared experience provides the platform from which we proceed to our goal of optimum reliability for a specific product.

Quality–Reliability, Is There a Difference?

Are reliability and quality the same thing? Is reliability part of quality? Or are they different concepts? We believe that they are different but have a very close relationship. We have all heard and probably used the expression "I know quality when I see it." We have read in many books, "Quality is in the eyes of the beholder." In shopping for a new car we walk around it looking for scratches, we check to see if the seams line up, we open and slam the doors to be sure that they fit together perfectly, we kick the tires, we turn over the motor, we peek inside the hood, we look in the trunk, we bounce up and down on the seats, and eventually we make up our minds if this is a quality car. Then, if the price is right, we may buy it. Reliability is a very different thing. We experience reliability every time we sit in our car and turn over the motor. Will it start? If it doesn't, we have reliability problems.

RULE 3:   Quality is observed.
Reliability is experienced.

But is it possible to have reliability without quality? Let's look at an example:

> Jim's old Lincoln is parked outside all year round. It has a broken parking light, torn leather seats, and dings on every door. Its headlight covers do not close anymore. Jim, what do you think about this car? "This is Old Reliable. I can leave it parked outside unused for three months, but when I turn the key in the ignition it's ready to go like a horse just let out of the barn and it still rides like new."

Truly the Lincoln's form, fit, and function may leave a lot to be desired. If you were looking at it to buy it, you would have a list of problems that would cover many pages; nevertheless, from Jim's standpoint this is a very reliable car. It was one of the major reasons that Jim purchased a new Ford product this year. In fact, you can have quality without reliability and you can have reliability without quality.

RULE 4   You buy based upon quality.
You come back and buy again based upon reliability.

Reliability, Not Quality, Is the Problem

It is not poor quality that is causing North America to continue to lose market share, it is poor reliability. We analyzed the mid-size passenger automobiles reliability data reported in the *Consumer Report Buying Guide 1998*.[5] We calculated an index by weighing the complexity of the unit from 1 to 3. We scored each unit's reliability rating as follows:

▶ Excellent   +2 points
▶ Very good   +1 point
▶ Good   0 points
▶ Fair   −1 point
▶ Poor   −2 points

The very best index a brand of automobile could get is 180. Using this index, we discovered that Japanese brands have an index that is almost 200% higher than North American brands. (Japanese brands index 113.8; North American brands index 60.9.) The two lowest reliability indexes were for two European cars. The Japanese Subaru Legacy had the highest reliability index, 133 out of a maximum possible points of 180. Only one Japanese car had a rating lower than 118 points, the Mitsubishi Gallant, which had a rating of 62. All of the North American brand autos index ratings were below 72.

The difference between Japanese and North American mid-size passenger cars is only five percentage points. It is so small that the consumer cannot detect the difference. It is the lack of reliability that is turning once loyal consumers of Ford, GM, or Chrysler autos to Toyota, Nissan, or Honda to get a car they can depend on. The result is that U.S. brands are continuously losing their market share in passenger cars even within the United States (see Figure 1-1).

If we cannot compete in our own backyard, how can we hope to compete internationally? If we do not wake up soon to the need for reliability in North

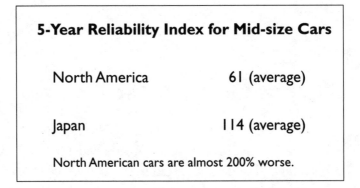

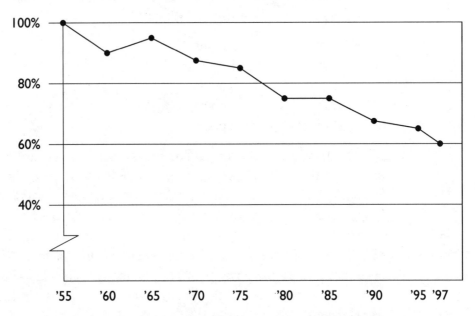

FIGURE 1-1.   **U.S. domestic brands' share of U.S. car sales**

American autos, the auto industry will follow the same path that our TV industry took.

It is more important than ever before that we develop our "Reliability Management System" to the point that our products reestablish themselves as the most reliable in the world. How long has it been since you benchmarked your Reliability Management System?

"These bones are 60 million years old. They are extremely reliable."

The Many Views of Product Reliability

Dd

This is a sample of the text for the definition, or these are more synonyms and usages that are commonly found in the English language.

Reliability is the probability of an item to perform its required function under specific conditions for a specified period of time.

(*Note:* A glossary of terms can be found in Appendix A.)

The archeologist above is not alone in believing that the dinosaur bones clearly fall within this definition of *reliability*. A prevalent observation is that *product reliability* in general is a vague concept with differing interpretations, especially to those not daily involved in product reliability activity. Following are other accepted definitions of *reliability*.

In McGraw-Hill's *Encyclopedia of Quality Terms and Concepts*,[2] *reliability* is defined as the study of the probability that a product or service will perform as intended under predetermined conditions and for a planned period of time (generally the longer the better). Other well-known quality management writers have defined it as follows:

Reliability is the probability of a product performing without failure a specified function under given conditions for a given period of time.
   —J. M. JURAN[3]

▶ *Product reliability is the ability of a unit to perform a required function under stated conditions for a stated period of time.*

▶ *Inherent reliability is the potential reliability that the designer conceptually designed into the item.*

▶ *Achieved reliability is the reliability that the item demonstrates under customer-consumer-usage conditions.*

▶ *Quantitative reliability is defined as the probability that a unit will perform a required function under stated conditions for a stated time.*[4]
   —ARMAND V. FEIGENBAUM[1]

The significant causes for this wide range of interpretations and applications of *product reliability* stem from two historical phenomena. First, the amount of product reliability content within products has great variation. At one extreme, government regulations usually specify that life-preserving and emergency products meet a standard of important product reliability. Commercial aircraft regulations also strive to attain the highest possible reliability. Fire extinguishers are designed to meet regulatory reliability standards. The high product reliability that meets governmental regulations provides an excellent example of successful product reliability science when applied to specific products. At the other extreme are products with little reliability content. These are consumer products whose reliability is not economically significant and, therefore, not considered a significant part of the business. We understand that airplanes must have high reliability and that lettuce and cabbages, as perishable commodities, perform their food function only once and contain minimum reliability content. Between these extremes are the many degrees of product reliability observed today. Most of us have been exposed to the lack of reliability represented by VCRs and copying machines. There is also a distinction between acceptable reliability and anticipated wear out of products. This distinction becomes very blurred when we discuss the reliability subject in detail.

Second, although optimum product reliability is politically correct and considered a basic ingredient to our future business prosperity, little formal education in product reliability is provided by our educational institutions. Product reliability has yet to form an extensive body of common science and familiar language. There exists an excellent example. Although the body of knowledge has been defined by the American Society of Quality (ASQ), and individuals are certified as reliability engineers, as of January 1997 there are fewer than 4,000 ASQ-certified reliability engineers in the world. This is less than 0.1% of the number of people who should have been certified. Presently, most business managers and engineers are untrained in product reliability.

Recent business trends point toward a future when reliability becomes increasingly important for survival of products in a competitive marketplace. The product reliability content of your products is evolving into a required factor in your competitive business strategy. This book allows you to correctly evaluate and optimize your product reliability without overwhelming you with detailed formulas and tables.

Let us present an example of the product reliability interaction within today's typical product that allows us to identify and summarize the significant reliability factors usually not recognized in common business transactions.

An umbrella is a simple example using a competitively priced consumer product. Umbrella prices range from $5.00 in a discount store to $50.00 in an upscale clothing and accessory store. So what does one get for the price? The $5.00 umbrella provides adequate initial protection in the rain, but it cannot withstand high wind due to its fragile design, has a one-year fabric life, and has a locking mechanism prone to failure. Most $50.00 umbrellas are better designed for a longer term of service (about five years), but features like carved handles are nonfunctional (not a performance adder), although they may create a substantial addition to product price. So what umbrella should I look for, or for that matter produce, to market from a reliability standpoint? I am not impressed by carved handles, so I look for a solid, basic umbrella, and by using a quick estimate, I would want to buy a good, reliable $20.00 umbrella that would be of best value to me.

The process used for purchasing an umbrella is quite inadequate for business decisions. It represents only a single, subjective estimate without knowledge from quantified data, describing the entire umbrella market. Our prime business objective is to understand the product market of which an individual customer/consumer has little universal comprehension. A common source for understanding the market (assessment) and the market data is not available. The seller is also incapable of determining your product business beyond his or her observed competitive sales volume.

Note that we did not explicitly mention umbrella reliability. This is because we often do not think of products in terms of reliability. We did mention fragile design, limited fabric life, and lock failure, but these factors are not expressed specifically as umbrella reliability. But if the identical umbrella mechanism were part of a lunar-landing craft antenna, those factors would be considered key reliability elements. The definition of *reliability* is not applied uniformly to products. We have many dinosaur bones and unlabeled reliability elements. Many organizations' reputations rise and fall based upon unspecified or uncalculated product reliability.

Now, what if you decided to produce umbrellas as a business? Your umbrellas need wide recognition in the market, and they need to meet all conditions to capture market share. Your product pricing activity will determine the profit margin based upon those product market conditions. One important condition is that your product exists in a competitive market with recognized superior reliability. That superior reliability is of real business value only when the product reliability value is perceived by the customer/consumer in addition to a competitive price. A product of superior reliability without a customer/consumer value does not result in a profit. In the case of the umbrella, more sales are made based upon the color or pattern than on reliability. Why? Because customers/consumers can easily see colors, and they are not provided with the reliability data they need to compare product costs and values.

Another factor is that most customers do not buy umbrellas based upon brand name, so poor reliability does not impact future sales to a great extent.

Customer—The person or organization that receives an output from a process. This person or organization may or may not be the consumer.

Consumer—The person or organization that is the end user of a product or service. (For example, a manufacturer sells a product to K-Mart, its customer, which sells it to the consumer, who is K-Mart's customer, not the manufacturer's customer.)

I have an unreliable umbrella.

Your customer/consumer requires an education in product reliability. Can you at this time educate the customer/consumer on the price versus reliability value of your present products and of the direct competitive products? In most cases, organizations do not even realize that reliability education is a significant factor to the customer/consumer. If the sales channel reports a customer/consumer education request for reliability and cost information, the organization likely does not have a mission for responding to the customer/consumer request. In addition, the organization may lack the education to exploit this explicit business opportunity. Unfortunately, this vague understanding of product reliability in business is prevalent today and is particularly noticeable in consumer products where product reliability is not explicitly determined, such as presented by the umbrella example. Someday, someone is going to make a lot of money by producing reliable umbrellas.

Due to lack of information, customers/consumers do not usually buy a brand because of reliability, but lack of reliability will keep them from giving the brand a second chance. To summarize the umbrella story:

1. Product reliability is often unidentified in the marketplace. Without customer/consumer perception of the value of product reliability, the product reliability content is not of significant profit potential, although lack of reliability can and often does affect future repeated sales.

2. Without explicit quantified product reliability data, subjective values enter the reliability value determination. Customer/consumer product loyalty is built on explicit product reliability. There are two reliability relationships involved in product loyalty.

Figure 1-2 may be unique for combination of producer and product, but it conveys the idea that product reliability can be controlled by the producer with an appropriate related cost.

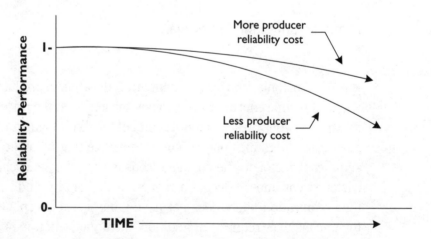

FIGURE 1-2.   Product reliability performance relationship to producer reliability cost vs. time

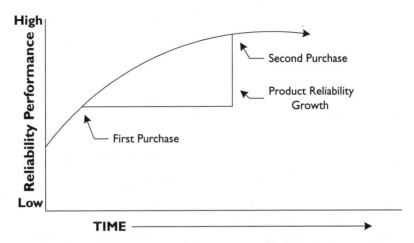

FIGURE 1-3.   Second customer/consumer purchase during reliability growth

The situation presented in Figure 1-3 is not an intuitive customer/consumer phenomenon. It occurs when a customer/consumer purchases a second of the same product at a later date and it has a significantly improved reliability. However, the customer/consumer did not have information about the alternate product reliability comparisons nor the absolute product average reliability improvement since the last purchase and has no idea that the product reliability has improved since the last purchase. Many customers/consumers switch brands unaware of improvements in the reliability of the originally purchased brand.

Significant customer/consumer product loyalty depends upon perceived incomplete or unknown product reliability information.

3. Product reliability should be defined in the product specification. Many products do not have a reliability specification. The reliability specification determines both your product reliability profit opportunity and your marketplace competitive position. Each organization should strive to specify their product reliability.

4. Many people do not think in terms of product reliability. However, when they purchase products they consider characteristics such as durability, ruggedness, and long-term performance in addition to cost and quality.

Note that even if an organization issues reliability data, they often cannot be compared with another organization's data due to the different evaluation method used by each organization.

A common observation is that product reliability has many perspectives within business organizations. These perspectives require understanding for each product. Readers of this book should consider putting up a sign in their office that reads "Think and Understand Reliability" or "Reliability: The Competitive Edge."

Reliability Program Implementation Perplexity

If product reliability is becoming an increasingly important business factor, why doesn't the business management properly respond to that demand for greater product reliability?

The problem with implementing the proper product reliability program within your business is not lack of intrinsic capability by your engineers and business managers. The problem stems from the inability of the entire business culture to respond to the changing marketplace demands for product reliability. A stunning example is the British automobile foreign business, which did not respond to the market demands for a reliable product, subsequently losing essentially all of its business.

Your potential inability to respond to the marketplace product reliability demands stems from two causes. First, your organization may lack educational and operational abilities. In general, the business importance of reliability is increased from a lower priority driven by customer/consumer demands or the competition's improved performance. Today, the more sophisticated customers/consumers place higher levels of priority on long-term reliability than on initial quality. The public is taking a long-term view of products and as a result is not just looking at the cost of acquisition but is placing an increased emphasis on the cost of owning the product. For example, the cost of a new VCR is less that $200.00 and a five-year maintenance contract is $425.00, a total out-of-pocket cost of $625.00, not $200.00. Plus an average of $125.00 cost to the consumer to return the VCR for repairs. To remain competitive, your business must be able to respond to this change. In another context, you need a business cultural change.

Second, even when an organization has the ability to respond to a product reliability requirement, it often lacks the tools to effectively achieve that requirement. The tools for achieving optimum product reliability are presented in this book. It is important that everyone involved in achieving product reliability be educated regarding the fundamentals of the operational product reliability tools and know how to apply the appropriate tools related to the assignment. This is the essence of your product reliability program execution. Communications are too difficult within an uneducated business organization.

The same inability presents symptoms that are observed as the perplexities of implementing the optimum product reliability program.

The symptoms exhibited by the inability of a business to adjust to new product reliability requirements are common observations. They are the frustrations and perplexities of many product reliability programs.

1. *Reliability-related costs should always be minimized since they add to the product cost.* Like most generalized assertions, there is an element of truth to this statement. However, management's view of the product's costs are seen from the eyes of the organization's controller, not the customer's/consumer's perspective. Management views product cost as their direct, out-of-pocket cost with no consideration given to the customer/consumer incurred cost or long-term business cost that results from loss of customer/consumer satisfaction. Financial analysis that does not take these two factors into consideration is not complete and should not be used.

The frustration symptoms occur when the reliability control function is reduced to zero or subcritical in the following environments:

A. The reliability program is deemed too costly to justify the proper level of reliability resource. Invariably, the reliability cost allocation is derived from the present budget priority instead of the product's customer/consumer demand for product reliability. The actual cost allocation may or may not be excessive. But sporadic reliability activity is frustrating, and unplanned response to field reliability problems is cost ineffective. The specific remedy is a management-approved, continuous, planned product reliability strategy. This does not mean that you need an organization solely devoted to reliability.

B. The business feels that it can respond to and correct any product reliability problem before the business is severely damaged. Therefore, the business has chosen a zero proactive reliability resource, and if one is lucky, the need for the product reliability organization may never occur. The specific remedy is overcoming the thrill of gambling.

This was an approach an organization could live with in the 1970s, when product cycles were measured in years. Today, however, no organization can afford to wait for the customer/consumer to identify weaknesses in their design and production processes because by the time the corrective action is completed, the product is replaced with a new one, and the organization's reputation is ruined. This will be even more important than it is today in the twenty-first century, when the product cycle will be measured in weeks, thereby placing increased emphasis on high reliability in the first products delivered to external customers/consumers.

RULE 5   Reliability is designed into the product, not tested into the product.

C. Reliability activity is just another form of business insurance. This is essentially true. The analogy of business insurance to product reliability is especially true when describing the two extreme conditions. The business can be "insurance (or reliability) poor" by applying excessive resources to that activity. The business can be at risk by applying insufficient resources to the business insurance (or reliability) activity. Both extremes are convenient to manage, but bad business. However, this convenient approach severely restricts thinking in terms of exploiting reliability for profit. The specific remedy is education.

2. *The uncertainty expressed in reliability is very uncomfortable.* The underlying cause for this opinion stems from the fact that all conclusions using reliability mathematical logic are presented as probabilities. This uncertainty creates an uncomfortable feeling for engineers and managers unfamiliar with these techniques. The entire language of reliability is uncomfortable. It

relates to product failures, to risk, and to impending disaster. "While the business is proceeding toward a goal of success, the reliability organization always is negative. They never have any good news."

Example 1: The Product Engineering Manager reports on a potential solution to a problem. "We have looked at the alternative, and this solution should solve the problem."

Example 2: The Reliability Manager reports on a potential solution to a problem. "We have tested the proposed solution to the problem on one unit and believe it has a 60% chance of correcting the problem. We will have to test it on 20 more units to be 95% confident, and that will take 20 more days."

In both examples the two managers have the same amount of information, but the Product Engineering Manager is not considering the risks, whereas the Reliability Manager has quantified them based upon the data that are available.

This specific factor can be reduced by communicating the reliability issues in an integrated business approach, thereby reducing the use of threatening rhetoric. Also, there is a real business exposure to the damage caused by product reliability data used in an improper manner. The solution to this exposure is not the suppression of all reliability data. The specific remedy is intelligent information control and education.

To date, there has been a great amount of talk about using statistical thinking to make management decisions, but it has been mostly talk. Management in most organizations fly by the seat of their pants or dress. They seldom take the time to quantify risks and probabilities of success related to their decisions. Often, important decisions are made based upon input data that are statistically meaningless. The probability of success between different alternatives is unknown. This free-wheeling attitude is in direct opposition to the effective reliability approach.

Quantification of business risks is imperative. Our studies indicate that when reevaluated 12 months later, only 5% of the decisions made in the board room are bad.

- ▶ 5%—bad
- ▶ 10%—best possible
- ▶ 85%—good but not the best

The reliability manager as viewed by management

In hind sight, 10% often were so good that the executives would not change anything. A whopping 85% of them were good and worked to some degree, but if they had a chance to do it over, they would do it differently. The effective use of quantified data can eliminate the bad decisions and increase the percentage of decisions that are just good but not the best.

3. *Doesn't the quality organization handle reliability? And aren't quality and reliability the same thing?* Reliability and quality are different by definition, although the product attributes overlap.

Dd
This is a sample of the text for the definition, or these are more synonyms and usages that are commonly found in the English language.

Quality product—Product that conforms to specification.

The product's quality is measured prior to the customer's/consumer's initial product use.

However, reliability differs from these qualities in a major respect: reliability is not an obvious attribute.
—DAVID K. LLOYD AND MYRON LIPOW[4]

Reliability is the probability of an item to perform its required function under specific conditions for a specified period of time.

Reliability is measured during the time of customer/consumer use either by time of operation before failure or by number of use cycles before failure. Quality and reliability are not generally related in any useful manner.

An example demonstrating the difference between quality and reliability is marriage in America. On all wedding days, the wedding couple truly believe that their mates are of perfect quality, the best in the world. But 50% of marriages end in divorce. As a result, initial perception of perfection does not last as anticipated. Marriages that end in divorce are good examples of high quality and low reliability. Other marriages turn out to be good examples of high quality and reliability combinations.

An effective organization often has the opportunity to trade off product quality for product reliability and create optimum business conditions. At the risk of stretching the wedding example beyond its useful limit, I would like to see less passion during the wedding day if it results in longer marriages.

A clear concept of your product attributes, quality, and reliability varies with each specific product. However, that distinction is acquired through education within your product reliability program.

4. *The reliability subject is too abstract for comprehension.* Reliability science uses nonlinear mathematics, statistical concepts, and simplifying assumptions as tools to model measurements and conclusions. The subject is too complex for a simple tutorial and too unfamiliar to establish logical boundaries. Reliability is for statisticians, not for real people with real problems. Keep them locked up and out of the real world so they cannot do any

"He's a statistician. . . ."

damage. A statistician is a person that takes so much time collecting data about a condition that, "By the time a statistician collects enough data about a situation to make a confident decision, the situation no longer exists." There is truth to some of these statements. One reason businesses use isolated reliability experts is to gain their perceived values while keeping the experts away from the decision-making process. Although the reliability methodology is complex, it is no more complex than the organization's financial methodology. If an organization cares as much about its customer/consumer as it does about its investors, the management team and employees will be trained and use both methodologies equally. The solution again is education.

The purpose of this book is to instruct you on how to estimate and exploit your product reliability. This book provides the assessment methods and operational tools required to achieve your optimum product reliability goal. It will assist you in reducing these product reliability symptoms from barriers to progress to manageable incidentals.

Product Reliability's Dark Side

There is a "dark side" to the product reliability business. When organizations practice poor reliability activities, they do not engage in a fair transaction. The corresponding business relationships with the customers/consumers are put in jeopardy. These activities stem from a short-term business perspective that promotes minimal product reliability costs and responsive actions to product reliability problems. This short-term business perspective may actually be effective where an organization is lucky enough not to have major reliability problems and the competitors are similarly deficient in product reliability knowledge. However, bad customer/consumer product reliability business eliminates the significant opportunity for obtaining substantial profits through an optimized reliability program. Some observations:

1. *Producers sometimes hide bad reliability data.* Bad customer/consumer reliability business occurs when the producers hide important product reliability information from the customer/consumer. This is done for a variety of reasons, such as to "buy" time to understand and resolve the problems and to prevent dissemination of harmful reliability data. Experience has shown that prudent caution is appropriate. First indications of problems are specious, and competitors do use unconfirmed product reliability data to their advantage. However, knowingly allowing a customer/consumer to purchase and continue to use defective product is dishonest. Appropriate and responsible communication with the customer/consumer is absolutely required.

2. *The reliability data may knowingly misrepresent the product.* A consensus feeling is that statistical data may often be used to misrepresent the true situation. This is a true feeling. Bad customer/consumer reliability business occurs when the producer supplies reliability qualification and warranty data based upon tortured data.

Tortured data is a label derived from the comment "If you torture data enough, it will say exactly what you wish." Unusual methods of arriving at product reliability estimates can cause problems with customers/consumers. Another common problem is to remove unfavorable data from the product reliability evaluation. This can be accomplished by throwing out data because they were classified as outrageous. In every case, the customer/consumer is a victim of a deceptive practice.

3. *The reliability data source is inadequate.* The inadequate data stem from a lack of valid reliability data for a specific product. In this case, the customer/consumer is not knowingly deceived, but the reliability specification is met using alternate supporting data that compromise the validity of a true product reliability similar product or upon customer/consumer product failure data that have an inadequate recording system and database. As a result, the product reliability never is validated within the present operating environment. The validation would identify an inadequate product reliability.

"Don't call them failures! Call them units not realizing their full potential . . . !"

The dark side of reliability programs based upon inadequate data is where a business knowingly uses the ignorance of product reliability to support the global business effort. The alternate product reliability data often lead to reliability problems that are too difficult to solve within the existing producer organization.

4. *While customers/consumers treat product reliability as a specified quantity, they fail to consider reliability costs of various producers during purchase negotiations.* Quality may be free, but reliability is not. The basic bromide of "you get what you pay for" is substantially true. Your house shingles that last for 50 years initially installed cost 60% more than the house shingles that last 20 years. In the long run, the less reliable roofing materials cost 500% more to own (see Figure 1-4).

This is a fundamental characteristic of the competitive market. A specific business game played by customers/consumers is to purchase product with superior reliability at an average marketplace price. You should never, never have to freely supply a competitively optimized reliability. If you have not quantified your product's and your competitor's reliability cost content, the customer/consumer will negotiate superior reliability at your expense. Customers/consumers need to be educated if they continually focus on products being too high in price and do not place a quantitative value on product

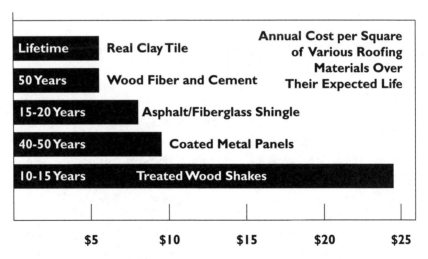

FIGURE 1-4. Yearly cost to own a roof/different roofing materials

reliability. The value of your product reliability in the market must be continuously assessed. The customer/consumer may be correct, and your product is not price and reliability competitive. However, the customer/consumer may be only trying to obtain superior product reliability without paying for it. For example, having a very reliable product and not advertising it is like selling a TV with a VCR but not telling anyone so that they will be pleasantly surprised after they buy the TV.

The markets should be assessed in terms of competitive products and customer/consumer motives. This is a prevalent practice of legitimate after-market business in replacement parts and generic products. The opportunity for compromising product reliability exists in many places in marketing and distribution. The customers/consumers should be educated and should understand in user-friendly terms what reliability means to them.

Dark side customer/consumer reliability business can be summarized as those activities that exist for motives other than establishing a quantified optimum product reliability program between the producer and the customer/consumer. It is sad to report that bad reliability business is a common observation. These activities need to be identified and eliminated before progress can be made toward the goal of realizing optimum product reliability. Realistically, you will have to proceed with your product reliability optimization while working within compromising situations.

Good Customer/Consumer Product Reliability Business

Meeting reliability requirements has become one of the major demands upon modern product technology. Buyers who once concentrated their purchases upon products that were primarily innovative or attention-getting now concentrate upon such products which also operate reliably.
    —ARMAND V. FEIGENBAUM, LEADING QUALITY EXPERT[1]

Good customer/consumer product reliability business is the ongoing process of a business relationship and partnership where reliability provides optimum profit for the producer and optimum satisfaction to the customer/consumer. This business relationship is established within the real world where "bad" business, as described earlier in the chapter, also exists simultaneously. Good customer/consumer reliability is not simply the absence of the "bad" reliability factors, for it includes three factors present in all successful reliability programs.

 1. *A managed product reliability program.* Product reliability is part of the business operating plan. The product business management has a working knowledge of the product reliability requirement. Management understands the product reliability of competitive products and the future reliability requirements, allowing the organization to remain competitive in the marketplace. Customer/consumer awareness is made possible through appropriate communications of this reliability program.

 2. *A good product reliability reputation.* Reputation requires time to be established. Advertising reliability claims do not relate directly to reputation.

"We have the best product. . . . Why do we need to exaggerate?"

Reputations are established by the customer/consumer based upon his or her perceived value of the product's performance over time. This often is encompassed in the concept of positive brand-name recognition. Reputation is established by proven superior reliability, on-time delivery of product, and excellent response and resolution of problems. A good reputation is very difficult to establish and requires only one bad incident to lose. Unfortunately, sales advertising has created a barrage of confusing invalidated claims to support or refute product reliability. This has given customers a more cynical attitude. The customers/consumers now seek expertise and quantified specifications to bypass the information barrage that is designed to influence their perception.

3. *Satisfied customers/consumers.* Good reliability results in high levels of satisfied customers/consumers. Satisfied customers/consumers are essential to your business. What are the characteristics of satisfied customers/consumers?

▶ The customer/consumer understands through experience that the producer always strives to exceed the specified reliability.
▶ The customer/consumer understands through the producer's actions that he or she is valued as an individual or organization.
▶ The customer/consumer understands through actions or proactive plans that the producer will be effective in solving any reliability problem if and when it occurs.
▶ The customer/consumer is comfortable with the producer's activities that monitor and communicate product performance.
▶ The customer/consumer feels comfortable in establishing some degree of partnership, sharing responsibility for business investments and benefits.

As customers/consumers, we all share many examples in the market of successful products based upon superior product reliability. Consider the present Sears Craftsman wrenches, Maytag washing machines, and Toyota automobiles. They and many other products have a well-managed product reliability program, a reputation for reliability, and a base of satisfied customers/consumers. In each instance, product reliability is an important part of their business. They are examples that represent the future of businesses where only optimal product reliability will exist in the marketplace. Consequently, we all share not only common product reliability experience but also the vision of a common goal for product reliability in the future.

Companies make their products more valuable to customers/consumers by making sure they are highly reliable and will perform as expected over a long period of time. Reliability includes four aspects that are of interest to engineers (and customers/consumers). These are (1) probability, which deals with how likely it is that a product will operate properly within a given time span; (2) performance, which deals with how well the product performs its assigned function for an employee or a customer/consumer; (3) time, which is about the length of time a product remains functional; (4) conditions, which deal with what kind of environmental considerations are required for a product to perform well.

—JAMES CORTADA AND JOHN WOODS[2]

Summary

Chapter 1 provides a comprehensive view of product reliability, in general, based upon our shared experience. Four common observations with product reliability form our initial perspective:

1. Product reliability principles are applied in extreme variations to products, depending substantially upon the requirement of the products to provide function with time of use. This extreme variation in application of reliability principles results in inadequate product reliability priorities and an inadequate education and awareness level among product engineers and managers. A significant amount of product reliability activities exists outside of the formalized product reliability organization but are not communicated in reliability terms. Products evaluated by consumers may be without important reliability principles. An example of ignoring reliability growth was presented graphically in Figure 1-3.

2. The management of your organization's product reliability is unique in the areas of financial justification and work product that features

uncertainty, uses unfamiliar concepts, lacks crisp definition, and communicates in abstract terms. This is a typical product reliability program with the associated frustrations. These observed symptoms of a product reliability program often create a communications barrier for business decision makers.

3. Product reliability focuses upon failure. The organization's ability to manage product failures easily leads to the negative behavior of concealment, misrepresentation, and deceit. Because of the potential of perceived bad product reliability ruining a reputation, the management of reliability data and information requires keen judgment.

4. A good reliability business occurs when the product continues to perform its function longer than anticipated by the customer/consumer, who then becomes loyal to the products, thereby creating an opportunity for profit.

These four common observations substantially generate the motivation for understanding product reliability. Product reliability is described by mathematicians in terms that produce fear in engineers and managers. This book, on the other hand, is a comprehensive resource of product reliability, helping readers to understand and not to fear reliability. Hence, this book explains the economic necessity, logical tools, and applied techniques for understanding and using product reliability science.

For business reasons, you should understand and not ignore product reliability. Chapter 1 describes the global observations of the average manager and engineer. It begins your journey to understand product reliability. Upon completion of this book, these pervasive observations will be understood as natural symptoms of a fundamental business factor rather than unnatural activities that are best to avoid.

The following is a list of important words and their definitions that will be used throughout this book.

This is a sample of the text for the definition, or these are more synonyms and usages that are commonly found in the English language.

Block diagram. A diagram that shows the operation, interrelationships, and interdependencies of components in a system. Boxes, or blocks (hence the name), represent the components; connecting lines between the blocks represent interfaces. There are two types of block diagrams:

functional and reliability. Functional block diagrams illustrate the flow of a system's subsystems and outputs, and how all relate to each other. Reliability block diagrams are similar, except that they emphasize factors that influence reliability of systems, processes, or items.

Flowchart. A graphical presentation of all the steps in a process. Relying on a technique used in software design, inputs, process, outputs, and decision are represented in blocks and other symbols. This is one of the most widely used quality tools because it allows one to easily document the flow of activities in a process.

External Customer/Consumer. A person or organization that receives a product, a service, or information, but is not part of the organization supplying it.

Internal Customer. A person or process within the organization that receives output from another person or process within the same organization.

Organization. Any group of people who, due to the management structure, are assigned to work together. (Example: A department, a function, a corporation, a team, a hospital, a government, or a university.)

Item. An item can be any output. It includes processes, products, services, equipment, and a computer program.

Product. A product is any output from a process, activity, or task. It can be hardware, software, or service.

References

1. Armand V. Feigenbaum, *Total Quality Control,* 3rd ed. (New York: McGraw-Hill, 1983).
2. James Cortada and John Woods, *McGraw-Hill Encyclopedia of Quality Terms and Concepts* (New York: McGraw-Hill, 1995).
3. J. M. Juran, Frank M. Gryna Jr., and R. S. Bingham Jr., *Quality Control Handbook,* 3rd ed. (New York: McGraw-Hill, 1974).
4. David K. Lloyd and Myron Lipow, *Reliability: Management, Methods, and Mathematics* (Milwaukee, WI: ASQC Quality Press, 1984).
5. *Consumers Report Buying Guide 1998* (New York: Consumers Union of U.S., Inc., 1997).

2

The Reliability Cycle

With an explosion of competitors, many of them new and without track records, reliability, rather than overly aggressive promises, is the most valuable strategic edge, especially for the mid- to long-haul.

—TOM PETERS[1]

Introduction

To provide a competitive, reliable item or service requires that the organization delivering the output understands and improves the processes that are used to design and build reliability into its output. Figure 2-1 represents a typical reliability cycle made up of eight phases.We have selected the word *cycle* because each generation builds upon the experiences and knowledge generated previously.

Phase I: Defining Reliability Requirements

The textbook approach is for the marketing organization to identify a product opportunity and to develop a product perspective that defines the cost, performance, and reliability requirements needed to service a specific market. Typical reliability measurements would be

- ▶ mean time to failure
- ▶ mean time between failure

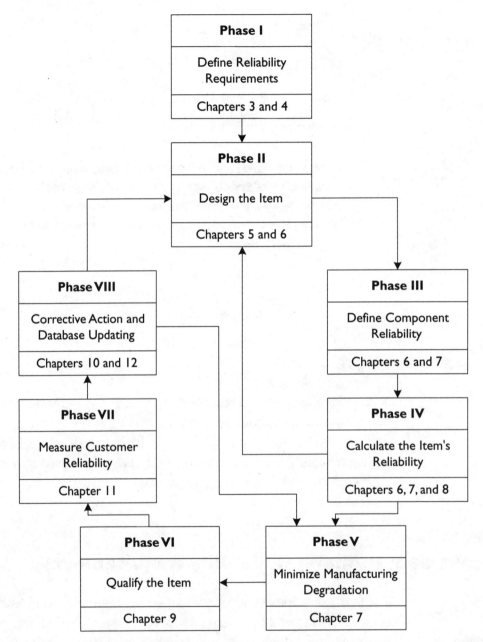

FIGURE 2-1.   The reliability cycle

▶ percent availability
▶ average downtime
▶ failures per 1000 hours of operation

Reliability measurements are discussed in detail in Chapter 3. This perspective should be based upon a detailed knowledge of the external customer's/consumer's need and environment plus a great deal of customer/consumer contact and potential customer/consumer inputs. The major value-added contents that a marketing group contributes to a product are the customer's/consumer's perspective, needs, expectations, and an expert projection of how these factors will change between the time the marketing group collected the research data and the date that the product will be available to the consumer. This is often a difficult task because many product development cycles are measured in years, not weeks, and technology is improving so fast that it is sometimes difficult for marketing's crystal ball to accurately project reliability requirements. On the other hand, there should be no one closer to the customer/consumer and in a better position to do it. A good marketing organization not only will understand the customer's/consumer's present and projected expectations but also will have a detailed understanding of the present technologies that are being developed that will drive further customer/consumer requirement.

Many organizations do not have marketing departments that fulfill this role. Instead, they function more like salespersons rather than doing the conventional marketing research work. This often occurs because organizations make the error of putting marketing and sales in the same function. If marketing is to be included with another organization, combine it with development engineering. However, we recommend it be an independent organization.

Using the product perspective as the product performance basic document, the product reliability specifications are usually developed by product engineering or R&D (Research and Development). Often the reliability specifications are more impacted by inherent reliability of the embedded technologies and competition than they are by customer/consumer expectations. In the better organizations, the consumer's reliability expectations are less demanding than the product reliability specifications. That does not mean that the reliability specification developed by R&D does not consider the customer/consumer requirements, because in most cases they do, but the engineer's thought process is very different. The engineer has a tendency to say: "The product's reliability is x, what percentage of the market will consider buying our product?" The marketing driven approach will state: "If you can provide product that will do this function, at this cost, and at this level of reliability, the market for the product would be y customers/consumers, and we should be able to capture z percentage of the market." It is then left up to R&D to design a product that will meet or exceed the market expectations. In reality, no organization is totally market driven. There is a lot of give and take between marketing and R&D before the reliability specification is finalized, as it should be. A key part of this interchange between marketing and R&D is defining what failures will be included in the reliability measurement. This may seem to be a very small point. In truth, it is not. We have seen organizations that claim to have product reliability performance that is 100% better than their competitors when both products' actual performance was about the same. At first glance, it would seem that a failure occurs whenever the customer/consumer has to get the product repaired. It would be so simple if it were that easy. Let us look at some examples that a computer customer/consumer would consider failures and return the computer but that the producer may or may not include in the reliability measurements:

- ▶ During the service check of the computer, it worked to specification and the customer/consumer could not get it to fail at the repair shop.
- ▶ The problem was defined by the repair shop as a software problem, not as a hardware problem. The software, in the example, was not produced by the organization that produced the computer.
- ▶ The return parts tested no trouble found.

It is very important to understand what types of failures will be included or excluded from the reliability measurement. It is easy to see that the reliability measurements could indicate that the product is performing much better than the customer's/consumer's real experience with the product, depending on what data are included in the reliability measurement. This is such an important point that we dedicated Chapter 4 to this important subject. Once the marketing perspective is complete and the reliability requirements are agreed upon, R&D has everything it needs to start designing a product.

The initial new-design control activity involves establishing the requirements for MTTF and whatever other reliability targets may be indicated to meet the reliability required for the product. To be meaningful, the reliability targets must be within reach at a planned date.
—ARMAND V. FEIGENBAUM[2]

Phase II: Designing Reliability into the Item

A major consideration in every design is the reliability requirement for the end item. The end goal of product design is to create a profitable business. Major considerations of design of an item are

- ▶ Cost
- ▶ Performance
- ▶ Reliability
- ▶ System Compatibility
- ▶ Availability
- ▶ Manufacturability

The item's intrinsic reliability is defined by the design. The design will dictate, for example, the materials selection, the item operating temperature, the structure of the item, the way it is maintained, and the way components of the item are used.

Of course, maintainability is part of reliability because downtime is a typical reliability measurement, and of course, easy maintenance has a big input on the customer's/consumer's cost of ownership.

Phase I is the most important phase in the reliability cycle because it starts the whole cycle going and defines the requirements for each of the other phases, but phase II runs a close second. Proper preventive maintenance may mask some of the reliability problems, but other activities like manufacturing, field repairs, and shipping only serve to degrade the intrinsic reliability of the design. Even preventive maintenance often has a temporary negative effect on the item's reliability.

A well-designed, preventive maintenance system removes components just before they reach their end-of-life points where the components' failure rates take off.

RULE 6   The item's intrinsic reliability is defined by the design.

In order for the R&D engineers to create an acceptable design, a great deal of component reliability data needs to be at their fingertips. In addition, they need to have an excellent understanding of reliability considerations (example: impact on components reliability when the component is used at derated values; impact of changing environmental conditions or where and when to use redundant circuitry). This subject is discussed in more detail in Chapters 5 and 6.

Software plays an important role in reliability.

The widespread use of computers and microprocessors in today's products, processes, and management systems has placed increasing emphasis upon quantitative measurement of the reliability of programmed logic, or software—which can be fully as important in many applications as the reliability of the hardware itself. Software reliability may be defined as the probability that a software system or component will operate without failure for a specified period of time in a specified environment.
—ARMAND V. FEIGENBAUM[2]

Phase III: Defining Component Reliability

Airplanes fail because units fail; units fail because assemblies fail; assemblies fail because subassemblies fail; subassemblies fail because components fail. A component's failure occurs due to weaknesses within the component or because the component was used in a manner that exceeded its specification. It is easy to see that the reliability of an airplane, or for that matter, any item, is determined by three factors:

▶ the component error rate over time
▶ its defined life span
▶ how the component is used

Based upon this fact, it is easy to see that the engineering departments need to understand the bathtub curve failure rates of all components if they are going to design a product that meets customer/consumer reliability requirements.

Bathtub curve—A picture of an item's failure rate versus time. It shows how the failure rate decreases during the item's early life to its intrinsic failure rate level and remains at that level until the item starts to wear out and its end-of-life failure rate begins to increase.

Establishing the bathtub curve error rates of all components is a critical part of a reliability program. Although early life and end-of-life failure rates are important design considerations, the most important consideration is the intrinsic failure rate. For a typical electronic component, the early life phase lasts anywhere between 100 and 200 hours of operation, and the end-of-life phase begins about 8 to 10 years after its first power on point. Some place between 1 and 7 years of the electronic component's life cycle, it will be performing at its intrinsic failure rates. It is for this reason that most reliability projects use only intrinsic failure rates in calculating the total item's projected reliability. This approach greatly simplifies the calculations. Unfortunately, the first thing that the consumer is subjected to is the high early life failure rates. As a result, consumer impression of the product is heavily weighted on the early life failures. "I just got this product and it already isn't working. I'll take it back and get another brand." A properly designed manufacturing process can do a lot to keep early life failures from reaching the consumer. There are many ways that intrinsic (inherent) component failure rate data can be obtained:

1. components' supplier databases
2. reliability data collected by clearinghouses
3. U.S. government databases
4. performance of the components in the organization's previous products
5. component reliability testing by the organization

When you use any one or all of the first three sources of information, be sure that you understand the conditions that relate to the way the data were collected. Pay particular attention to the failures that were excluded from the database.

When you are using your own database (source 4), be sure that you understand the data. It is important that returned components be failure analyzed to determine if they were defective, no trouble found, overstressed, if the failure was an early life or end-of-life failure, or if it was an intrinsic failure.

The last and most expensive way to get component data is to test the component in a life test or stress test condition. These types of evaluations are often necessary when specialized components are developed for a specific application and no reliability data are available. Often, it is less expensive to stay with your present components that have an established database than take the risk of causing a reliability problem in the field. Frequently, component reliability testing is done at the assembly level to increase the amount of information related to a number of components at the same time. (Example: A set of circuit boards could be tested as an assembly or unit.) This type of approach often limits the usefulness of the data when it comes to applying it to another assembly or unit. The subject of reliability component data is discussed in detail in Chapters 6 and 7.

Phase IV: Calculating the Item's Reliability

There are two ways to calculate an item's reliability:

- ▶ testing at the completed item level
- ▶ testing at the lower levels and calculating the item's reliability

Usually, a combination of both these approaches is used to give a maximum level of confidence at minimum cost. Testing the completed item in a simulated customer/consumer environment provides the most accurate data, but it is expensive, very time consuming, and often impractical. For example, if the product's life expectancy was 10 years, the organization would have to test a very large sample of the item for 10 years before they could publish reliability figures. For this reason, stress testing and accelerated life testing of small samples of the product is most frequently used to support shipment to customers/consumers. This approach makes all of your customers/consumers part of the organization's product reliability test sample. To minimize the change of not meeting the reliability specifications in the customer's/consumer's environment, the final item's tests are supplemented and verified by mathematically combining testing at the lower levels of the item (component, assembly, unit, etc.). This is the best way to estimate the item's reliability during the design stage of the item's life cycle.

Once the error rate for the individual components is determined, the reliability of assembly can be calculated. In order to accomplish this calculation, the engineer must understand how the components are used and what environmental conditions they will be subjected to. An assembly's reliability can be calculated by mathematically combining the reliability projections for the components that make up the assembly once they have been adjusted to reflect the way they are used. Assembly reliability can be combined mathematically to define unit estimated reliability. The unit reliability estimates, in turn, can be combined to estimate the item's intrinsic reliability. This data usually do not take into consideration any degradation that would occur as a result of the manufacturing and servicing activities. If the reliability estimates do not indicate that the product will meet the reliability specification, phases II (Design the Item), III (Define Component Reliability), and IV (Calculate the Item's Reliability) will be repeated (see Figure 2-1).

Chapters 5 and 6 of this book cover the mathematics related to projecting reliability, and Chapter 8 covers test considerations related to the reliability projections.

Phase V: Minimizing Manufacturing Degradation

As we have already stated, the item's intrinsic reliability is defined by the design. The manufacturing process can only degrade the item's performance from this intrinsic reliability value. Typical manufacturing things that could cause degradation of the item are

- ▶ Stresses that are applied to the component during manufacturing that exceed the component specification or expected use, but the unit does not stop functioning. (Example: A flow soldering machine that is set too high can cause damage to many flow solder joints within the components and the connections on the circuit board without causing them to completely fail, but it could greatly decrease their mechanical integrity, increasing the item's failure rates after it is delivered to the customer/consumer.)
- ▶ Tests that do not functionally test all the conditions that the customer/consumer will apply to the item. This is referred to as "Test Coverage" when applied to electronic systems.
- ▶ Assembly errors. (Example: a wire pulled too tight around a sharp edge that results in cold-flow causing the unit to short out.)

▶ Workmanship problems. (Example: loose screws, poor solder joints, etc.).

▶ Contamination. (Example: dust inside the disk drive, debris that drops between contacts, or metal filings that short circuit electrical contacts or circuit boards.)

▶ Missing parts. (Example: missing weld joints that cause fatigue to occur or missing retainer clips that allow connectors to open.)

New manufacturing processes should be qualified to minimize the degradation they have on the design. Typical points that would be considered during a manufacturing process qualification activity would be as follows:

▶ Are the documents complete and understandable when used by the manufacturing operators?

▶ Are the tools and test equipment capable of producing products that repeatedly meet the engineering specification?

▶ Are the controls in place to ensure that out-of-specification conditions can be quickly identified, preventing the escape of deviant product from the process?

Process control requirements that should be analyzed are as follows:

1. Process capability studies would be complete. The process should be capable of producing product at a C_{pk} of 1.4 minimum. World class C_{pk} is 2.0 or six sigma.

2. Accuracy or precision assessment should be completed on all pieces of equipment, and measurement error should be considered when the manufacturing acceptance specification limits are developed.

3. The test equipment must be capable of testing the product to the engineering specification with proper guard bands built into the test results.

4. Each operation must be characterized.

5. Training procedures must be established for all operators and inspectors. The training requirements should be documented as part of the individual work instruction.

6. Nonconforming material procedures must be established and working effectively.

7. Yield targets must be met.

8. Product traceability must be established throughout the entire system.
9. Quality performance data system must be in place and operating.
10. Change control for all manufacturing and engineering documents must be in place and operating.
11. Equipment must be calibrated and on a recall cycle.
12. Workmanship standards should be defined so that there is no confusion between good and bad products.
13. Purchase components must come from approved suppliers whose components have been evaluated by the reliability organization.
14. All critical materials that come in contact with the components that make up the item must be identified, have engineering specifications released, and be procured through a controlled system.
15. The process must be capable of working without off-spec from any of the engineering requirements.

The subject of minimizing the manufacturing impact on decreasing the product's reliability is discussed in detail in Chapter 7.

Phase VI: Qualifying the Item

To qualify an item, two factors have to be evaluated:

▶ The product design needs to be evaluated to ensure it is capable of meeting its design requirements, called *design verification*.

▶ The manufacturing processes and their support processes need to be evaluated to ensure that they do not degrade the basic design to an unacceptable level, called *manufacturing process validation*. (Sometimes there is also a Manufacturing Product Validation.) The FDA requires these activities for controlled products.

Design Verification—An evaluation of the product design to determine if it is capable of meeting the design requirements.

Manufacturing Process Validation—An evaluation of the manufacturing processes and their support processes to ensure that they don't degrade the basic design to an unacceptable level.

Manufacturing Process Certification—When an acceptable level of confidence has been reached that the operation or equipment is producing products to the requirements when the documentation is followed. Typically, this will require that the process capability be a minimum of plus or minus 4.0 sigma.

Manufacturing Product Qualification—An evaluation to ensure that the product or item meets the design specification.

Once the design has been released and the item's production process has been certified, the item should be subjected to a qualification test to determine if the theoretical reliability estimates were correct and to provide a minimum degree of assurance that the specified reliability performance has been designed and built into the item. At the components and small assemblies levels, the sample size may be large enough for the organization to have confidence that the reliability projections will be met. For large, complex assemblies and items (example: cars, planes, computers, etc.), it is often too costly and time consuming to evaluate a large enough sample size to have a meaningful level of confidence that reliability projections can be met. To offset this risk, many organizations conduct a number of evaluations throughout the product development cycle in order to gain a higher level of confidence that the item will meet reliability expectations in the customer's/consumer's environment. For example, IBM's new-product cycle includes a number of performance and reliability assessments that are performed by an independent organization called Product Test throughout the development cycle. Typical end-item tests are

- ▶ **Engineering validation test.** This test evaluates development-level hardware that contains pilot line components to determine if the product can perform to its design objectives and reliability requirements.
- ▶ **Design verification test.** Components and assemblies that are used for this test are built on a preproduction line using released engineering documents. The test may start using components built on a pilot line, but they must be replaced with components built on a qualified production line before the end of the evaluation. Products sub-

mitted to this test will reflect the latest manufacturing-released documents. The purpose of this test is to ensure that the design is complete, that the product meets final functional specification and external customer/consumer needs, and that the product can be manufactured and serviced effectively.

▶ **Manufacturing verification test.** This is a test of a large quantity of products manufactured on the production line that will be used to ship products to customers/consumers. The purpose of the test is to see if the product can be produced in volume and still continue to meet expectations during the first 30 days of operation.

Although the three tests take place during different portions of the product cycle and the hardware used was manufactured on different processes, they basically have the same common objectives:

1. Identify and resolve reliability problems.
2. Validate conformance to function and engineering specifications and to applicable standards.
3. Determine conformance to performance specifications including service, manufacturing ability assessment, and reliability projections.

These tests often use stress tests and accelerated life test techniques to reduce the time required to obtain the necessary results. These techniques are discussed in Chapter 9.

The most important reliability tests are those applied to the system or end product as a whole; however, many tests may be conducted at the part, sub-assembly, and assembly levels prior to receipt of hardware for system tests. It is not feasible, from cost and schedule viewpoints, to conduct statistically significant tests at all equipment levels. Accordingly, it is suggested that major emphasis be placed upon tests at the component-part level and the complete-system level.

—J. M. JURAN[3]

Phase VII: Measuring Customer/Consumer Reliability

Once the floodgates are open and the product is being delivered to the external customers/consumers, the true reliability of the item can be measured. Unfortunately, the customer/consumer sees reliability as a black and white consideration. For example, a person gets into the car, and the car starts or doesn't. He or she puts on the brakes, and the car stops or doesn't. The customer/consumer doesn't care if it is an early life failure or end-of-life failure or whether he or she was using the item as it was intended to be used or not. The customer/consumer just expects it to work each time he or she wants it to operate. Now, the real test of your reliability system is put on the line. It is very important that systems be put in place to collect these data in a way that will allow the reliability problems related to the item to be corrected and to provide information that will allow future items to benefit from the correc-

It's very reliable! You can depend on it not working.

tion of detected mistakes made on this item. It is a lot easier to say that the data system should be put in place than it is to make it work.

In today's fast-reacting environment, it is absolutely essential to have pertinent information available to the total organization on an ongoing basis. Today's best practices put the repair action data from yesterday's failures on the president and other key executives' desks today. IBM's field reporting system is an excellent one to benchmark.

The subject of collecting and analyzing customer/consumer data is discussed in further detail in Chapter 11.

Phase VIII: Corrective Action and Database Updating

The database that is developed in phases III through VII is established for three purposes:

- ▶ to measure current product reliability
- ▶ to correct current reliability or perceived reliability problems
- ▶ to collect component and assembly error rate information for future use

The key to good corrective action is defining the root cause of the problems. In most cases, this means the suspected component needs to undergo a detailed failure analysis activity where it is characterized and very often dissected. We like to be able to re-create every external failure condition. When you can take a good component and get it to fail in exactly the same way that the component under study failed in the field operation, you have gained true knowledge of the failure mechanism and can solve the problem. In most cases, a good failure analysis system is a key ingredient of an effective corrective action cycle, but correcting the problem is only the start of the total cycle. Truly, you need to prevent problems from reoccurring on the current process and all future products. In this case, we need to look at what an effective preventive action cycle is. Seven critical ingredients that are required in any long-range plan to permanently eliminate problems are

1. *Awareness.* The employees and management must be made aware of the importance of eliminating errors and the cost of errors to the busi-

ness. In many companies, eliminating errors could reduce costs by more than 30%.

2. *Desire.* A desire to eliminate errors must be created. No one wants to be wrong; just give them a chance to do it right.

3. *Training in problem solving.* The individuals working to eliminate the problems need to be confident problem solvers. They need to do more than just correct problems; they need to define the best-value solution of each problem. They need to assemble a number of alternative solutions and then select the very best one.

4. *Failure analysis.* A system is needed to translate symptoms into a precise understanding of what caused the problem (failure mode). Without this type of data, many problems can only be solved by very expensive trial-and-error methods that take too much time and cost too much.

5. *Follow-up system.* A system to track problems and action commitments is an essential part of the total preventive system. It should also provide a means to evaluate the effectiveness of the preventive action.

6. *Prevention activities.* Once you have solved the problem on the current product, you are ready to start your prevention activities. You need to ask yourself why the problem occurred. Then, define how the process that allowed the problem to occur needs to be changed to prevent the problem from reoccurring in future items. For example, if the problem was caused because a Teflon-coated wire shorted out because it had too much pressure applied to it as it was routed around a right-angle metal edge, the R&D design rules should be changed to state: "If Teflon-coated wire is used, all metal parts that could come in contact with the wire must have $\frac{1}{16}$" radius corners."

7. *Liberal credit.* Credit and recognition should be liberally given to all who participate.

Let's change the way we look at problems and think about each problem we face each day as an opportunity to contribute to making the organization more successful. As these opportunities arise, we need to have a systematic way of addressing them so that they are not just put to bed, but buried. If you put a problem to bed, it can and will get up some time in the future to cause the organization more disruptions. It may be next week or next month or next year, or perhaps five years, but it will come back unless the process that allowed the problem to occur initially is error proofed. When you have error proofed the process that allowed the problem to occur, then and only then have you buried the problem so that it will not come back. That's what the "opportunity cycle" is all about (see Figure 2-2).

For more detailed understanding of the opportunity cycle, read *Total Improvement Management* or the book in this series called *Performance Improvement Methods,* both published by McGraw-Hill.

When teams follow these six steps defined in the opportunity cycle, their life becomes much easier. Unfortunately, the more experienced the teams become, the more likely they are to take shortcuts. Process shortcuts have probably led to the demise of more teams than can be counted. When a team elects to circumvent the correct problem-solving process, it automatically reduces its ability to function in a continuous improvement environment. The team may ultimately be successful, but its success will be by accident, not by design. As reliability problems are identified and a corrective solution is defined as a change to the design, phases II through VII will be

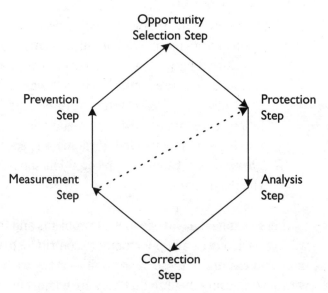

FIGURE 2-2.   **The opportunity cycle**

repeated as they are related to the design change. If a manufacturing process solution is involved, only phases V through VII will need to be repeated (see Figure 2-1).

Another important ingredient in the opportunity cycle is cycle time. The clock starts running in the opportunity cycle at the time that failures occur in the customer's/consumer's environment and runs until the change has been implemented in all of the items that are being delivered and the items that are exposed to failure in the field. In most organizations, this cycle time should be reduced by about 70%. The average opportunity cycle was defined in the 1980s and has not been streamlined to meet the reduced product cycle windows that we are living with today. Even if your opportunity cycle has been decreased by 70% in the last 10 years, it will need to be cut in half again by the beginning of the twenty-first century.

The other way that field reporting data are used is to update the component failure database. This is an extremely important part of the total reliability cycle as it builds the integrity of the next item's reliability projections. In order to make effective use of this rich source of information, there are a lot of supporting data that need to be collected. The measurement system that was designed to support phase VII has to include these key considerations.

Establishing and maintaining a database to support the organization's reliability systems is discussed in detail in Chapter 10.

Summary

The reliability cycle (Figure 2-1) depicts the process that every item whose reliability is of concern to the customer/consumer and management should go through. You will note that each cycle is triggered with a new reliability requirement and that the cycle is short circuited when an item's calculated reliability does not meet reliability requirements or when the products' actual reliability performance fails to meet consumer expectations.

In a pure service environment, the reliability cycle needs to be modified to focus upon the processes that produce the service. In these cases, a fault-tree-analysis type activity becomes very important. Too often, management believes that reliability is a hardware measurement and does not apply to the service industry. Nothing could be further from the truth. The five traits that are most important to having customers/consumers return to a service provider are

- ▶ accuracy of information provided
- ▶ timeliness of service
- ▶ responsiveness of personnel
- ▶ reliability of organization's process
- ▶ physical appearance

Reliability can be your competitive edge. Is your Reliability Management System up to it?

References

1. Tom Peters, *Thriving on Chaos* (New York: Alfred A. Knopf, 1988).
2. Armand V. Feigenbaum, *Total Quality Control,* 3rd ed. (New York: McGraw-Hill, 1983).
3. J. M. Juran, Frank M. Gryna Jr., and R. S. Bingham Jr., *Quality Control Handbook,* 3rd ed. (New York: McGraw-Hill, 1974).

CHAPTER | **3**

Product Reliability Economics

There is a certain product-reliability level that provides the most economical device to meet customer/consumer needs.

—Armand V. Feigenbaum, Leading Quality Expert[1]

Introduction

Managers should read Chapter 3 to understand the fundamentals of making a profit from product reliability. Managers are shown how to estimate their product's reliability cost content and how to optimize their reliability cost to customer/consumer demand. These are relatively new activities to most managers but will be fundamental activities for survival in the future marketplace.

Engineers should understand the principles of product reliability economics so that they support an optimal product reliability strategy in a cost-effective manner. Your product reliability specification can be established only through this business optimization process.

Our ultimate goal is to achieve the best business economics for our product reliability. Quantifying the economics of your product reliability is the most significant activity directed toward product reliability management and control.

49

If product reliability is too low, actual total costs to the customer/consumer may be high because of excessive repair, maintenance, and out-of-use costs. If an unduly high reliability level is evolved, total cost may still be excessive to the customer/consumer because of the higher price caused by unique requirements for components and assemblies.
—ARMAND V. FEIGENBAUM[1]

Reliability Economic Models

There are three models that summarize the reliability economics views of most organizations. These three models represent a good, better, and best representation of reliability economics.

Reliability—The probability that an item will perform its required function under specific conditions for a specified period of time.

Once this definition of product reliability is presented, what remains is the difficult application of the definition to all products. A good way of viewing product reliability is to realize that products provide functional operation during their initial use by the customer/consumer but will probably fail to provide function operation with time and functional use cycles. Figure 3-1 contains this view of reliability and represents the following:

1. The product has an intrinsic reliability based upon the functional materials, design, and physical specifications that were part of the product functional specification, which is the initial value of the x axis. This is the product reliability that comes with the product without any effort and cost directed toward the product reliability.

2. Intrinsic reliability in the functional product can be improved by effort and cost directed toward improving product reliability, which is the Producer Reliability Cost of Figure 3-1. The reliability cost content of any product becomes exponentially higher with reliability improvement when we require very costly techniques to realize smaller improvements at high reliabilities. Reliability is never perfect.

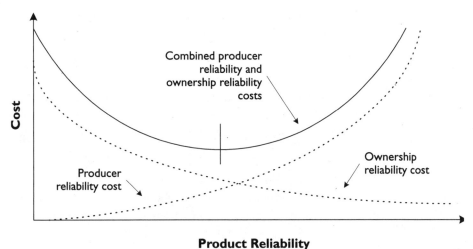

Product Reliability

FIGURE 3-1. **A total cost reliability (TCR) economic model**

3. The improved reliability will reduce the cost of ownership by the customer/consumer as presented by the Ownership Reliability Cost of Figure 3-1. These reduced costs of ownership are mainly fewer replacement parts, less service and maintenance, and less work interruptions.

4. Note that the combined cost of producer reliability and ownership reliability does produce a minimum overall cost as indicated by the vertical line in Figure 3-1. That point is where the amount of cost spent to improve a product's reliability is balanced with the amount of savings realized by that improvement. This point is most apparent when producing something for your own use.

The TCR is a good economic model for product reliability. It presents the concept that best business is neither to ignore nor to spend too much money on product reliability. This is a good guiding principle that should be understood by your entire organization. The TCR is inadequate as an operational product reliability model for the following reasons:

1. The producer reliability cost and the ownership reliability cost do not occur at the same time, and accurate accounting systems to evaluate the minimum overall cost do not exist.

2. It does not distinguish between reliability failure and anticipated wear out. The ownership cost of product includes wear out. This anticipated cost is often confounded with product reliability performance.

A common example is automobile tires. A tire may be purchased with an explicit mileage rating, and the purchaser anticipates that usage until wear out. In the same purchase, the tire is under warranty for manufacturing defects and also insured for road hazard catastrophes. By definition, only the manufacturing defects are considered for product reliability. Today, most tire failures result from environmental use (alignment, low air, etc.) or catastrophic episodes (nails, rocks, etc.). Some of us remember a major manufacturer's reliability problem when it ventured into the new product of radial tires.

Appliances have standard warranties that define the producer's liability for a reliable product. What is confusing is that extended warranties are issued that under contract define liability as a cost. The nature of extended warranties is to include anticipated product wear-out costs in addition to the usual product failure costs. With age, the extended warranty evolves into a service maintenance contract. This activity is done without ever defining random product failures and product wear out.

3. It does not address the role of social intervention into the reliability of life-sustaining products. The minimum point in combined producer and ownership reliability costs does not occur for many products. Airworthiness, fire safety, medical device effectiveness, and air bag effectiveness are familiar examples of product attributes that drive reliability to socially acceptable levels rather than simply economic optimization. Products with socially driven reliability attributes are usually government certified. These products still require reliability techniques to achieve their certifications.

4. It does not address two categories of products: (1) product that fails to function the first time, which may or may not be classified as a reliability failure, and (2) product that is specified to function only once during an emergency, for example, fire extinguishers and airplane oxygen masks. These products are tested for function periodically prior to their anticipated emergency use. Whether that test is a reliability test has ambiguous interpretation. (This book does not expand upon the one-time-use product reliability; it presents reliability as a function of time or multiple use.)

5. Finally, it does not address products such as personal computers and telephone equipment where the replacement due to economics and improved function greatly outweighs replacement due to unreliability.

The TCR model is a good reliability economic model for establishing a communications base or principle. However, as demonstrated by the examples, and many other cases, it does not apply to all products.

The Business Product Reliability (BPR) model (see figure 3-2) presents a common economic model of product reliability that is based on quantified data. When warranties for product failures are used, the BPR model is frequently used. It quantifies the producer cost during the warranty period. We believe that the BPR model is better than the TCR model for the following reasons:

1. The BPR model is a product reliability model based on two real economic variables: the average failure rate of the product and the time period of warranty.

Average Warranty Failure Rate of Product—The total number of failures during warranty divided by the total number produced during warranty. This relates to the total producer's direct cost of product reliability.

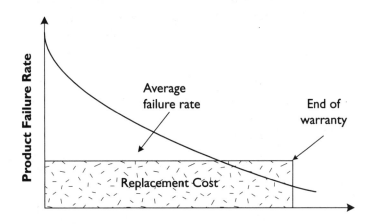

Time of Product Use

FIGURE 3-2.   **The business product reliability economic model covers only the warranty period**

The time period of warranty is chosen to provide customer/consumer economic relief for product failure but limits that relief to less than the anticipated product wear out during specified use conditions.

2. The BPR model may not be conceptually understood by your entire organization, but it is specifically quantified in planned out-of-pocket warranty costs and does explicitly provide economic relief by reducing your average product reliability. In this sense, the BPR model is a dynamic model that drives product reliability specifications to gain an economic advantage.

3. With a little adapting, the economic model in the BPR model actually has the problem of universal application to all products noted in the economic model in BPR.

The BPR is a superior model because it demonstrates product reliability in terms of failures and warranty times. Both failures and warranty times are quantified parts of your organization's management and control activities, not abstract relationships. The BPR is a better reliability economics model. However, it does have some shortcomings.

- ▶ The reported failures during use are an unknown fraction of all product failures. This creates an uncertainty in determining the actual product reliability from the reported warranty-related failures.
- ▶ Only failures are reported, which most often does not identify a failure mode. This prevents product reliability improvement through the process of identification and elimination.
- ▶ The product warranty is based upon competitive positions in the marketplace and historical warranty cost. These two factors are so subjective that they normally do not motivate a directed product reliability effort.
- ▶ The customer's/consumer's incurred cost of failures during the warranty period and after the warranty period is not considered. The only cost that is included is the producer's cost.

The BPR model presents a product reliability economic model based upon real economic considerations. It is a better model but not quite as intuitive as the economic model in Figure 3-1 nor as universally understood.

Figure 3-3 is a very sophisticated product reliability model called the Reliability Worth Economic model that accounts for customer/consumer and

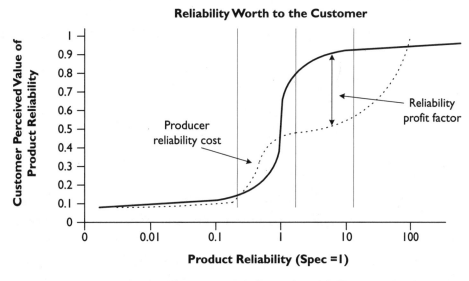

FIGURE 3-3. The Reliability Worth Economics (RWE) model

marketing economics as well as product reliability cost content central to optimizing all reliability programs. It is unique for each product. It contains the concept that product reliability by itself may be the key to the economic success of your business. This is the economic model we prefer. This chapter leads you step by step, in a logical method toward quantifying these sophisticated concepts for your product.

The RWE model presents a relationship central to all product reliability economics. It is the reliability specified by the customer/consumer versus the customer's/consumer's perceived value of your product's reliability content. That relationship includes all factors presented in Figures 3-1 and 3-2 along with the following factors that are understood by very few organizations:

1. The customer/consumer not only asks for economic relief caused by your product failures but also values you as a supplier of reliable product. You will be a preferred supplier if you provide good product, on time, and at competitive prices. A preferred supplier gets premium prices and increased profits.

2. The perceived value of your product depends upon the customer's/consumer's almost subjective judgment. The fundamentals of communication, understanding the details of your product reliability, and demonstration of product administration and control are critical to that process.

3. The product reliability cost content is nonlinear and difficult to accurately determine in most situations. However, the relationship between your reliability cost content and your product competitiveness may be the most important relationship in your business.

The RWE model requires a large amount of work to develop the degree of accuracy required for product reliability in today's marketplace. It would be irresponsible to say that this is an easy task, even when presented in a book called *Reliability Simplified*. However, it would be blatantly negligent to ignore this task of presenting product reliability in terms that will result in the greatest economic rewards for your business.

It is not an impossible task. The future of your organization rests upon your understanding of the RWE model for your specific business. And remember, this process is no more difficult than the financial process of your business.

Developing Your Product Reliability Economic Strategy

This chapter directs itself toward developing a sophisticated view of product reliability economics as shown in Figure 3-3. This is the level of sophistication that will be required for businesses in the future.

The several steps in quantifying the product reliability economics are the same for the many different products made by the readers of this book. The extent of applying these steps into your business also is a clear measure of the maturity of your business reliability strategy.

A graphic presentation of these steps is shown in Figure 3-4. Each step is essential in achieving a reliability program capable of determining your best product reliability.

FIGURE 3-4.   **Reliability program maturity**

Step 1. The tentative evaluation of your product's reliability cost. The reliability cost content of all products has a broad distribution of values. This step will tentatively assess the intrinsic worth of reliability in your product. In a quick method, you can approximate the reliability value within your product. The prime value of this step is to determine what profit opportunity exists by effectively managing your specific product's reliability.

Step 2. Reliability prices based upon customer/consumer demand. This section describes the product reliability demand price. This will determine what the product reliability is worth in the competitive marketplace for your specific product. This activity is a minimum requirement for all managed product reliability.

Step 3. Competitive reliability analysis. Building upon the quantification of your product reliability prices developed in step 2, step 3 outlines the procedure for analyzing your product reliability prices versus your competitors' reliability prices in the marketplace. An analysis of competitive reliability in the marketplace should be an integral part of business self-evaluation and planning.

Step 4. Product reliability strategy. This step demonstrates by example how all product reliability cost and price data can be integrated into a strategy to migrate (or maintain) your product reliability in an optimized business condition.

Step 1. The Tentative Evaluation of Your Product's Reliability Cost

An extremely simplified model of product cost content would be a development cost and a manufacturing cost that results in a product. The product is specified to provide functional use in a specified use environment. The product can have one use or repeated use (as measured by cycles or time) during its life. A certain cost (functional) is expended to attain the specified functional use. Additional cost (reliability) is expended to attain improved repeated use before failure of the product.

Product reliability cost content—The percentage of the product cost explicitly expended toward lowering the product failure rate during usage.

The functional and reliability cost contents of products are difficult to separate due to business cost-accounting practices. Beyond accounting practices, the state-of-the-art or naturally occuring reliability of products creates products with implicit reliability. As a result, the product reliability cost content definition depends significantly upon the word "explicit" (or identified).

Reliability cost content of a product's sale price—The percentage of the sales price due to the explicit expenditure toward lowering the product failure rate.

The first step toward managing the business of product reliability is to determine approximately the product's reliability cost content. The first approximation of reliability cost content in common products is from approximately 0 to 25% of the retail sales price. This is the amount of the customer/consumer sales price that is attributed to reliability cost content of the product. The reliability cost content of 0 to 25% has been observed in evaluations of retail products and will be demonstrated in an exercise later. All products and services do not have a significant reliability content. If the product and service reliability cost content is intrinsically low or zero, then the potential for exploitation of the product reliability for profit is also low or zero. It is not possible to improve the reliability of apples; so that is not an idea with potential profit. Therefore, it is best to first estimate the reliability cost content of your specific product. Your first estimate establishes the upper limit of potential reliability profit.

The approximate method of evaluating your product or service reliability cost content is extremely simple and effective. It is called the *Telephone Yel-*

Let your fingers do the walking through the yellow pages

low Pages evaluation. This is an introductory method of estimating reliability cost content. It does not have the rigorous detail to be of immediate value to your business. It is a quick, memorable, and realistic orientation to the reliability cost content evaluation. Every location has a consolidated product and service advertisements in the local Yellow Pages. It represents a broad distribution of product offerings to the business and consumer buying public. By sampling a variety of product offerings, one can quickly create the following list of products and services listed by approximate percent of reliability cost content. The list is divided into categories that help to characterize the products. Remember that this list does not require accuracy beyond a quick mental approximation.

 Here is a sample list. Take 10 minutes to form your own list from your Yellow Pages. This quick simplistic view will make you feel comfortable with the concept of product reliability cost content. Remember the definition: reliability is the probability that an item will perform its required function under specified conditions for a specified period of time.

- ▶ Perishable products and services (reliability cost content ~0% of price; because of the one-time use)
  —Bakery goods
  —Car wash
  —Pizzas
  These are goods and services that are utilized immediately, substantially, without any reliability cost content.
- ▶ Expendable products and services (reliability cost content ~1 to 5% of price; because of the extended one-time use, this results in a reliability factor)
  —Attorneys
  —Diesel fuel
  —Air filters
  —Signs
  These are goods and services that are utilized in time but intrinsically exhibit little loss in intended function during use.
- ▶ Warranty products and services (reliability cost content ~5 to 15% of price; clearly demonstrates failure rates with time and cycles of use)

—Automobiles

—Computers

—Earthquake insurance

—Shingles

These are products and services that explicitly have a reliability cost content that is often reflected in the specific warranty that financially backs the producer's reliability claims.

▶ Life-preserving and emergency products and services (reliability cost content >15% of price; life-sustaining products with lowest possible failure rates during usage)

—Airplanes

—Fire alarm systems

—Medical emergency transportation

—Oxygen delivery systems

These are products and services in which reliability is an explicit factor in the cost of product and market price. Usually, the reliability cost content is not precisely known but integrated into the cost of manufacturing, cost of delivery, and price structure of the products and services.

How about your product? Where does it fit in the categories of this tentative evaluation? After you have produced this global list from the Yellow Pages, determine in which category your products presently should be included:

▶ If your product falls in the "Perishable" category, only the quality of the product at the time of delivery to the customer/consumer is important to your business.

▶ If your product falls in the "Expendable" or "Warranty" categories, the evaluation suggests continuing on the path toward a product reliability strategy. You should understand all aspects of evaluating the reliability profit potential.

▶ If your products fall in the "Life-preserving and emergency" category, product reliability by definition is an integral part of your business. This book provides tools for meeting your specified requirements.

The product reliability external standard often minimizes competitive reliability profit exploitation.

The Yellow Pages exercise is a unique way of introducing product reliability. The process may seem to be a trivial game, but this first step toward managing your reliability reinforces the concept that product reliability is an integral part of every business. The following response came from an individual instructed to form the same list to quickly determine the percent value of their product's reliability.

The understanding of reliability became immediately clear to me. I can never again think of any product or service without including an estimate of the reliability content. The relationship of producer, customer/consumer, and the value of customer/consumer loyalty has been frozen in my mind. This exercise should be done by everyone, producers and consumers.

If you are in the expendable and warranty categories (1 to 15% reliability content in price), continue to the next step of quantifying your product's reliability worth to the customer/consumer. If you are in the perishable and life-preserving and emergency categories, your reliability cost content is already explicitly determined. However, this book provides, beyond this reliability cost content evaluation, the skills and tools required to preserve your defined reliability program.

Step 2. Reliability Prices Based upon Customer/Consumer Demand

How much is your specific product's reliability worth to the customer/consumer? It would be unusual if that amount were systematically evaluated and accurately understood in your business at this time. Step 2 is to quantify the reliability cost content within your product and the reliability value or worth of your product to the customer/consumer. These two amounts are the essential values required to effectively control your product reliability on a business basis. The following approach will assist in determining these essential values and ultimately in communicating your reliability strategy to your organization and your potential customer/consumer.

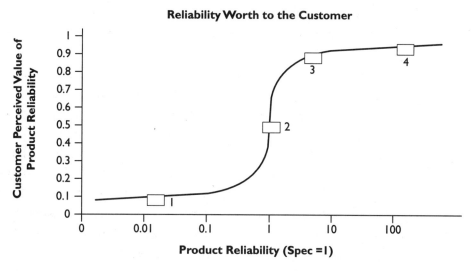

FIGURE 3-5. The intuitive customer/consumer reliability relationship

Figure 3-5 displays Product Reliability in the *x* axis (scaled by the customer's/consumer's product reliability specification) in relationship to the Customer/Consumer Perceived Value of Product Reliability in the *y* axis. The initial relationship is plotted to demonstrate graphically the concept of the fundamental customer/consumer financial response, which is the key to all product reliability financial evaluations.

This is the most important paragraph to understand in Chapter 3. Figure 3-5 presents a *y* axis scale of only the customer's/consumer's perceived reliability value content, not the customer's/consumer's perceived value of the entire product. This is the product's reliability value content to the consumer (typically 1 to 15% of product cost). There also is a producer's reliability cost that is part of the cost of production. The consumer's perceived value of reliability content and the producer's reliability cost are typically not known but are embedded into the product cost and price structure. The purpose of Chapter 3 is to assist you in quantifying the product reliability customer/consumer value and producer costs. Your product reliability cannot be controlled unless you quantify these economic factors.

Figure 3-5 is a loose quantitative relationship of the marketplace price a customer/consumer is willing to pay for the product's reliability. This plot is unique for each product and each customer/consumer. The *x* axis is a logarithmic scale of reliability, where 1 is equal to the customer's/consumer's product reliability purchase specification. So an *x* value of 0.1 is 1/10 of the specified customer/consumer product reliability and an *x* value of 10 is 10 times the specified customer/consumer product reliability. The *y* axis is the perceived value by the customer/consumer of the product reliability content. The *y* axis value range is the decimal percentage of the maximum amount that the customer/consumer will pay for reliability. This figure only applies to one customer/consumer per plot, since customers/consumers have varying product specifications and perceive the same product's reliability with different absolute values. These customer/consumer values are a result of use experience and sampling evaluation techniques.

The product reliability cost originates with the customer/consumer. The customer/consumer will pay for a required (specified) product reliability the same as he or she will pay for product performance. That concept is intuitively familiar and understood by most people. It is best presented as Figure 3-5 with the variable Product Reliability (as specified) related to Customer/Consumer Perceived Value of Product Reliability.

Several characteristics are displayed by Figure 3-5:

1. Figure 3-5 is an example of a graphic plotting of quasi-subjective relationships. It requires quantification to be of any use. To repeat, it is unique for each product and customer/consumer.
2. Point 1 is where the product reliability is 100× less than the specification. This product cannot be used by the customer/consumer due to inadequate reliability, and therefore, the product is of little value to the customer/consumer. When a product does not meet the customer/consumer reliability specification, the customer/consumer perceives the product reliability content to be of little value and also finds the entire product of little value due to the inadequate reliability.
3. Point 2 is the specification and operating point of the customer/consumer business and occurs when a customer/consumer has specified a reliability for the product. Whether that reliability specification it-

self is correct for the customer's/consumer's product is not part of this evaluation.

4. Point 3 reflects the price the customer/consumer is willing to pay to purchase the superior product reliability, which satisfies all of their specified reliability goals, has an excellent history of supplying reliable product, and has an established reputation for product reliability. This is consistent with the concept that certain products have superior reliability (products with outstanding reputation), are worth a premium price to the customer/consumer, and create a profit for the producer.

5. Point 4 occurs when the customer/consumer has reached the limit of paying anything additional for better product reliability because he or she feels that there is no value added. In every case, the customer/ consumer does not consider the producer cost of reliability, but only the product's measured reliability and the specified reliability requirement.

Figure 3-5 presents the producer/customer/consumer product reliability relationship as a function that describes the intuitive concept, but it is only the first step toward specific reliability management and control. However, it is an excellent step that is used to widely communicate your product reliability activity.

Figure 3-6 presents the same basic customer/consumer product reliability economics by enhancing the relationship established in Figure 3-5. First, we establish economic zones of operation. The reason for assigning zones is to easily communicate the producer/customer/consumer relationships regarding product reliability. These zones ultimately define in simple terms where your current reliability business is and where to deliberately migrate to optimize your reliability profit.

In Figure 3-6, the zones of customer/consumer product reliability business are overlaid directly upon Figure 3-5. Figure 3-6 is valid for all the various business environments that exist that comprise the scope of the reliability business. The *x* axis is segmented into four zones:

▶ Zone 1 presents the condition where the product reliability is determined by the customer/consumer to be inadequate to meet the speci-

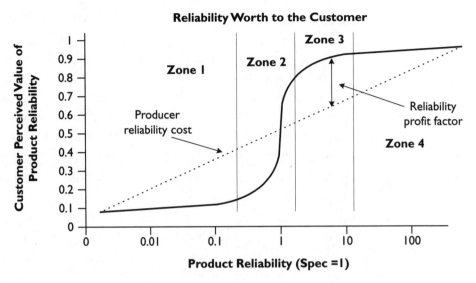

FIGURE 3-6.   Zones, producer costs, and Reliability Profit Factor
(RPF)

fied reliability requirement. Product in zone 1 does not sell due to inadequate reliability.

▶ Zone 2 presents the condition where the customer/consumer has specified the product reliability for his or her best business interest. The
product will be tested to determine if it meets the customer/consumer
specification prior to accepting the initial shipment and on an ongoing
inspection plan.

▶ Zone 3 presents the condition where the customer/consumer has complete confidence that the product reliability will never be a cause for
business concern. The customer/consumer will pay for a premium for
this superior reliability.

▶ Zone 4 presents the condition where the customer/consumer has
reached complete confidence in the product reliability but will no
longer pay a greater product price for unnecessary reliability improvement. The price that the customer/consumer is willing to pay remains constant while the cost of reliability increases.

A dotted line labeled Producer Reliability Cost is included in Figure 3-6,
which hypothetically presents that variable for demonstration purposes. The

producer reliability cost is unique for each product, nonlinear with product reliability, and rarely is accurately known for all zones.

In the center of zone 3 is the Reliability Profit Factor (RPF) arrow that represents the difference between the consumer perceived value of product reliability and the producer reliability cost. The arrow is placed in zone 3 where the difference is a maximum. The value of understanding your specific potential or realized RPF is that it represents the upper maximum profit point from your product reliability.

Figure 3-6 presents the concept that if enough money is spent on product reliability, it can be improved to almost any specified amount. It also presents the concept that the difference between product reliability manufacturing costs and price paid for that product reliability may be an expense or profit. It may be negative, even, or positive. Figure 3-6 qualitatively summarizes the entire business profitability of product reliability.

Figure 3-7 displays a quantified graphical presentation of a hypothetical unique product reliability economics. Every business with products that have a reliability content should generate and understand such a quantified relationship. The greatest difficulty for all product reliability programs is to generate and establish universal acceptance of this quantified relationship,

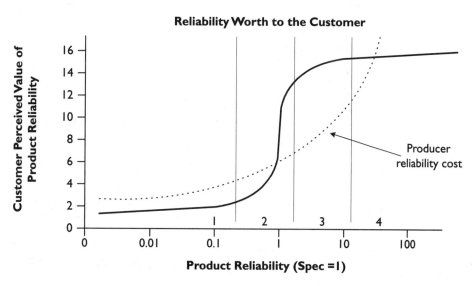

FIGURE 3-7.   Example of reliability economics of a specific product

and the greatest benefit is the use of this relationship to graphically present the reliability business function of your product.

The initial estimate used to quantify the relationship in Figure 3-7 may be inadequate to confidently manage changes to optimize your product reliability business. In your specific situation, you may have to reiterate the quantification process until a management consensus is reached about the validity of your information. The initial data used to generate the information presented in Figure 3-7 are typically vague; do not allow this situation to terminate this evaluation. Remember, it is impossible to optimally manage your product reliability without understanding the relationships presented in Figure 3-7. The better the relationships are quantified; the better the decisions are made in your reliability management. Ask yourself a key question. How can one effectively manage your product reliability without the information presented in Figure 3-7? Quantifying your reliability economics is difficult, but there is no alternate effective process. The example in Figure 3-7 was specifically quantified in the following manner. Your product reliability economic quantification will use all available data, following the general guidelines of this example.

The *y* axis displays a scale of the anticipated product reliability content at the customer/consumer specified acceptance level and the maximum that the customer/consumer will consider paying for superior reliability. In this case, the initial product sales price is approximately $100, and the maximum that the customer/consumer would pay for the product reliability content is determined to be $16 (Figure 3-7, *y* axis).

The first input information in evaluating the *y* axis came from a conversation with the customer/consumer. The customer/consumer was quite definite in the additional amount paid for superior reliability above the required specified reliability, which is $8.00. Apparently, this value had been determined earlier as a business decision to purchase from an alternate source. The customer was willing to share the information based upon our efforts to manage our reliability. This represents the top portion ($8.00 to $16.00) of our *y* axis scale. However, the customer/consumer product program manager had a difficult time even imagining the reliability cost content of a product that does meet the required reliability specification. The customer's/consumer's response was: "We pay for a complete specified product, any reliability cost elements that are part of the complete specified product are known only by you, the supplier." It is obvious that the embedded cost of our product reliability is of a considered, but unknown, value to our customer/consumer.

The second information source was our own organizations. Initial evaluation of product reliability cost content will have a broad distribution of values estimated from various sources proximate to our product's manufacturing and accounting organizations. We conclude that this broad distribution of values of product reliability cost content is actually a symptom of our inadequate product reliability program. Since the customer/consumer premium was clearly defined at $8.00, we estimate that it is reasonable to assume that another $8.00 of value content is implicit by the customer/consumer in the cost of meeting the basic customer/consumer reliability specification. In this case, the value of $8.00 falls reasonably within our own estimate distribution. So the y axis scale is $8.00 of reliability content value to meet the customer/consumer specification with an additional $8.00 of premium paid by the customer/consumer for superior reliability product. This agrees, in the first evaluation, with our best customers'/consumers' and our own organization's economic inputs. Therefore, we have established a $16.00 y axis scale.

Figure 3-7 also has an estimate of Producer Reliability Cost. We estimate this value next. This line was generated by matching the existing organizational reliability costs (allotted money) through zones 1 and 2, and then projecting an estimate of additional costs required for product reliability in zones 3 and 4. The estimate shows that the product reliability cost content is approximately equal to the customer/consumer perceived value of product reliability for product reliabilities up to the product specification. This is true only for this unique example. The cost of product reliability improvement increases rapidly for product reliabilities greater than the product specification (zones 3 and 4). The basic input is that additional procedures are required to improve the current reliability tenfold, and that would essentially double the cost of product reliability. This input was excellent because it came from part of the yearly engineering planning that considered a high-reliability product. For the example presented in Figure 3-7, we have completed the first iteration of a quantified evaluation of our product reliability economics. Usually, certain segments of the curve are better known, as stated in this example. Although the values of the first iteration of Figure 3-7 are relatively inaccurate and represent unfamiliar independent product reliability economics, they are often used for management input and action. The second iteration will result in better evaluations.

This book describes only the procedure to quantify an example (presented in Figure 3-7) of product reliability economics. We cannot hope to address the semi-infinite number of difficulties encountered by those attempting this evaluation in all products. However, this example is described to highlight some key elements common to all product reliability evaluations:

1. The information is gathered from several sources. Initially, ulterior motives bias the input values from these sources.
2. Expect that arbitrary management and territorial control will inhibit the establishment of product reliability economics. Executive management involvement either aggravates or alleviates difficulties.
3. Important business information quickly emerges from combining various input data as in the example of Figure 3-7. In this example, assuming that we are supplying a product reliability to meet the customer/consumer specification, a fivefold reliability improvement would allow a marketplace reliability price increase in zone 3. This is potentially a significant profit enhancement. On the other hand, if the customer/consumer changes the product reliability specification requiring a tenfold improvement, our product will not sell without adding extensive producer reliability cost. This is a potentially dangerous business situation. Figure 3-7 presents a dynamic chart that identifies business problems. What frequently happens is that your initial charted product reliability economic estimate will become utilized as a tentative business input in a positive manner.
4. The initial completion of Figure 3-7 forms the basis of future product reliability economics validation. The next iteration of this evaluation will be much easier. All input parties, including customers/consumers and producer product managers, will be interested in these business data. Your goal is to motivate action, if required, to optimize your business economics. Figure 3-7 is a tool toward achieving that goal.

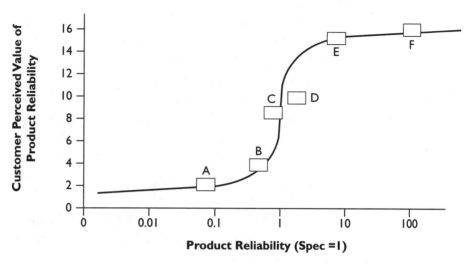

FIGURE 3-8. Customer's/consumer's view of available product reliabilities

Step 3. Competitive Reliability Analysis

Figure 3-8 is the customer's/consumer's view of the total marketplace of product reliabilities. It is the marketplace competitive offerings of a product. It also is the basis for the customer's/consumer's general perceived product reliability value versus specification relationship presented in Figure 3-5. The source of data comes from your most significant customer/consumer. Don't modify your customer's/consumer's perceptions, just record and plot the data. The following supplier product reliabilities have been identified:

▶ **"A"** is a supplier with a perceived reliability of less than 1/10 the specified reliability. It is felt that this product has unacceptably low reliability, and a product purchase offer was not even extended for that reason.

▶ **"B"** is a supplier whose reliability has been evaluated quite extensively by the consumer/customer, being a major supplier of a former product. Recently, some product was used due to parts supply shortage without any current reliability feedback. The reliability of one-half of the specified reliability seems about right from known field failure data. This is typical of product suppliers with reliability needing improvement to meet the latest reliability specifications.

▶ "C" and "D" are both suppliers with product reliability evaluations that meet the customer/consumer specified reliability. They are relatively new suppliers but have an extensive reliability evaluation of this product. The price content for the new reliability was determined in the product purchase price analysis. That amount is about $7.00 for producing reliability to specification. This agrees with our estimate of an $8.00 product reliability cost for Figure 3-7. It is reasonable to assume that competitive product reliabilities should have approximately the same reliability cost content. They both also have a replacement warranty of 3 years.

▶ "E" is a supplier who obtains a premium price of $8.00 for product reliability content. This supplier has for 10 years been the prime producer for this high-reliability product in industry applications. They have a reliability organization that communicates well to customers/consumers throughout the product life and is the undisputed reliability leader in that product. The reliability function of supplier E is already an integral part of that company.

▶ "F" is a supplier of the same product in government projects that furnish another order of magnitude of reliability. The reliability is achieved through extensive design and environmental stress screening. There is no question that this is the most reliable supplier, but the reliability of 100-fold specification adds little value to the customer/consumer product, and the supply volume from supplier F can only satisfy 10% of the requirements during the projected peak production.

It is important to mention that the reason the customer/consumer was sure about the $8.00 premium when we quantified Figure 3-7 was because that was the amount that supplier E was realizing and the amount that supplier F was offered to supply the superior reliability product above the price of the product, just meeting the minimum reliability specification. At this point, we have acquired significant understanding of our reliability business.

In Figure 3-8, you may be represented by any supplier in the customer's/consumer's perception. Figure 3-8 presents an initial view that E is in zone 3 and is probably enjoying a profit from the product reliability. A and B need to evaluate if the potential profit in migrating to zone 3 would be good business. C and D are already suppliers but will realize profit improvement by migrating into zone 3. These secondary suppliers have on occasion a lot of profit to gain from a small change in the customer's/consumer's reliability perception. F needs to evaluate the correct product reliability for the marketplace and reduce the product reliability cost. Consider that you can legitimately be in any of these business positions.

This competitive analysis may be oversimplified, but even in early iterations, it brings to your organization a sense of understanding, communication regarding your competitive business position, and hope to optimize your business profits. In terms of profitability, it is not unusual that the reliability profit factor (RPF) from the supplier with optimum product reliability management realizes a greater profit from the RPF than the average net profit for products realized by all competitors in the market. This is a great incentive for you to optimize your RPF.

Figure 3-7 quantified your reliability relationship of your greatest single (or average) customer/consumer. To achieve a complete step 3 level of reliability business evaluation, you must complete and consolidate this process for all of your customers/consumers. It may not be possible to integrate into a single summary all your quantified reliability customer/consumer relationships. The prime problem is that customers/consumers have a wide variation in evaluations of the same producer, which is why we only evaluate one customer/consumer (and his or her perceptions) at a time. Another fundamental problem is that customers/consumers have varying reliability specifications for your product; therefore, the specification is not a point, but a distribution of points.

RULE 7   In summarizing the quantified customer/consumer evaluations try to reduce all evaluations to a single graphic relationship. This will involve several simplifications:

1. The customer's/consumer's perceived order of supplier reliability should be approximately the same because they rely on approxi-

mately the same validated test data. If this is essentially the case, then consolidate all customers/consumers into a single graphic relationship.

2. The exceptions to the order of supplier reliability among all customers/consumers require some understanding. Is the perceived reliability difference based upon incidents or test data? Are the customers/consumers honest in sharing reliability data? Are they really comparing the same reliability specifications? Your organization should understand these details because they affect the business environment of your product.

3. If your product reliability is perceived to have a broad distribution, you have identified an immediate problem. Your customer/consumer requires education, and your product requires a reliability fix as soon as possible.

The simplification process required to consolidate the entire product reliability market for competitors will identify problems, but these problems must be identified and solved by an effective business organization. The steps of determining your product reliability economics will uncover problems that require action by your business.

Use Figures 3-5 to 3-8 as communications tools. It is beneficial for anyone in the continuing process of reliability business optimization to use for communications the graphics of Figures 3-5 and 3-8 for others to observe and submit their comments. The amount of input questioning the process (particularly the quantified data) will be substantial. This is a natural uncertainty that is prevalent within reliability evaluations. However, this observation and comment process in itself is valuable because it provides a direction toward the understanding, consensus, focus, and action needed to migrate toward optimum product reliability.

Step 4. Product Reliability Strategy

The basic strategy to optimize your product reliability business is easy to articulate but difficult to execute. Figures 3-6 and 3-7 present the concepts that certain "zones" of product reliability are of more value to the customer/consumer and that the customer/consumer views all potential product and service suppliers as a distribution across those zones. Figure 3-8 is a generalized presentation including all suppliers of a customer/consumer. For a specific customer/consumer, your product is one in the distribution.

The optimal business strategy is to migrate your product reliability position into zone 3, where all customers/consumers are willing to pay a premium for your product reliability yet your business is providing a minimum adequate reliability cost. Many examples of products in this category exist in the public and commercial markets. Usually, the profit for existing in zone 3 is so substantial that directed efforts are made to maintain and exploit that position.

From the perceived product reliability business status (Figure 3-7) or the actual evaluated business status (Figure 3-8), you only have to honestly assess the business position of your product and determine the value of migrating to a different competitive reliability position. Remember that reliability is only one business factor to be considered. Again, the case for improving your reliability profit needs a continuing process of refining the justifying data for that improvement.

Figure 3-9 displays data already presented in Figure 3-8 but only details strategic actions of producers D and F. When producers D and F change their

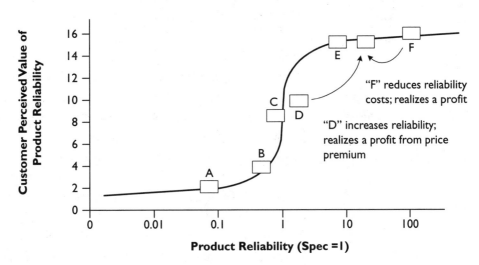

FIGURE 3-9.   Product reliability strategic actions

product reliability (and product reliability cost content) to the position on the curve next to E, they will both be in a position to compete with producer E in an optimum profit realization for their product.

Producer D requires an investment to improve his reliability tenfold. Then D needs to demonstrate, to the customer's/consumer's satisfaction, that the improved reliability places the product in the same zone 3 position with E. This is not difficult within an environment of open communications, honest evaluations, and true concern for the customer/consumer. The additional profit is realized in time by pricing a superior product in a competitive market. It can be quantified and determined as a return on investment (ROI).

Producer F requires a reduction in cost content to compete with a superior product in a competitive market. For producer F to change to the same zone 3 position on the curve and realize a maximum RPF, there must be a reduction in product reliability cost content. The easiest technique is to increase production and spread the fixed cost of product reliability across more units. A second technique is to apply the costs of present product reliability superiority to future products in an investment potential of capturing future profits. A third technique is to engineer a less reliable product to meet the market requirements. This, for example, could include elimination of a final stress screening process that contributes to the present outstanding product reliability. This may seem radical to some devoted to reliability improvement, but remember, we strive for the best business that may not coincide with the highest product reliability.

Strategic changes within a business require excellent data, with clear logic that results in significant information. For strategic reliability changes, the significant information must be accompanied by confidence in your reliability data and personal performance. Do not be frustrated by the fact that most businesses operate with very little understanding of the detail required for a strategic change. This is the prime importance of communicating with graphics similar to Figures 3-5 through 3-9. Repeated presentations of such graphics is the best way of achieving a common consensus and strategic business operation. Figure 3-9 is the basis of strategic action.

Figure 3-9 presents the idea of investing $2.00 per unit to increase the product reliability of E by a magnitude of tenfold. Figure 3-9 also presents the idea that this tenfold increased reliability results in a potential increase in sales price of $7.00. The change to this new reliability would result in a $5.00 profit per unit, which is very substantial. The bad news is that the $5.00 profit cannot fully be realized until the superior product reputation is established in the marketplace. A coordinated sales and customer/consumer education effort assists in establishing a superior product position. The good news is that the tenfold increase in product reliability requires only unit testing costs and control, not large capitol investments up front. This means that a mistake in strategic action is reversible without a substantial business loss.

The strategic goal of F is to sell the product for $1.00 less per unit while spending $6.00 less in the product cost of reliability. F would then realize a net profit of $5.00 per unit. F actually executed this strategy by maximizing the output volume, eliminating two product stress-screening steps, and keeping specific accounting on this product's reliability cost. The specific accounting reduced the shared reliability costs generated by other products in company F.

Are those profits there? Yes they are. There is no trickery in this evaluation. They are the profits resulting from business execution of the optimum product reliability. D and F are changed to the optimum RPF in zone 3. Of course, this is a dynamic situation. D and F are now in direct competition with E and the resultant market shift toward higher product reliability (reliability growth). This is a continuous process, and we can forget about A, B, and C, left behind as noncompetitors in the market.

The product reliability strategy solidly rests upon credible data. It is as important to manage the data input to the strategic decision as managing the strategic decision itself. Some key elements needed in data are

1. For it to be based upon customer/consumer input upon present status and future market forecasting. In the example presented in Figure 3-9, it is crucial for supplier D to understand the potential market volume before committing additional money into the product.
2. For it to be quantified to the greatest extent. The profit potential is in dollars. Try to assess all factors as resulting in dollars.
3. For it to be derived, for greatest credibility, from an ongoing process of reliability business analysis. Manage your reliability business by a set of charts (such as Figures 3-5 to 3-9), that consistently and logically communicate the reliability business economics.

4. For it to be simply presented and understood. Figures 3-5 and 3-6 are not combined because they become too confusing for effective communication. Many excellent ideas are not communicated due to confusing complexity.

The product reliability strategy is a direct response to your business position as presented by Figures 3-6, 3-7, and 3-8. Credible input data to Figures 3-6 to 3-8 is crucial. A common scenario is that the business opportunity for realizing substantial reliability profit is observed, but the strategic move to capitalize upon this opportunity does not occur because the data are not compelling. Within this section, it is assumed that the basic data are accepted as valid through the diligent work of the responsible reliability organization. It is not cynical to say that the key product reliability decisions are typically made during times of product reliability problems. We can't pick a worse time. It is recommended that the process of quantifying the product reliability business as presented by Figures 3-6 through 3-8 be a continuing effort and that strategic decisions be made during the tranquil times. We can also anticipate some of the problems that reduce product reliability evaluation credibility enough so that one would not risk major business actions.

1. The same product may be made to two levels of reliability. The best example is semiconductors made to military and commercial reliability specifications. A continual purchasing dialog existed and exists today about cost optimization of product produced at two established reliability levels.
2. A small segment of your market may be a customer/consumer demanding a comparatively high reliability. The decision to meet that demand is based upon specific business factors. These exceptions are difficult to contain in a simple uniform strategy.
3. Reliability growth is generally prevalent in the business. Old product reliability evaluations tend to understate the product reliability.
4. Customers/consumers may have several product reliability specifications for their applications. This is hard to optimize.
5. The customer/consumer may continually buy products whose reliability is less than the specification. This causes a fictitious product reliability specification.

6. Semantics may blend into uncertainty. Some customers/consumers buy to a product reliability level rather than a product reliability specification. This sometimes results in subjective interpretation of reliability values.
7. Some producers are so willing to stay in a low product reliability market that they do not care to evaluate optimal reliability profit.
8. Some producers feel that the customer/consumer should adjust to the present product reliability specification rather than ask for improved product reliability.

This is a small sample in a great list of policies, practices, and subjective conclusions without supporting valid data that will inhibit the process of establishing the correct strategy for optimizing the product reliability business. All specific problems will have to be presented and considered along with any strategic data. This is extremely important because management's view on missing business factors is not that of effective presentation but of inadequate work quality.

Summary

Product reliability economics motivates organizations to manage and control product reliability in an optimal fashion. In the past, the primary motivation in product reliability economics was the fear of populating the customer/consumer with failing product that would ruin the financial stability and reputation of the producer. This fear of producing bad product generated a global perception that product reliability should be equated to business insurance. In the future, product reliability will become a dominant marketing factor based upon competitive excellence. The fear of producing bad product is still justified, but that aspect will be only a minor factor in future business. What will dominate the marketplace is appropriate reliability for the customer/consumer along with a balance of cost and performance. One of the intentions of *Reliability Simplified* is to motivate product reliability based upon market economics. An entire book could be devoted to that subject.

Chapter 3 presents a universal view of reliability economics, a cost view of reliability known by organizational accounting and a template pattern for quantifying reliability economics as required for management and control of an effective reliability program.

This chapter also greatly expands the market-driven economic view of product reliability because that demonstration is most significant to the average reader of this book. You will probably need to improvise within the demonstrated steps to apply this information to your specific product. As noted, this process never ends and only becomes effective in business through detailed and diligent work.

However, the rewards of quantifying your product reliability, if possible, are extremely lucrative. The superior business positions of companies that understand their product reliability relationships with customers/consumers are not due to luck but are deliberate efforts to understand and exploit the product reliability area of the business. This chapter presents an initial example of developing strategic business moves in product reliability that result in significant profit.

For those organizations that are successful by marketing brand names synonymous with reliability (Timex, Maytag, Toyota, etc.), the steps to quantifying their market position may not be exactly as presented, but the equivalent intent and process are practiced in every case. It is the authors' hope that we all can learn from this observation.

You can spend too much or too little on reliability. Don't do either.

Business Economics is the prime motivation for product reliability.
  —Dr. Les Andersen

References

1. Armand V. Feigenbaum, *Total Quality Control,* 3rd ed. (New York: McGraw-Hill, 1983).

CHAPTER **4**

Interpreting Product Failure Data

You know you are in trouble when your data look good and your customers are frowning

—H. J. HARRINGTON

Introduction

Managers should read Chapter 4 to acquire an understanding of basic product failure dynamics. This chapter presents how product failures are generally understood only through oversimplified measurements. Many management decisions are made using oversimplified product failure measurements that often lead to bad decisions. You will be taught the right questions to ask so that the best possible decision can be reached.

Engineers should read Chapter 4 to grasp the importance of understanding product failures in detail. They will also learn to understand the priorities of failure-mode elimination, the business benefits of specific failure-mode elimination, and how to audit existing efforts to balance product reliability improvement efforts with the validated field failure modes. For the engineer,

understanding failures is essential in providing priority and direction to product reliability efforts.

The misunderstanding of your physical product failures (reliability) is a primary cause of bad product reliability management. In existing products, reliability improvement relies heavily on the identification and elimination of product failures. Product reliability efforts typically proceed without a complete specific understanding of the present product failures or a projected optimum goal for product failures and failure rates appropriate for the application. The purpose of Chapter 4 is to provide an understanding of the various basic aspects of fundamental product failures. This clear understanding of product failures is required to attain optimum product reliability. The use of graphics to communicate product failure data and information is presented in this chapter. Communication tools are required for successfully implementing a meaningful reliability program in an organization.

Product Failure Concepts

Failure Rates during Product Use Time

Every group of business managers and engineers has an intuitive understanding of reliability. That intuitive understanding is substantially correct; however, it cannot be directly applied to most reliability issues at hand. A lack of expertise is observed in the understanding of product failures. This section bridges the gap between the general intuitive feeling of product reliability (failures) and the workable business definition of your product reliability (failures).[1]

Figure 4-1 shows the product failure-rate "bathtub" curve, so called because its shape resembles a bathtub. The early time failures are also called initial failures, early life failures, etc., and the random failures are often called normal operating period, stable period, etc. In this book, the segments of the bathtub curve are consistently labeled as presented in Figure 4-1.

Figure 4-1 presents a plot of product failure rate (failures/time) versus time. It is recognized by most business managers and engineers. This is a failure rate model generalized to all products. The curve makes intuitive sense and agrees with these general observations:

1. Initially, the product failure rate starts at a high level, primarily due to failures caused by product design that occur in early customer/con-

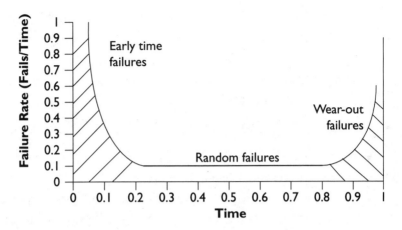

FIGURE 4-1. The "bathtub" curve

sumer usage life, intrinsic manufacturing defects, and product defects that initially escape detection at final test. The classic example is the returning of a new automobile to the dealer to fix problems. Fortunately, effective effort by automobile manufacturers has reduced this practice to a memory. The failure mode in the initial product operating use period, plotted in Figure 4-1, is called early time failures (ETFs). The ETF failure rate declines with time as the ETF defect population becomes depleted.

2. A second mode of product failure appears (actually hidden within the ETF from the beginning of customer/consumer usage) when the ETF failure-rate curve decreases into a constant failure rate with time curve caused by random defects in the product population. This failure mode, plotted in the middle of Figure 4-1, is called the random or the flat part of the bathtub curve.

3. Eventually, in addition to the random failure rate, the product population exhibits failures caused by physical wear out of the product. The failure mode is called wear out.

In Figure 4-1, which has universal recognition, we encounter misunderstood concepts caused by not defining in detail the common relationship:

▶ Figure 4-1 is commonly called the universal product reliability curve or the bathtub curve. However, it is not a product reliability curve, which would be a measure of surviving (and failed) product with time. Figure 4-1 is actually a product failure-rate curve.

The **product failure rate** can be defined in two ways:
1. As the ratio of failed items to the initial amount of items (in time).
2. As the ratio of failed items to the surviving amount of items (in time).

In defining the plot, have we measured failures (and rates) including or not including replacement of failed items?

This overlooked factor can make a significant difference in values of the product failure-rate data. For purposes of Figures 4-2 to 4-5, we consider that the product failure rate is a ratio of failures (in time) to the initial amount of items.

The importance of each of these misunderstandings may not be crucial to your product reliability activity. However, these poorly understood, ambiguous interpretations contribute to a broad superficial view of reliability. These are typical examples of how conceptual confusion originates.

Figure 4-1 provides an introductory concept into the subject of your specific product reliability. It explicitly presents that product will fail initially with a high ETF failure rate, settle down to a lower random failure rate, and eventually will fail due to wear out of the intended product function. This is good common sense based upon general experience.

Figures 4-2 to 4-5 are relationships that modify Figure 4-1 for application to your specific product failures. Figures 4-2 to 4-5 provide a better description of your specific product failures for communications and action.

Figure 4-2 is a product failure-rate curve representing products of relatively low failure rates and essentially infinite product use lifetimes. Infinite lifetime means that the product will never reach wear out during its designed operating lifetime. A wear-out failure mode is not present in Figure 4-2. Some solid-state electronics products perform according to the curve in Figure 4-2. Figure 4-2 presents a category of initial or installation product failures along with the ETFs. These initial or installation failures require management, even though they were missing from our intuitive bathtub curve (Figure 4-1).

Figure 4-3 is a product failure-rate curve typified by relatively high failure rates with designed wear out. An example is an incandescent light bulb.

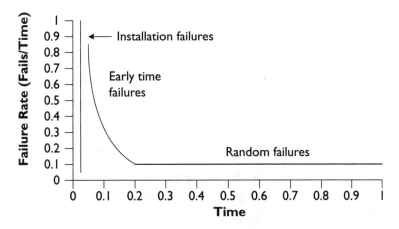

FIGURE 4-2. **Product that doesn't wear out**

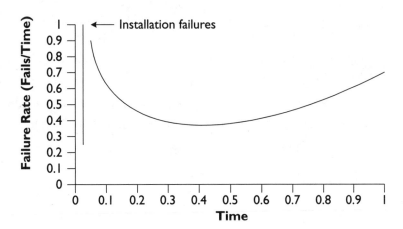

FIGURE 4-3. **Product designed for complete wear out**

The bulb, designed for optimum luminescence to power efficiency, will wear out in about 1,000 to 1,500 hours. The designed efficiency determines the product reliability. The reliability curve has a short ETF and random failure period to about 900 operating hours. After 900 hours, Figure 4-3 presents a wear out increase of failure rate with time until about 1,600 operating hours (in this example). At 1,600 operating hours, the entire bulb population has failed. There isn't anything wrong with this reliability curve. In many cases, the optimum business is to design the product unreliability. In the case of incandescent light bulbs, the customers/consumers have created a compromise between a light bulb designed for efficiency and a light bulb produced for maximum lifetime of operation. The current incandescent light bulbs are produced to an optimum specification responding to customer/consumer requirements.

Figure 4-4 is a product failure-rate curve that represents a product with extensive reliability content, using all available techniques to prevent failures. A good example is an aircraft. The aircraft is engineered with safety as a prime objective. Techniques for improved reliability such as redundant systems and safety mechanical maintenance factors are utilized. Programs of inspection for defects and periodic maintenance is strictly enforced. The aircraft reliability is maintained through a continuous effort of identified effective techniques. The reliability record of commercial aircraft has been commendable. It is truly riskier to drive to the airport than to fly on the plane.

The aircraft example provides several unique factors to consider:

▶ The airline passengers are discreetly denied reliability data as airline operating procedure. Passengers cannot consider nor compare alternate aircraft reliabilities.

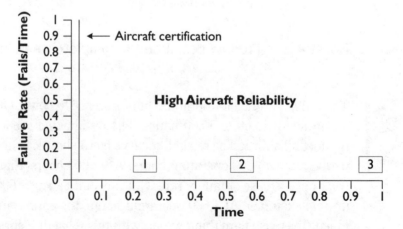

FIGURE 4-4.   Product with a very low failure rate

▶ The total aircraft reliability effort, considering the complexity of the aircraft function and operation, attests to the effective success of product reliability engineering.

▶ Reliability maintenance, a subject not explicitly included in this text, is a significant part of reliability in some products.

Figure 4-4 presents a failure-rate versus operating-time curve with no ETFs or wear out. It can hardly be understood in terms of the product failure concepts of Figure 4-1. The failures are really considered as a series of incidents, rather than a failure rate.

Now it is your turn to generate a failure rate with time graphic for your specific product. Several examples of various products are presented in Figures 4-2 through 4-4. Figure 4-5 is an example that represents a product typical of the commercial market where an average failure rate is plotted to reduce the product failure behavior to a single value. Figure 4-5 is appropriate for the vast majority of commercial competitive marketplace products.

Note: It is in your best interest to know exactly what your product failure-rate curve is, and communicate your unique product failure rate with time relationship rather than superficially manage according to the intuitive concept (Figure 4-1).

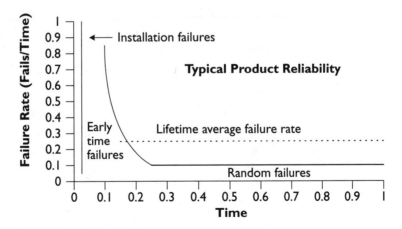

FIGURE 4-5.   An example of your product failure rate with time

This step seems so elementary that it appears to be trivial. There is nothing further from the truth. The ultimate success of your product reliability program depends upon a consensus agreement of basic failure dynamics. A clear descriptive model, like Figure 4-5, is key to communication of a reliability program and provides an introduction to the required fundamental concepts presented in the remainder of this chapter.

Reliability Growth

The initially shipped products often have a higher failure rate than ones shipped later in a production cycle. This section will focus on the product changes with time that improve product reliability.

Product modifications improve reliability with production time and experience for several reasons:

1. It is rare that all failure modes, which can only be eliminated after valid identification, can be identified in the product prior to actual customer/consumer use. Changes to products based upon identification and elimination of early customer/consumer failures will improve product reliability. Operating experience is required to identify and eliminate these failure modes.
2. The manufacturing process may introduce product failure modes never identified in the product development process. Engineering changes in products should be made immediately after identification to eliminate manufacturing-induced defective product.
3. The variations in customer/consumer environment may induce failure modes never anticipated nor tested during product development. These environmental factors are minimized by "ruggedizing" the product or creating the suitable product environment.
4. New components, with a higher reliability, will be used rather than those initially used for manufacturing. This will improve the actual product reliability during the production cycle.

These four conditions frequently occur to improve product reliability when a product development and manufacturing cycle is proceeding in a normal manner. These main four conditions (and others) to reliability issues cause the observed phenomenon called *reliability growth.*

Figures 4-1 to 4-5 do not define whether the failure rate with time represents a projected average for an entire anticipated production of items, a projected amount for a specific vintage of product, or a value based upon customer/consumer use of specific product. Reliability growth is another source of fundamental failure-rate misunderstanding. When creating or interpreting a product failure graphic, be very sure how the graphic was generated and what product the graphic does or does not represent. The graphical communication of product reliability rarely explicitly states the vintage of product represented by the product reliability graph. This in turn leads to immediate bad assumptions and conclusions.

The typical product failure rate versus time relationship for the typical initial four production quarters of manufacturing is presented in Figure 4-6, which shows

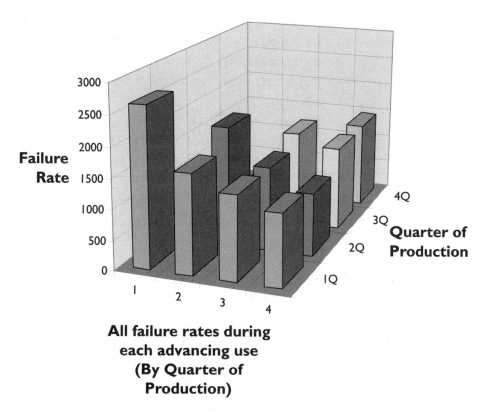

**All failure rates during
each advancing use
(By Quarter of
Production)**

FIGURE 4-6.   Reliability growth of a product (as a failure rate)

▶ Failure rate in the z axis (scale: 0 to 3,000 failures/quarter)
▶ Quarter of production in the y axis (scale: 1Q to 4Q)
▶ Quarters of customer/consumer product use in the x axis (scale: 1 to 4)

What is being measured is the failure rate from each quarter's product during periods of use. Figure 4-6 is a three-dimensional graphic that presents the first four quarters of product (vintages) and their failure rates during customer/consumer use periods (up to four quarters). Note the following detail:

1. The product with the highest failure rate during operation is the product made in the initial quarter of production. Consumers know that the initial production has high failure rates. The initial quarter of production has the least reliability improvements (reliability growth) and is subject to the maximum ETF.

2. Compare the failure rate of the product made during any quarter of production in its first quarter of use with the failure rate of that made in the next quarter in its first quarter of use. The trend toward lower failure rates (reliability growth) is apparent. The product failure rate improves with time as the product design and manufacturing process becomes "debugged."

3. The total product failures at any point during a product cycle is (failure rate of a certain product for a time period) × (the volume of the same certain product during the same time period) integrated over all time periods.

4. Figure 4-6 exhibits a common phenomenon regarding the reliability of product vintages shortly after all reliability improvements have created substantial reliability growth. The failure rates are plotted at one year by quarter of production (vintage). Note that a relatively higher failure rate occurs from product from the first quarter of production, due to initial problems still present in the product, and from product from the last quarter of product, due to its higher ETF rate on a normal reliability versus time plot. This creates a "saddle" in the failure rate after one year, as observed in Figure 4-6.

5. Fortunately, the volume rate of manufacturing product usually increases simultaneously with the reliability growth. This results in a relatively small fraction of product in customer/consumer use that has

the initial high failure rate. The initial product reliability is improved through failure-mode identification and elimination. A relatively few unreliable items, initially produced, may negatively influence the customer/consumer. This phenomenon must be clearly understood for your new product when you negotiate with your customers/consumers regarding product reliability. Orient your customers/consumers to the specifics of your product failure rates with a chart like that in Figure 4-6. This is critical, since reputations are made during the marketing review of early products.

Figure 4-6 is a three-dimensional product reliability curve plotted for specific vintages of product, so that it can include the reliability growth of that product in one presentation. This figure, and particularly the numbers used to generate the plot, is a vast improvement over the simplified concept of the bathtub product reliability curve. There is nothing complicated about Figure 4-6. All that is required is a definition of a product failure and an accurate collection and projection of failure data.

What initially appears to be a simple concept of your product failure rate quickly becomes complex and requires diligent focus to obtain key measurements required for management. It has been observed that measurement numbers are frequently used without an understanding of the detailed product failure process. Note that this exercise of clearly understanding failures can be completed with little or no quantified data or with the use of mathematical tools. It has been observed that product reliability management often believes that the mathematical application of reliability principles eliminates the need for understanding the fundamental failure details. Prepare yourself for a disaster!

Interpretation of Mean Time before Failure (MTBF)

The acronym MTBF may be used in many texts to indicate mean time between failures.

The classical meaning of **Mean Time Between Failures** is the average time to failure of a repairable product plus the average time to repair or replace the product (return function to system).

MTBF is becoming more understood as a measure of average time to failure of nonrepairable product with zero repair and replacement time. In *Reliability Simplified,* MTBF is mean time before failure, assuming only operating product time. If MTBF is used to indicate something different than mean time before failure, it will be stated at that time.

The MTBF is the universal measure of product reliability. It is a single value used widely as a measure of product reliability for consideration by the customer/consumer. Product reliability, the true measurement by definition, is not commonly used to express its own value. MTBF is used as simply the average time to failure:

$$\text{MTBF} = \text{Total time of use/Total failures}$$

$$\text{Example: MTBF} = 20,000 \text{ hour/12 failures} = 1,667 \text{ hours}$$

MTBF is the simplest single value that represents your product's reliability to the customer/consumer. MTBF is a concept so simple that the MTBF number of a specific product has an aura of accuracy. It avoids the complexities of the measurement of product reliability with time by introducing a simple linear relationship that never accurately represents, without introducing supporting detail, the product reliability. This allows the measurement of MTBFs to be only an artifact of underlying conditions. The following examples will illustrate deficiencies in the MTBF measurements:

1. *Total time of use is an undefined variable.* An automobile may have an MTBF of 880 hours per failure. However, the MTBF during the automobile's first 3000 hours of operation depends upon many factors. Does the time relate to when the engine is idling or when the automobile is moving? Many taxicabs have substantial engine idle time. Does the time relate to active driving or storage conditions? If the automobile exceeds 10 years in age, failures occur due to rubber seals and chemical corrosion independent of the use time. Does the MTBF time depend upon use in stop-and-go driving relative to freeway driving? Wear out, a very familiar phenomenon, is absent from this calculation. So an automobile MTBF is meaningless unless the conditions of the use time are understood and properly measured. The variables

are so great that an MTBF is not available for automobiles, although advertising stresses product reliability in an abstract manner.

Semiconductor products have significant MTBF variation in use time. The greatest variation in MTBF stems from the fact that the same semiconductor product operates within a system in several different applications in varying degrees of active switching. It is not really the system power-on time that influences MTBF, but the failure mechanisms of each application caused by stress during actual circuit switching. The main stresses are temperature causing increased atomic diffusion and mechanical stress. Therefore, it is not use time, but application that determines MTBF. Major variables are start-and-stop stress cycles, where the semiconductor operates within a voltage and temperature environment, and voltage and radiation tolerance. So a semiconductor MTBF is also meaningless unless the input variables are understood. The use time alone does not produce an MTBF of value. Because of the great variation in use of MTBF during applications, the consumer designers are aware of and account for application equivalent use time.

2. *Total failures is an unspecified variable.* Most people have a general idea of what constitutes a product failure but have extreme difficulty in defining specific failures.

A reliability product failure by definition is that product is no longer performing its specified function. It has failed! Now let's look closer at failures returned from the customer/consumer.

A. The failure may be a physical condition that prevents the product from performing its intended function under anticipated use environment. A product may be mechanically broken or worn beyond specified operational tolerance. It is the open circuit in a burned out electric bulb or a broken valve within an automobile engine. The physical failure condition is usually defined as catastrophic. However, the failure is considered definitely as catastrophic only if it occurs within about the first half of the anticipated (and advertised) product lifetime. If the failure occurs in the last half of product lifetime, the failure is usually considered as part of the distribution of normal product wear out. This is the origin of product warranty considerations. Notice that there is a "gray" zone of uncertainty that separates catastrophic product failures from anticipated product wear out. Not everyone considers a wear out an MTBF specified failure. MTBF does not address this issue.

B. The failure may occur during or after the product is operating outside of its designed environmental limit. A home computer being used within a paper mill with the presence of reactive chemicals, on the average, will fail more often than if used within the home environment for which it was designed. A drill designed for occasional home use will fail more often and wear out sooner if used daily in construction work. The product reliability is directly related to the use environmental conditions. It is not rare to observe differing failure rates among customers/consumers for this reason. What is the MTBF?

C. The failure may occur because the product does not perform within a system in which the system component interfaces are not specified. This applies when your product is part of a larger operating system. A plastic structural product may not work because it swells upon being exposed to the chemicals of the system. An electronic interface circuit causes errors in signal flow because of undefined electrical noise in the system. However, these explanations for failure are mute because this product has no measurable problem. An agonizing situation exists when some products work and some don't within the system, and there is no measurable difference in the product functional tests. There are situations when switching only one component will make both systems function properly. These are the pseudofailures that are labeled no trouble found (NTF). You may encounter NTFs as a significant contributor to your product failures.

D. Another factor that can give misleading results occurs when an error in another part of a product causes undue stress to be applied to a component causing it to fail, or worse still, weakening it so that it will fail in the near future. Typical examples are a short that can weaken a solder joint in another part of the machine or a transient mechanical failure that can bind up a gear train, causing one of the shafts to warp.

E. Administrative error is a significant contribution to the number of defined failures. In the case of a system, your product may be included in a mass replacement technique used to restore system function. The priority is to return the system to operation. The components (your product) are considered a failure by default, although that fact has not been validated. You will therefore have an NTF failure due to nothing more than administrative procedure. Another administrative error occurs when your product is damaged during maintenance and repair of the customer's/consumer's system. Another administrative error occurs when your product is deemed unacceptable for a portion of the customer/consumer usage, then ruled defective for all applications.

Another form of error not well categorized (we will call it administrative) is when incorrect functional product is sent to the customer/consumer due to lack of controlling engineering levels or not reviewing the changing customer/consumer demands. The reason for the product failing is that it is the wrong functional product. That really has nothing to do with product reliability as we understand the subject; yet these are considered failures. Are all of these failures part of your MTBF?

The MTBF is the prime measure of product reliability. Figure 4-7 presents an example of types of failures within a commercial product. It is convenient for a producer to adjust his MTBF value by excluding a Figure 4-7

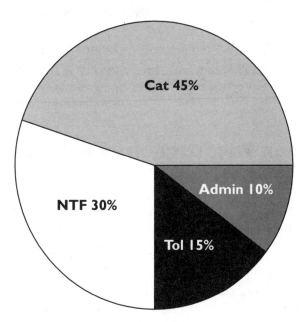

FIGURE 4-7. Composition of product failures

category as unimportant without the consumer knowledge. This makes MTBF values, and especially comparisons, less than worthless unless the precise details involved in the MTBF calculations are known.

MTBF is a prevalent measure that communicates product reliability in an overly simplistic manner. There are many detailed inputs that influence the validity of any MTBF number and must be understood before MTBF can be used in a rational, controlled, product reliability program. As a reliability-conscious engineer and manager, you should ask the following questions to learn about your product failures:

▶ Do we have an MTBF for our product?
▶ Why do we need an MTBF?
▶ What are the details of total time and total failures used to define our MTBF?
▶ Is there an organization-wide consensus about MTBF product failures?
▶ Do we have an idea about the variation of failure rate (and failures) with time that reflects reliability growth and the proper product reliability curve (Figure 4-6)? The reliability growth variation in your product may invalidate the use of an MTBF number.

These questions probe qualitative details that are relatively simple in concept. The answers are required if you are going to measure your products using MTBF as a key performance indicator.

Information Your Organization Should Know

In the last two sections, we focused upon the fundamentals of product failures and MTBF measurements. The reason for investigating these basic product reliability factors is that you probably will have more difficulty changing your organization's culture that is based upon established oversimplified concepts than implementing all of the mathematical tools and physical techniques presented in *Reliability Simplified*. What is required to establish an optimum product reliability program is to re-evaluate your old product failure and MTBF concepts in a detailed manner to effectively characterize your product. This re-evaluation must be communicated to all individuals affecting your reliability program. This establishes a common platform for all to initiate your optimum product reliability program. In our opinion, this is the most difficult task for any reader of *Reliability Simplified*. But if you bypass this aggravating, and seemingly unimportant step in establishing your product reliability program, your final goal of optimum product reliability will never be achieved due to lack of full organizational support.

We strongly suggested that you use graphics such as Figures 4-5 and 4-7 to communicate the consensus values of your product failure rates and MTBF. An organizational consensus of product failure types and MTBF details is crucial in making the correct decisions about your product reliability. You can expect some disagreement and ulterior motives directed toward these very fundamental values. This is just part of the path toward establishing a better product reliability program that will provide profits to the business.

In addition to the re-evaluation of your product failure rate and MTBF, it is an opportunity to present some additional fundamental information to your organization. This information may not directly apply to your specific business operation and probably has not been articulated within your business organization. However, these basic product reliability concepts should be clearly understood by people concerned about reliability.

Figure 4-8 presents a graphic that is very useful in determining the common consensus of all factors affecting your product reliability. This figure is

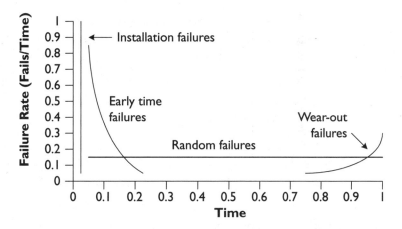

FIGURE **4-8.**   **Your product with separated failure modes**

an example of a current estimate of the entire product's (past, present, and future) failure rate with time fit into a bathtub curve with distinct early time, random, and wear-out failures. It provides an initial platform from which to understand your product failures. It is quite effective in summarizing the divergence of opinion within your organization by forcing everyone to estimate failures by individual failure modes. Figure 4-8 is a graphic with numbers in the x and y axes. We are beginning to quantify our established concepts, which is exactly the reason for using this chart. It will convey an initial estimate of your specific product reliability and will prompt the next step of input of accurate data to substantiate an accurate graphical relationship. Remember that everyone gets to see this operational chart.

The random failure events presented in Figure 4-9 can be due to many unrelated variables causing the failures during customer/consumer use. However, a distinct problem with bad lots of manufacturing product can hide within the random failure portion of the product reliability curve. An all-too-common phenomenon of product reliability occurs as failures over the random portion of the reliability curve with the root cause of failures occurring in a short manufacturing period of time. These bad lots or segments of product are referred to as "maverick lots." Figure 4-9 presents a bad product day. An example would be when the key process rinse to remove corrosive chemical was omitted. The rinse process step was only absent one day, but the re-

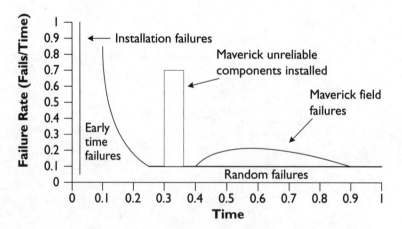

FIGURE 4-9.   The results of maverick lots

sulting product failures during customer/consumer use may spread over a period of several months. Without a failure analysis, the maverick lot would remain undetected, and failures would be random in time. Does your organization recognize this failure dynamic? Do you have indications of maverick lots with significant failure rates within your shipped product? What fraction of your random failures do you attribute to maverick lots? Maverick lots can only be detected with an appropriate database and failure analysis. Very similar to ETFs being significantly a problem of product failure-mode identification, maverick lots may be plaguing your manufacturing reliability throughout the product manufacturing period. Your manufacturing operation may be very sensitive to such an evaluation; so this topic is best introduced at a fundamental review level.

Figure 4-10 is the final evolution of the Figure 4-1 generality. Figure 4-10 expresses the contributions of our product reliability fundamentals. Yours will be unique to your product but will still contain specific significant contributors. The operation benefit of Figure 4-10 is amazing. In one chart, the rationalization of MTBF and the significant contributors to product failures are presented. Within an organization such a chart usually creates heated discussion and always prompts for active response by responsible organizations. What product program manager wants to pay for a warranty that is primarily based upon NTFs and administrative error? The product program

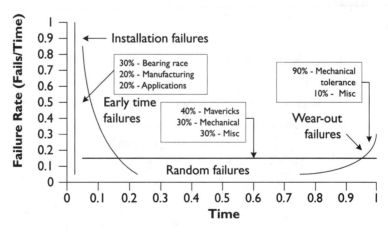

FIGURE 4-10.   Unbundling your product reliability

manager will pay only for the "real" failures and will demand that the business unit fix their "business" problem. What executive would defer action when he or she suspects that the product reliability problem may stem from maverick lots caused by inadequate manufacturing control? He or she should evaluate the customer's/consumer's failures to establish the true situation and take corrective action. What manufacturing organization continues to operate at poor yield to perpetuate a poor product reliability design? An engineering change to fix the problem is requested. These are all business issues that become active when the details of your present product reliability are investigated. This process leads directly to mathematical tools and physical techniques required for problem solution. Your required reliability program is actively initiated by analysis and communications of problems.

The information graphically presented in Figures 4-7 to 4-10 is so elementary and so basic that it is typically bypassed in product reliability development in favor of working with abstract concepts of reliability measurements or action programs based upon undefined goals. As stated at the beginning of the chapter, the inability to understand the details of product failures is the number one reason for bad reliability decisions. Knowing and understanding the details of failures is a necessary condition for control of product reliability.

Summary

The subjects critical to the clear understanding of product reliability are presented in the following:

▶ The universal product reliability bathtub curve is developed into a specific communication tool for your product reliability. This graphic display of your specific product reliability is essential for communication and organizational agreement of present product reliability status and future product reliability goals.

▶ The subject of product reliability growth is addressed to clarify this commonly misunderstood subject. Again, it is recommended that a graphic presentation (e.g., Figure 4-6) be used to explain your reliability growth factor to people in your organization unfamiliar with the subject and to customers/consumers specifically interested in your total reliability during the production cycle.

▶ MTBF is often a single value used to measure a product's reliability. The underlying complexity of determining that single MTBF is explained using familiar examples. Your clear understanding of the input variables used to calculate MTBF is required to confidently use the MTBF number as input to product reliability decisions.

▶ Interpreting product failure data is prioritized by quantification of all failure modes, even if the first estimate is derived from a distribution of opinions. Also, the insidious existence of maverick manufacturing lots is presented for all not familiar with this phenomenon. Finally, an assignment of failure cause and effect is presented as the most effective (and the most controversial) method of interpreting your ongoing product reliability.

There were no new concept nor difficult practice presented in this chapter. However, unless the product failures and associated reliability measurement techniques are understood in detail, your product reliability program will lack optimum effectiveness. Remember: This is the most frequent problem relating to inadequate product reliability management and control.

References

1. Armand V. Feigenbaum, *Total Quality Control,* 3rd ed. (New York: McGraw-Hill, 1983).

CHAPTER

5

Product Reliability Mathematics

Reliability is a probability concept.

Introduction

Managers should read this chapter to learn the fundamentals of product reliability mathematics. The abbreviated descriptions of common distributions are useful as quick references to product reliability mathematical applications.

Engineers should understand all of Chapter 5 to establish fluency in using the mathematics of product reliability. The mathematical description of product reliability is based upon probability and statistics and expressed by probability distributions. Chapter 5 will assist in specifying your own product reliability and provide understanding required to formulate proper inquiries into the product reliability of your suppliers. The understanding of probability distributions to properly characterize your product reliability is required for all engineers affecting your product reliability.

Distributions

Product reliability uses the mathematics of probability and statistics, which is expressed in probability distributions.

Distributions are required for measuring and controlling product failures and understanding the value of failures through sample measurements rather than fixed values.

The use of distributions, probability, and statistics often creates an aura of unfamiliarity and misunderstanding related to product reliability. In this section we will provide a comprehensive view of the fundamental distributions used to define and communicate our product reliability. Understanding of the fundamentals of distribution is required for the applications presented later in this chapter and later chapters.

Variation *in product quality must be constantly studied within batches of product, on processing equipments, between different lots of the same article, on critical quality characteristics and standards, in regard to the pilot runs of a newly designed article. This variation may best be studied by the analysis of samples selected from the product lots or from units produced by the processing equipments.*
ARMAND V. FEIGENBAUM[1]

The Bernoulli Distribution

The primary building block of probability is the Bernoulli distribution, as represented in equation 1:

$$p(x) = p(1 - \mathrm{p})^{1-x} \quad x = 0,1 \tag{1}$$

The **Bernoulli distribution** specifies that the probability $p(x)$ is related to the occurrence of x only for the values of $x = 0$ and $x = 1$. Equation I represents the simplest case of where a result is not certain but has two probable outcomes.

An example familiar to everyone is traveling by automobile to the same destination by the same route. You will stop at every stoplight depending upon the color of the stoplight. Now, consider leaving your home by automobile by the same route and approaching the first stoplight. The light is only green or red. We can mathematically represent the green light as a "1" and the red light as a "0." The decimal percentage distribution (value) of the variable "0" and "1" for the first stoplight is called the random probability distribution given by equation 1.

Note that the light can be only green or red ($x = 1,0$), that the total probability is 1.000 (the light has to be either green or red), and that $p(x)$ is always given as a decimal fraction. A single event (e.g., approaching light) is called a *Bernoulli trial*. The outcome of many Bernoulli trials can be presented as a distribution shown in Figure 5-1.

Figure 5-1 represents a Bernoulli distribution of an outcome probability of a single event. All we have said is that the outcome of a single event can be represented by a probability distribution of a random variable.

Now, where do we get the probability from? It comes from three sources:

1. It is based upon a large number of observations (trials) in an analogous situation. In this example, maybe we assume that the probability distribution of green and red lights is the same as another route.
2. It is based upon physical determination. In this example, maybe we know the city has a timer set for the green light to be on 0.20 of the time.

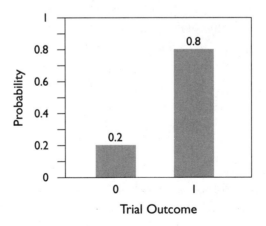

FIGURE 5-1. **The Bernoulli distribution**

3. It is estimated from a small sample (statistic). In this example, maybe we observe the first 10 approaches to the light and estimate the probability of a green light from that sample.

The Binomial Distribution

A single Bernoulli trial sort of just states the obvious. However, a sequence of a fixed number of Bernoulli trials is very interesting and useful. It is called the binomial distribution.

$$P(x) = \frac{n!}{x!(n-x)!}(p)^x(1-p)^{n-x} \tag{2}$$

Where x = number of successes in a sequence of n trials, n = fixed number of single trials, and p = probability of success of a single trial. The parameters of the binary distribution are p and n. The binomial distribution is called a discrete distribution because it can only represent integer values.

Assume that we drive toward that same stoplight five times a week. How many green lights can one encounter in a week? One can deduce that the observed value of green lights for one week can only possibly be 0, 1, 2, 3, 4, and 5. In equation 2, this is the number of successes in a sequence of n trials. What is the probability that I will have one of these outcomes (values) for one week? I cannot say anything with certainty about a specific week, but I can determine, to a degree of confidence, the probability of observing these values when observing many weeks by use of equation 2.

The binomial equation, and the following probability distributions, use mathematical principles to quantify the uncertainty inherent in physical systems. Distributions are the only way to measure and control uncertainty. Remember that the nature of product reliability is that the failure time (reliability) of a single item is uncertain, but the distribution of time to failure of many items can be determined and used to manage the product reliability.

Using the binomial equation to generate the probability distribution, Figure 5-2 represents a distribution of values for green lights in each week when the probability of a single green light is 0.20.

Figure 5-2 is a graphic of equation 2 presenting the distribution of values of a weekly number of green lights and their probabilities randomly encoun-

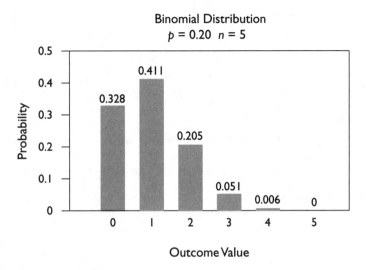

Binomial Distribution
$p = 0.20$ $n = 5$

FIGURE 5-2.   A binomial distribution

tered at the first stoplight. Its powerful application comes from the ability to detect an unnatural occurrence to this distribution even though the individual events do not occur with a certain outcome. For instance, what if your spouse tells you that this stoplight has been observed to be green for the last three straight weeks? Based upon Figure 5-2, we know that a single week of five green lights occurs less than one time in a thousand weeks. So the three straight weeks of green lights is very unnatural. Probably something is wrong. The stoplight's green probability may have changed (e.g., a defective switch), the event is no longer random (e.g., the light has a greater proportion of green in the morning), or maybe your spouse is not properly reporting the data. So don't believe your spouse's assertion until the data are validated.

Figure 5-2 and all binomial equations have the following rules:

1. The probability distribution is for a fixed number (n) of identical trials.
2. The trials are independent.
3. Binomial means each trial has only two outcomes.
4. The probability comes from an external estimate.
5. The probability is the same for every trial.

The importance of a binomial distribution is that it is easily understood, is a common-sense introduction to the many rules of probability and statistics, and is generated often by physical constraints. Gambling—whether in the form of throwing dice, playing cards, or spinning a roulette wheel—is easily understood by binary statistics.

You may encounter the binary distribution in applications where the product may be considered $p(x)$ to fail or to survive $[p(1 - x)]$.

The Poisson Distribution

The Poisson equation describes the binary distribution at conditions of high n and low p.

$$P(x) = \frac{\lambda^x}{x!}e^{-\lambda} \tag{3}$$

Where $\lambda = np$, $x =$ number of successes in a sequence of n trials, and $n =$ fixed number of single trials.

The **Poisson distribution** is a discrete probability distribution of values $p(x)$, obtained in randomly selecting a sample of n items from a source with a fixed value of x. The application of this distribution to sampling of product to detect failure levels is extremely important.

The classical example of the Poisson distribution is presented in Figure 5-3. It is a graph of the probabilities of values when one randomly samples a huge jar of jelly beans where exactly 2% of black (licorice) jelly beans are randomly mixed within the jar. How many black jelly beans can one expect to observe in samples of n size?

1. Let us have a sample size of 100, and with a 2% level of black jelly beans; we have a lambda of 2.0 for use in our equation.
2. The number of black jelly beans can be 0, 1, 2, . . . , 100. The maximum black beans in our sample is 100. We intuitively would not expect to pick 100 black jelly beans at random.
3. So all we do is calculate the probable value (equation 3) for each discrete value of black jelly bean and plot in Figure 5-3. We stop at $n =$ 6 because of the meaningless low probabilities for obtaining at ran-

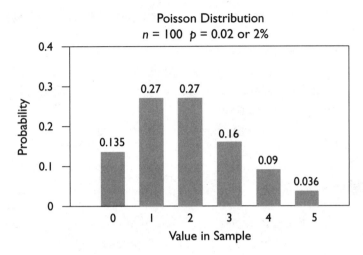

FIGURE 5-3. **A Poisson distribution of jelly beans.**

dom more than six black beans in any sample. That coincides with our intuition that randomly picking more than six black jelly beans is quite rare.

The powerful applications of the Poisson distribution are derived from its ability to detect unnatural deviations in the expected distribution. For instance, say that we were mistaken, and actually 10% of the jelly beans were black. The event of drawing at random six or more black jelly beans is less than 2 times in 100 when the black jelly beans are 2% (Figure 5-3) but now will occur in about 90% of the samples. So we can statistically determine, by sampling , a change in the expected value and expect that change to probably be present in the bulk population.

The Poisson distribution is similar to the binomial distribution for samples of low p and high n. Note that the shape of Figures 5-2 and 5-3 are very similar. Again, certain application rules apply:

1. The lambda is a determined or assumed value.
2. The measured item is randomly mixed within sampled composition.
3. The model presents a mathematically exact distribution in samples.

The Gaussian or Normal Distribution

The most widely used distribution is the **Gaussian or normal distribution**. It is useful because it closely represents the natural distribution of variation in values when many small random effects interact to influence the measured outcome.

The following equation generates the Gaussian or normal distribution.

$$p(x) = \frac{1}{\sigma\sqrt{2\pi}}e^{-(1/2)[(x-\mu)^2/\sigma^2]} \tag{4}$$

The parameters of the normal distribution are the Greek letters μ (mu) and σ (sigma). The parameter values are generated from the measured data points comprising the distribution and represent the average value μ and variability of the data distribution sigma.

The argument of equation 4,

$$\frac{1}{\sigma\sqrt{2\pi}}$$

normalizes the equation so that the entire distribution of frequency probabilities is equal to 1.

The normal distribution is a continuous function, rather than a distribution of discrete values such as presented in the Bernoulli, binary, and Poisson examples. Since the total value of the integrated normal probability distribution is 1.00, the probability between any two x values (x_1 and x_2 in Figure 5-4) can be simply calculated by evaluating, as a decimal fraction, the integrated area of the normal distribution function between the two x values.

The normal distribution is important in product reliability because it furnishes a mathematical tool that we use to establish control over products and processes that already possess a natural variation.

It is not the purpose of *Reliability Simplified* to investigate in detail the properties of these distributions that are models for our product's behavior. You can expand your knowledge with further education. However, these distributions model the behavior of our product and are commonly used as tools to achieve product reliability control.

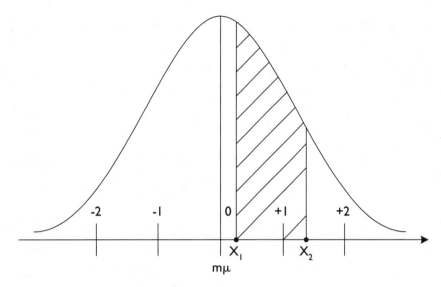

FIGURE 5-4.   The normal distribution

The Bernoulli, binary, Poisson, and normal distributions closely represent the real product reliability behavior. Each is a special perspective of the same physical phenomenon based upon probability. In fact, when the discrete distributions (binary and Poisson) have a probability of 0.3 and a sample number of 30, they closely match with the normal distribution. This is to be expected, because they all describe the same physical phenomenon.

The Exponential Reliability Distribution

Introduction

A note is required here about nomenclature. What is referred to as the "exponential distribution of reliability" in this book is also referred to as "exponential distribution of failures" in other books. Most often it is referred to as just the "exponential distribution." This variation in nomenclature should not cause difficulty, since the only exponential distribution widely used does not have viable alternates that could create confusion.

Dd

This is a sample of the text for the definition, or these are more synonyms and usages that are commonly found in the English language.

The **exponential distribution** is the mathematical model that universally quantifies product reliability. The greatest benefit of using the exponential distribution to quantify product reliability is that everyone requiring product reliability information uses a mutually understood number to plan their future work activity.

The exponential distribution equation is

$$p(x) = e^{-x/\theta}$$

The exponential equation has only one parameter, θ (theta), which can be understood as the average time to failure (MTBF) of a product.

The good news is that from this single mathematical model the values of failure rate, total failures with time, and failures from the remaining survivors of the initial set or group of products can be calculated. The bad news is that we have to severely constrain the application conditions of our product reliability in order to utilize this mathematical model.

Conditions for an Exponential Distribution of Reliability

The exponential distribution is a mathematical model for product reliability under the following conditions:

1. The product is a finite number (set) starting in functional use at the same time (time zero). (An example would be 4,000 parts sent out on March 20.)
2. The product failures occur at a constant rate and are random with time. The constant rate by definition means that the probability of each unit of product failing in time is equal. This does not mean that failures occur at constant time intervals.
3. All products in the set have the same failure rate. So the entire product set is composed of individuals with the same failure probability.
4. Failed product is not replaced within the set.
5. The product use environments do not affect the failure rate.

The exponential distribution allows a single number to represent the entire product reliability under these specified conditions. But, even with these restrictive conditions, the exponential model with a single value (MTBF) has been successfully applied to many product reliability descriptions.

Exponential Distribution Mathematics

The exponential distribution, which plots product survivors and failures as a decimal fraction, is presented in Figure 5-5.

When $t = 0$, 1.00 of the items are survivors, and when $t =$ MTBF, 0.37 of the items are survivors. Note that we cannot predict which items do survive, but we can describe with adequate accuracy the number of failures within the group.

The following set of mathematical definitions and relationships apply to the exponential distribution:

1. Reliability is the probability of an item to perform its required function under specified conditions for a specified period of time. Product reliability is exactly described as the survivors with time by the exponential distribution.
2. Survivors plus failures = 1 for all time.

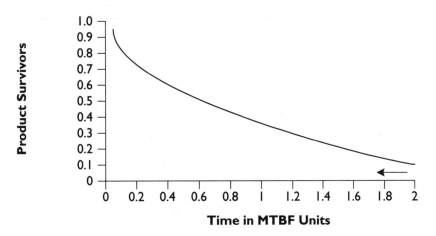

FIGURE 5-5.   The exponential distribution

3. MTBF = theta = mean time before failure.
4. Failure rate is failures/time.
5. Failure rate is symbolized as λ.
6. MTBF is the reciprocal of failure rate (FR) (lambda) (for a constant FR).
7. MTBF $\times$ FR = 1.
8. MTBF = 1/FR.
9. FR = 1/MTBF.

MTBF can be considered a constant with product operating time only under these restricted conditions provided in the exponential distribution model.

The universal application of the exponential distribution to represent product reliability allows us to calculate several needed values:

1. The number of survivors with time (stated as a decimal fraction).

$$S(t) = e^{-\lambda t} = e^{-t/\theta} \tag{1}$$

Where λ is the failure rate, θ is the MTBF (reciprocal of lambda), and t is the time of operation.

$S(t)$, survivors with time, is the exact, universal definition of product reliability. It is based upon this exponential relationship with the failure rate (or MTBF).

2. The number of failures with time (stated as a decimal fraction).

$$\text{Since survivors}(t) + \text{failures}(t) = 1; \quad \text{failures}(t) = 1 - e^{-\lambda t} \tag{2}$$

Again, lambda is the failure rate.

3. The total failures of a set of product with time.

The total failures with time is the integration of the failures(t) over time.

$$F(t) = \int_0^t f(x)\,dx = 1 - e^{-\lambda t} \tag{3}$$

$F(t)$ is called the cumulative distribution function.

Note: It has to be the same as $1 - S(t)$ shown previously.

4. The number of failures per unit time of the survivors.

This is explicitly the constant failure rate times the surviving product.

$$f(t) = \lambda e^{-\lambda t} \tag{4}$$

f(t) is called the probability density function.
5. The definition of constant failure rate.

From the basic definition of failure rate, at any point in time it is the $f(t)$ (failures) divided by the $S(t)$ (operating units).

$$\lambda(t) = \frac{f(t)}{S(t)} = \lambda \tag{5}$$

This mathematically restates the condition that lambda is a constant.
$\lambda(t)$ *is sometimes called a hazard function.*
6. MTBF in the reliability exponential distribution.

The MTBF of all products measured by the reliability exponential distribution is the point in time where the exponential factor $\lambda t = 1$. By definition, it is the point in time where $e^{-1} = 0.37$ of the product has survived.

All of these mathematical functions receive great attention from mathematicians applying these concepts to practical product reliability problems. Many references are available for your use. However, it is important to remember that the value of the exponential distribution model relates directly to how well the underlying conditions represent your product.

Your Product's Exponential Distribution

The use of the exponential distribution is relatively simple. Your big problem is how to accurately represent your own product. *This can only be done by fitting empirical data to a representative mathematical curve.* The input of FR or MTBF comes from an independent calculation or by directly fitting an exponential curve to the actual failure data.

This "best" fitting of an exponential reliability distribution to actual data is most often done on a computer. The computer will calculate the "best" exponential curve to fit the random failure data. The data can also be manipulated with success without a computer. Although this book does not address curve fitting in detail, two predominant problems demand mentioning:

1. It is obvious that the constant failure rate of a product can be based upon a relatively few number of failures. In fact, the exponential reliability distribution can be established with one failure. However, 30 failures are needed to determine with confidence a number that represents the failure rate. If you have fewer than 30, check with a statistician as to the confidence of the data. (How sure are you of the failure rate?) The number of failures used to generate an exponential distribution is a primary problem of product reliability data.

   The use of the exponential reliability distribution does not increase confidence in the input data. The higher the number of data points, the higher the confidence.

2. The assumption that the failures are constant and random forces the real reliability (Figure 3-6) to be plotted as a convenient single mathematical function (Figure 5-5). That process will forever lose data such as reliability growth, ETF, and wear out during the specified (and not often mentioned) evaluation period. That detailed data can never be recovered from the generalized exponential product reliability distribution. Be very careful.

   The best way to determine a failure rate, without a statistical correction for failure number and confidence, is to do a simple calculation based upon total failures of about 30 and the total operating time (to 30 fails) of the product set. The failure rate can be inserted directly into the exponential function to calculate any desired parameter of the set.

Examples Using the Exponential Reliability Distribution

The exponential distribution is often used to derive information. Here are three typical calculations:

Example 1: A company has 400 units of a product operating with a failure rate of 2×10^{-4}/hour. What is the number of failures requiring replacement in the next 500 hours?

Answer:

$$S(t) = e^{-\lambda t} = e^{-(2\times 10^{-4}/\text{h})(500\text{h})} = e^{-0.1} = 0.904$$

Since the decimal fraction of survivors is 0.904, the total survivors are $0.904 \times 400 = 362$. The failures are $400 - 362 = 38$. Note that, beyond the unfamiliar use of exponentials, the calculations are simple.

Example 2: Fifty thousand units of product X was sent to the field. After six months it was determined that 156 failures had occurred with an average estimated operating time of 730 hours. How many of these units will fail in the first 3,000 operating hours?

Answer: Given the failure data, notice that an approximation must be given to calculate total operating hours, since the precise time at failure is not known for each failed unit. Because there are few failures (156 out of 50,000), the total operating hours will be estimated as 50,000 units times 730 hours.

$$\lambda = \frac{\text{Total Fails}}{\text{Total Operating Time}} = \frac{156}{36.5 \times 10^6} = 4.27 \times 10^{-6} \text{ Fails/h}$$

This value of failure rate is typical for a high-reliability electronic device.

Now, from the exponential function, calculate the decimal fraction of survivors at 3,000 hours.

$$S(t) = e^{-\lambda t} = e^{-(4.27 \times 10^{-6} \text{ Fails/h})(3,000 \text{ h})}$$

Evaluating the exponential, $S(3,000 \text{ h}) = 0.987$, or $50,000 \times 0.987 = 49,350$ will survive after 3,000 hours of operation.

This means that $50,000 - 49,350 = 650$ units will have failed by that time. So the answer to the original question is that 650 units will fail by 3,000 hours of operating time.

This model provides a convenient method for all parties to obtain the same failure estimate from the failure rate. It is also reasonable to predict that 650 units from the set would fail by 3,000 hours because 156 units were known failures in the first 730 hours. At small fractions of failures, the exponential function produces an almost linear value with time.

Example 3: If we shipped a total of 10,000 units with a failure rate of 0.056/KPOH, how many units can we expect to be failing between the 7 and 8 KPOH of operation?

The number of fails is the failure rate (per KPOH) times the number of survivors at 7 KPOH of operation.

$$S(7 \text{ KPOH}) = e^{-(0.056/\text{KPOH})(7 \text{ KPOH})} = e^{-0.39}$$

Evaluating the exponential, $S(7 \text{ KPOH}) = 0.67$ or $10,000 \times 0.67 = 6,700$ survived to 7 KPOH.

The probability density (which was really asked for) is $\int(t) = \lambda e^{-\lambda t} = 0.056/\text{KPOH} \times 6,700 = 375$ units will fail between 7,000 and 8,000 power on hours.

Note that the absolute frequency of failures has substantially decreased since only 6,700 units are still in operation. This is not a good product reliability, assuming that the failures were truly random.

Exponential Distribution Conclusions

The exponential distribution is the most common product reliability model in use. In applications, it has obtained success in both communicating the product reliability values and in measuring product reliability improvement. By definition, it is limited to the reliability description of the random portion of the classical reliability bathtub curve. It does not represent early time failures nor wear-out failures.

An advanced mathematical treatment of product reliability that accounts for change with time of failure rate (and MTBF) is the Weibull distribution. A summary treatment of the Weibull distribution is given in Appendix B.

The Pseudo-MTBF Calculations

The use of MTBF to indicate product reliability in the marketplace is universal. Also, MTBF numbers rightfully receive skepticism due to their ambiguous nature, which is addressed in this section.

Typical advertised values of MTBF in the marketplace are

1. 1,500 (operating) hours of a light bulb
2. 50,000 (operating) hours for an aircraft control system
3. 10,000 (operating) hours for electric power delivered to homes
4. 800,000 (operating) hours for an electronic data storage device
5. 100,000,000 (operating) hours for an electronic integrated circuit

In these five examples, the MTBF is calculated from validated data by the simple formula

$$MTBF = \frac{\text{Total Operating Time}}{\text{Total Failures}}$$

Now let us look at the origins of two MTBF numbers.

 First, let us determine the MTBF of a particular automobile battery. Ten batteries sold by an auto dealer were evaluated at 50 months. One battery failed at 27 months, two at 38 months, one at 47 months, and one at 48 months. The remaining five batteries were known to be in operation. What is the MTBF of the automobile battery?

Answer:

$$MTBF = \frac{\text{Total Operating Time}}{\text{Total Failures}}$$

$$= (27 + 38 + 38 + 47 + 48) \text{ months} + (5 \times 50 \text{ months})/5 \text{ failures}$$

MTBF = 448 months/5 failures = 89.6 months

Note that this was by definition a legitimate calculation. However, the predominant failure mode is wear out. These auto batteries are starting to wear out in 4 years. Observe that there were no failures in the first 24 months; but there were four failures in the past 12 months. Now, what if two failed in the 51st month and the last three failed in the 52nd month? The MTBF would be

$$= (27 + 38 + 38 + 47 + 48 + 51 + 51 + 52 + 52$$
$$+ 52) \text{ months}/10 \text{ failures}$$

MTBF = 456 months/10 failures = 45.6 months per failure

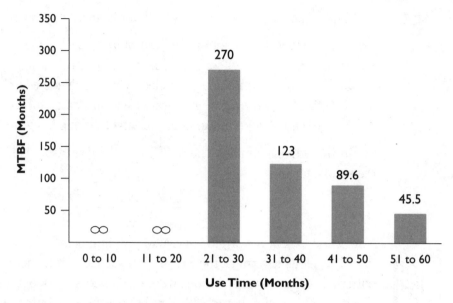

FIGURE 5-6.   MTBF of automobile batteries

The MTBF changed significantly in two months. The MTBF of the entire product set of 10 batteries is 45.6 months. Figure 5-6 plots the MTBF as a function of time of product operation. Note that MTBF is only calculated when a failure occurs. It is not unusual for MTBF to be calculated on product to substantially represent the wear-out failures. The underlying concept of importance is that the MTBF varies with time.

Second, let us investigate a semiconductor component that has incurred 35 failures in 1.5 billion hours of operation. The MTBF is 42.9×106 hours. From the failure data, a large number of these items were observed operating for extensive periods of time, and only a small fraction (>1%) failed. ETF failures are not apparent, and wear out in this product does not occur. The failures are randomly distributed around a constant failure rate value. In this case, the linear approximation of the constant failure rate satisfies the conditions specified for the exponential distribution of failure. Notice in this case that MTBF only measures the random failure mode, not ETF or wear out. Figure 5-7 plots the region of the failure rate that represents the product failures during use. The MTBF value describes accurately the product reliability.

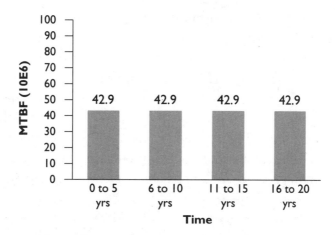

FIGURE 5-7.   **MTBF of a semiconductor component**

The MTBF implied for models using the exponential distribution is a constant that substantially represents the random failure mode. The MTBF often used in the marketplace represents ETF and wear-out failures of a product. There is nothing right or wrong about these calculations. Just realize that MTBF is an ambiguous concept.

Two prevalent misunderstandings of MTBF occur in product reliability when the reliability model does not follow the universal exponential distribution. The implied MTBF value is inaccurate in both cases.

1. The entire product's failure rates (vintage and operating time), as presented in Figure 5-6, are averaged into a single failure rate and are used to create an exponential distribution. This averaging does not properly account for ETF, wear out, and reliability growth of a product. Planning of warranties, product reliability optimization, and customer product-failure response, based upon such an MTBF, are highly inaccurate.

2. As plotted in Figure 5-6, the MTBF is a time variable useful to the knowledgeable customer but should not be considered as represented by the exponential model to calculate, manage, and control the product reliability, unless you understand the variable MTBF in detail.

These two methods of oversimplifying data cause continuing problems. In this section, they are referred to as pseudo-MTBFs. In Chapter 3 we emphasized the importance of understanding the details of MTBF calculations. In the process of quantifying your product reliability (MTBF), you may lose your understanding of detail and ability to control and manage.

The only MTBF that has universal recognition mathematically is that MTBF that exists within a legitimate exponential distribution. All others require extensive detailed explanations. It is left to you to review the list of advertised MTBFs at the beginning of this section. How do you think these MTBF values, indicative of product reliability, are flawed? For more information on the Weibull reliability distribution, see Appendix B.

Summary

Entire careers are devoted to the mathematical treatment of product reliability. In this chapter, only the fundamental nature of reliability mathematics is presented so that basic understanding of future mathematical applications of sampling, controlling, and establishing a failure-rate model can be achieved. It must be emphasized that although some mathematical reliability treatments often seem unduly complex, the underlying mathematical rationale is no more complex than that presented in this chapter.

The significant advantage of mathematical tools to manage product reliability is that quantified data are generated that permit businesses to be controlled in a rational manner. Mathematical models are convenient descriptions of physical reality. Distributions are the fundamental models of reliability. The uncertainty and unfamiliarity with distributions is not a characteristic of the mathematical models but of the physical reality that the models describe.

The Bernoulli, binomial, Poisson, and normal distributions are logically developed for use as tools in later chapters of this book. It is important to understand the fundamentals and limitations of these mathematical expressions. Enough information is provided so that an inappropriate use of the mathematics can be recognized before bad information, followed by bad conclusions, occur.

The Poisson and normal distributions have extensive use in modeling product reliability. Those mathematical functions will be used later based upon their rudimentary knowledge.

Originating with the observation that product reliability is an outcome described by the random probability of failure, an exponential distribution can be used as a model to universally communicate product reliability and calculate reliability functions for each product. This simplified and workable approximation is excellent for business planning and communication. The fundamental measure of product reliability, MTBF, is based upon the exponential distribution.

An extensive explanation of mean time to failure (MTBF) is presented because it is the most frequently used and most frequently misunderstood measure in product reliability. Examples are given to demonstrate the origination of these misunderstandings.

Reference

1. Armand V. Feigenbaum, *Total Quality Control*, 3rd ed. (New York: McGraw-Hill, 1983).

6

Reliability Design Development

The excellence of the item's design defines how reliable the item can be.

—H. J. HARRINGTON

Introduction

Managers should primarily read Chapter 6 to understand the business aspects of their product reliability specification. The product reliability specification of a product determines the product reliability cost content as a function of resources and planned activities, the strategic position of the product in the marketplace, and the product development direction and goals for managing to an optimum business operation. Chapter 6 also presents reliability design by demonstrating examples of the design techniques that can be used to achieve the desired specific reliability goal. Redundant systems design is included, although that design technique may not be required for attaining the reliability specification of your product. Redundant reliability design techniques are frequently part of discussions during business decisions.

Engineers should read Chapter 6 to understand the details of product reliability specification and prediction. That understanding should at least be at a generalized level among all product development engineers. The summary of typical reliability design parameters is given as an initial guide to those unfamiliar with fundamental product reliability design techniques. Redundant systems design is presented because of the high interest in that subject by many engineers.

Chapter 6 presents the three major topics in product design development that are often unfamiliar to many professional engineers and business managers:

1. How to specify appropriate product reliability.
2. How to design to a specified product reliability.
3. How to apply redundant designs to improve product reliability.

This chapter has sufficient content to explain these three design activities. However, the abbreviated descriptions presented primarily provide background for understanding product reliability development activities and assisting better communication. Many excellent texts have been written to augment this introduction to fundamental product reliability design processes. Those texts are recommended to further your understanding of your specific product reliability development.

A view is often expressed that "if the product were designed correctly, there should be no product failures." It is better to express the view that "if the appropriate reliability is included in the design, the optimum profit for the product will be realized." The first view is a worthless platitude, and the second is a valuable guide. The purpose of this chapter is to provide an understanding of the tools to achieve an appropriate product reliability design.

A fundamental truth related to reliability is that the product can never be better than the designed reliability. Both production and repair detract from the intrinsic design's reliability. The one exception to this is that an effective preventive maintenance can create the illusion of product reliability being greater than the product's designed reliability.

Common practice of managers and engineers is to search reliability design topics in order to find a specific "magic bullet" or easy solution to their specific product reliability problem. Chapter 6 explains the basic concepts of controlling product reliability specification and reliability prediction, some generalized rules for controlling electrical and mechanical product reliability, and the design of functionally redundant systems to control the product reliability. The key words are "control reliability," which is the operational mission of product development. These three topics were chosen because they represent important product reliability development activities most unfamiliar to the managers and engineers outside of the product design reliability activity. It is doubtful if you will find a magic bullet within this chapter.

Reliability Specification and Prediction

Introduction

Inherent in the establishment of reliability requirements is the need to estimate or predict reliability in advance of manufacturing the product. This prediction is a continuing process which takes place at several stages of the progression from design through usage.
    —J. M. JURAN[1]

Reliability is (1) the probability of an item to perform its (2) required function in a (3) specific environment for a (4) specified period of time. Reliability is the survivor rate of product under defined performance functions and a defined environment.

Your product reliability is of economic interest to you and your customers/consumers. So it is in your best business interest to develop an appropriate product reliability. The product reliability specification itself is the explicit documentation of items (1) to (4) in the reliability definition.

Product reliability specification is required for your business mainly in three activities:

1. *Development of new products.* Development of new products always considers the reliability of that new product. In documented form, that is the product reliability specification. The customer/consumer requirement, based upon a competitive business marketplace, is the

usual input for new product reliability specifications. The reliability development choices made to achieve that new product reliability specification are based upon similar existing product's reliability performance and component level reliability data that contribute to the total product reliability.

The initial new-design control activity involves establishing the requirements for MTTF and whatever other reliability targets may be indicated to meet the reliability required for the product. To be meaningful, the reliability targets must be within reach at a planned date.
—ARMAND V. FEIGENBAUM[2]

2. *Evaluation of engineering changes (ECs).* Development also has the proper resources for validation of the reliability impact of ECs to existing product. Most ECs are directed at improvement of product performance or product cost reduction.
3. *Validation of reliability problem resolutions.* On occasion, the EC will be primarily directed toward product reliability improvement. These are the reactionary product reliability activities that correct serious product reliability deficiencies.

The entire scope of development product reliability, upon closer inspection, is actually the same business process applied to product at different times during the product cycle, and in every case, the data required for product reliability determination are the keys to that process's effectiveness.

How Did You Arrive at Your Product Reliability Specification?

Reliability Simplified is not written to ignore the realities of the present reliability business process. In many instances, the reliability specification has been determined with a minimum of data and a maximum of business intuition. Usually, the motivation to specify a product reliability stems from competitive product's reliability claims in the marketplace. In the competitive marketplace, the more favorable product reliability creates a product sales advantage. However, the intelligent customer/consumer will demand that the product reliability claims be backed with liability responsibility, most often written into a warranty. These warranties are becoming more and more directed at financial retrieval of losses suffered due to product failures. So in a competitive environment, the product reliability specification is based upon a dynamic equilibrium between sales advantage and warranty cost.

In many businesses, this process of determining the optimum product reliability specification is accomplished without a quantified reliability analysis. In fact, the reliability specification may be determined at a meeting without anyone educated in reliability in the room. In most cases, an effort is made to collect all data possible to support the product reliability determination. However, when a reliability data system is not adequate, the available data require significant subjective interpretation. When an operational reliability database is in place, a more ideal scenario occurs where validated product reliability values are used to determine the product reliability for the business.

You must have awareness of the range of your capabilities to provide an accurate product reliability specification. Great care should be taken to ensure that your product reliability specification is reachable. A reliability specification that is generated substantially upon marketplace competitor specifications and warranty costs, without proper consideration of the physical reliability of your product, will eventually economically harm your business. The effective communication of all pertinent information related to a potential new product reliability specification is extremely important. Use visual presentations, such as Figures 6-1 and 6-2, to maximize the impact of your existing information (based on hard data) upon the predicted product reliability specification.

Figure 6-1 is a modified Figure 3-10. It is used to communicate quickly the overall scope of product reliability specification. Note the following:

1. The average failure rate and end of warranty period are determined. This is our goal.
2. The installation failures and wear-out failures are mentioned but explicitly excluded, in this case, from the product reliability specification. That point has to be clear.
3. The intuitive ideas of ETF and random failures are assigned. This is not an abstract exercise.

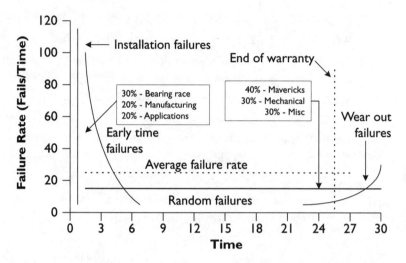

FIGURE **6-1.**   **Input information to a product reliability specification**

4. The significant contributors to failure are mentioned. Responsibility for failure origin is the basis of business success.

What is not presented is reliability growth, which would make the presentation too complex. For the product reliability specification and warranty, only consider the average failure rate projected for the entire program product volume to the end of warranty or explicit product life.

FR = Unit failures per 1,000 hours (× 1 million) = ppm/KPOH

Figure 6-2 presents the future projected product reliability specification along with the best existing reliability of an existing similar product. It is

Product	Catastrophic	Tolerance	No Trouble Found	Adminis- trative	Total
Existing	1,650	300	750	300	3,000
New	1,050	150	225	75	1,500

FIGURE **6-2.**   **Summary of current and projected product failures**

generated to communicate and obtain consensus agreement regarding the existing product failure modes and the reliability projected for the new product. It is required to bridge between existing known product reliability and the new product reliability specification. It is also the master chart for directing action toward product reliability specification in your business. Figure 6-2 should exist for every business.

Fault tree analysis (FTA) is a tree diagram that shows failures and/or defects in increasing levels of detail. It helps to narrow the root cause and focus on preventions.

The fault tree analysis (FTA) presented in Figure 6-3 is a popular presentation containing the entire projected failure summary in a convenient format. The failure information is structured as a tree with trunk, branches, twigs, and leaves. Figure 6-3 contains the "new" information presented in Figure 6-2 and, in addition, has the contributions of the catastrophic failures.

FTA is a prominent method of presenting information. The compelling message of an FTA presentation is that the entire spectrum of failures (and reliability) has been investigated. The focus upon understanding product failures in Chapter 3 was directed precisely at the issue of detailed understanding of product failures when the product was in customer/consumer use. In general, the greatest deficiency with FTA presentations is that the presented data may not have adequate analysis and understanding. FTA of failures should prompt inquiry into the source data.

Your optimum product reliability specification can only be attained by evaluation of the existing data. The participation and communications from product reliability experts is crucial in this process.

Data Sources for Product Reliability Specification and Prediction

The previous section is a plea to utilize existing data to determine your product reliability specification. It is important for you to systematically obtain data for your new product reliability prediction based upon all available sources. The data sources typically are

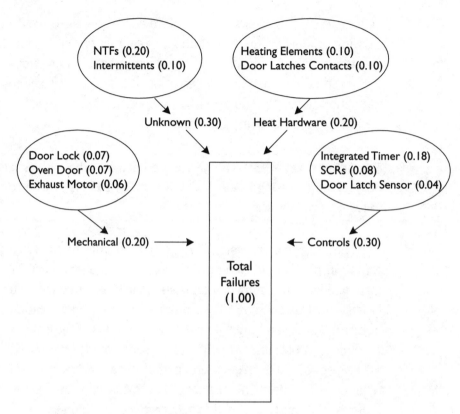

FIGURE 6-3.   Fault tree analysis, warranty product failures. Example's product is a hypothetical stove

1. *Existing customer/consumer product reliability data.* The existing prior customer/consumer failures provide the most accurate data on the product reliability. Through failure analysis, each failure can be traced to a root cause. The elimination (or significant reduction) of failure root causes is the basis of product reliability growth.

The **Failure root cause** is the primary physical or environmental condition within a system that logically initiates a path to system failure.

2. *Product accelerated life tests.* Product accelerated life test (qualification) data generation is explained in Chapter 8. The new product is operated

to the equivalent of its anticipated operating life in a time-accelerated manner. The failures are determined both qualitatively and quantitatively. The accelerated testing often will not exactly replicate customer/consumer use conditions. However, the qualification test in general is an excellent method for obtaining reliability data.

3. *Materials test data and basic physics.* At the component material level, many reliability science factors have been developed to predict the reliability of the component. The factors that are well characterized, such as electromigration, are assumed to be correct for design in any component application. They are only subject to reliability validation within a specific design.

4. *Component reliability test data.* The components themselves may have been tested to a reliability specification. The reliability data for the component can be used in the product reliability prediction. Often, these data can be obtained from the supplier.

From these four data sources, the single component reliability and product reliability are determined. The product reliability is predicted as a summation of the reliability of each component.

The data we typically use to predict product reliability is based only upon catastrophic failures with root causes being physical defects. This is only part of our product reliability (and specification) as presented in Figure 6-2. Failure modes such as wear out, NTF, and administrative actions are optional and not often considered directly in product-failure predictions. Predicted failure modes, other than catastrophic, are only estimates of existing modes as presented in Figure 6-2. The reason for referencing to total product failures at the system level at this point is to emphasize that reliability prediction can only effectively occur for catastrophic component failures. This fact is repeatedly overlooked in the reliability planning of new products. Failure data available for prediction from customers/consumers may not contain a complete set of failure modes; so be very careful.

Product Reliability Prediction Procedure

The first approximation of a product reliability prediction (as a failure rate) is estimated from the summation of the component failure rates. Several formal procedures for reliability prediction are available. The MIL 217-(—) procedure has created a common approach to the reliability prediction activity. Also, the Bellcore TR-xxx-000332 is an excellent guide primarily for reliability prediction for electronic equipment. Both procedures are proven to be effective and recommended for operational and reference purposes. The reliability predictive sequence is as follows:

1. A list of components is determined for the product (usually the product bill of materials). A search for all components used in the bill of materials is made in the four sources listed in the last section. The component reliability data for evolving products is usually already in place.
2. A reconciliation is needed among the differing values established by the various sources. The reconciliation problem may be as simple as the definition of the component to an actual disparity in failure rates by different sources. A tentative (and eventual) accepted value for each component must be determined.
3. The various operating stresses projected for the preliminary design and customer/consumer operating conditions must be factored into the failure-rate prediction for each component. Bellcore 332 has these stress factors already predetermined for electronic components. Examples of stress factors are temperature and voltage. Various stress factors may be generated in unique product applications as a meaningful factor in the failure rate.
4. An actual summation of the total product reliability must be generated that results in a product level estimation of the reliability. Figure 6-3 is an example of a reliability prediction based upon the summation of catastrophic failures. Note that it has the features of prioritizing existing failures. This procedure, when applied repeatedly to new evolving product,
   —becomes an accurate indicator of unreliable components in the new products,
   —becomes an accurate indicator of total system reliability determined by catastrophic component failure, and
   —becomes the historical document of product reliability.

COMPONENT	UNIT FR	NUM	TOTAL COMP FR	STRESS FACTOR	FR ESTIMATE
Line Drivers AB 456783	12.6	24	302	1.2	362
D – Caps 27956743-xx	1.35	168	227	0.8	181
PCB Connector	90	2	180	1.0	180
Input MUX 456455-55	23	4	92	1.0	92
PCB Card (TBD)	90	1	90	1.0	90
Systems Switch (TBD)	45.0	1	45	2.0	90
DRAM 458222	6.0	4	24	1.0	24
AC – Caps 279000-03	0.90	36	32	0.5	16
SCSI Interface 456200-20	2.0	2.0	4.0	1.0	4.0
Resistors 279455	0.01	36	0.36	1.0	0.36
TOTAL					**1,039**

FIGURE **6-4.** **Product reliability predicted from component data**

Figure 6-4 is an abbreviated example of a product reliability projection for a product based upon catastrophic failure modes. It is consistent with Figure 6-2. Figure 6-4 can be specifically modified to include any new contributing factor to product reliability such as stress caused by heating, loading factor, power-on time, and mechanical vibration. Figure 6-4 provides the basic concept of quickly producing a working document for product reliability specification and prediction.

If your product requires a product reliability specification, it requires an accurate estimation of current and projected reliability values. Frequently, it is observed that a product reliability based only upon projection of component failures results in a fairly accurate prediction of the total product failures. This situation is the result of two deficiencies: (1) inadequate failure reporting understates the actual failures at the same time that (2) catastrophic failures understate the projected total failures. A case where two wrongs almost make a right! This situation is operationally adequate but inadequate for a managed response to reliability control.

A component level synthesis of a product reliability is recommended for all serious product designs. The process becomes more accurate with repeated use and will evolve into the reliability design communication tool for your business. The failure-rate prediction presented in Figure 6-4 is an excellent example, since printed circuit boards (PCBs) have extensively used this technique to predict product reliability. However, any failure factors can be used to synthesize a product failure rate.

Every serious product reliability control program has a documented product reliability activity that provides the specific details and focus for the ongoing development program. The scenario where the same mistake was repeated (twice or more) is all too common in the newly developed product. This is especially true in cases where design limits have reached the physical limits of operation. Without a documented history, new personnel do not effectively use the acquired experience.

Reliable Design

The overall subject of reliable product design cannot be adequately addressed in this chapter. The vast numbers of products and reliability techniques established to date would require a large library to contain the proper text to properly document the subject. The initial recommendation is to search for literature specifically pertinent to your product. The second recommendation is to obtain the current product reliability information through the periodicals listed in Appendix C. In *Reliability Simplified,* the subject will discuss methods using the frequently used engineering techniques as examples. The techniques presented may not include options that are available to specific designs. This procedure will establish intent and direction for your specific product reliability design.

Electrical Reliability Design

Nine techniques to improve reliability in electronic functions are listed in Figure 6-5. The list of techniques is commonly used to design a specific reliability specification.

1. Temperature—keep the operating temperature as low as possible. This can be accomplished through the evaluations of product heat-transfer models using the physical techniques of reducing power, providing heat sinks and thermal conduction and radiators, providing packaging with optimum airflow, and specifying the operating (class) environment. As a general rule, the failure rate increases about twofold for every increase of 10°C of the product operating temperature.
2. Derating—derate the components used in the circuit. *Derate* means to stress the components with only a fraction of their designed capacity.

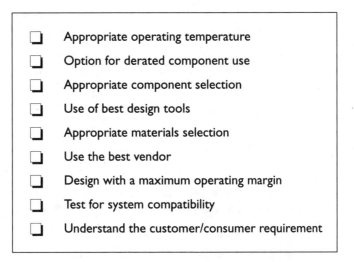

> ❏ Appropriate operating temperature
> ❏ Option for derated component use
> ❏ Appropriate component selection
> ❏ Use of best design tools
> ❏ Appropriate materials selection
> ❏ Use the best vendor
> ❏ Design with a maximum operating margin
> ❏ Test for system compatibility
> ❏ Understand the customer/consumer requirement

FIGURE 6-5.   Checklist of significant electrical reliability design factors

Use a 50-V-rated capacitor in a 10-V application. Use a 1-W rated resistor in a $\frac{1}{4}$-W application. Use a 5-W-rated magnetic switch in a 1-W application. The decrease in failure rate by derating is normally available from the component suppliers tests. For active components such as discrete transistors and integrated circuits, the reliability is specified at the operating voltage. Therefore, a derating opportunity may not exist.

3. Component selection—purchase appropriate reliability components. These components will have been environmentally stress screened to achieve a higher (and specified) reliability. Some components demand a higher price, but they will significantly reduce the failure rate in the product. The trends in reliability in the 1980s and 1990s have provided the electrical designers with excellent competitively priced options of purchasing high-reliability components.

4. Design tools—use computer-based circuit layout capability that will minimize electronic noise and maximize electronic voltage margins in the circuit physical design. Noncomputerized layouts are not adequate for modern PCBs.

5. Physical choice of materials—use materials that tolerate a higher level of temperature, humidity, and chemical corrosion resistance. These materials, which can almost be considered a mechanical factor, are implicit in the PCB and component structures. An example would be designing the use of a tantalum capacitor rather than an electrolytic capacitor to decrease failure rate and increase operating life.

6. Component purchasing—it may seem cloying, but reliability can on the average be enhanced by buying from a vendor with proven reliability history. We are now the customer/consumer paying the RPF explained in Chapter 3. Use electronic device components whose reliability can be depended upon to exceed the specified reliability. In the design phase, you are the customer/consumer for your suppliers. You should intelligently balance the impacts between cost and reliability. Buy a component with reliability that makes you feel comfortable.

7. Operating safety margin—develop the highest operating margin possible for your product. Give the product preliminary tests at condi-

tions beyond the margin extremes (voltage and temperature) experienced by the operating customer/consumer. Test time constraints do require accelerated tests (Chapter 7), but remember that the highly accelerated tests may present artifact failures that do not reflect the product's true reliability.

8. System compatibility—the electronic product must receive all specified inputs possible in system use and only produce valid outputs specified in system use. The electronic design is tested for two major system compatibilities: (1) that a true electronic fault is not propagated undetected within the system and (2) that the timing of the electronic information flow is in synchronization to that of the system. Although this factor is often considered to be one of product functionality, realize that the result is a product failure. Inadequate electronic fault detection and correction, and inadequate electronic timing are measured during product qualification testing. They are significant contributors to product failures.

   Note: Often, your customer/consumer will use your product in an unspecified manner and not inform you how it was being used when a failure occurred, causing unnecessary improvement expense.

9. Communication—improving product reliability may only involve communication with the customer/consumer to determine the appropriate product reliability. Don't proceed toward the goal of perfect and costly reliability with your product, only to use that reliability as a "lost leader" in negotiating with customers/consumers requiring a much lower reliability from your product.

Figure 6-5 provides a checklist approach for reviewing the reliability aspects in product design. Each unique product will have its own list.

Mechanical Reliability Design

Mechanical reliability design factors are familiar to most people. Products fail when they break (strength, fatigue), do not operate after mechanical stress (shock), and do not operate due to operational tolerance (thermal design, materials design, wear out). The specific product mechanical reliability specification is established to represent the requirement of the product in use.

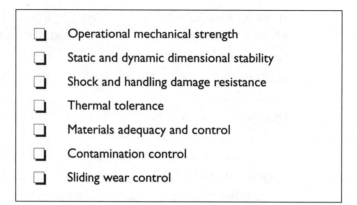

- ❏   Operational mechanical strength
- ❏   Static and dynamic dimensional stability
- ❏   Shock and handling damage resistance
- ❏   Thermal tolerance
- ❏   Materials adequacy and control
- ❏   Contamination control
- ❏   Sliding wear control

FIGURE **6-6.** **Checklist of significant mechanical reliability design factors**

That same mechanical specification also is the reliability design goal for that product.

A checklist of typical mechanical design factors is given in Figure 6-6. It is recommended that a list of mechanical design factors, similar to those presented in Figure 6-6, be generated to characterize your product.

It seems reasonable to expect that your list of significant design factors would be quantified and become part of your product reliability specification. The value of such a checklist is that it produces a focus upon the failure modes in the design phase of the product cycle.

The top seven techniques to improve mechanical reliability are listed in the following. These provide a variety of methods for achieving the product reliability as specified for the product.

1. *Strength and ruggedness.* The product should have sufficient operational mechanical strength to survive the peak mechanical stresses in the operating use environment with mechanical integrity. This requirement for a rugged product usually requires extensive design effort. Current products are marvels of mechanical reliability design. The ability to design high-strength products with minimal weight has been enhanced by the products for outer-space applications. The use of the computer in finite analysis to calculate the stress and strain relationships of complex physical geometries has

aided immensely in optimizing the mechanical design and allows accurate evaluations of multiple mechanical structures without actually fabricating any of the design options. The choice of materials used for mechanical design increases with time, allowing optimum design to meet the required product mechanical specification.

Knowledge is the combination of education, training, and experience.

Knowledge is the key to using the tools previously stated. The process has become too complex to be properly completed in an unprofessional manner. Reliability problems in this factor invariably are traced to unprofessional mechanical design.

A specific mechanical reliability factor in many product applications is the safety factor designed into the product. Figure 6-7 presents the mechanical safety factor as two distributions, one is the distribution of product strengths to failure, and the second is the distribution of environmental stresses in time that are anticipated to impact the product. The design should first consider the two distributions and then include a stress safety margin appropriate for the specific product. An example would be an operation stress of 10 lb./sq. in. (sigma = 2 lb./sq. in.) and a designed strength of 40 lb./sq. in. (sigma = 4 lb./sq. in.). In this example, the stress safety margin

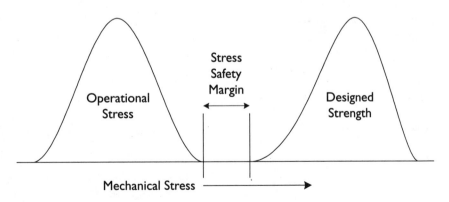

FIGURE 6-7.   **Operational stress and designed strength**

value, the difference between the 3-sigma upper operational stress and the 3-sigma lower designed strength is 12 lb./sq. in. The design balance is between the higher reliability inherent in larger stress safety margins and the cost of achieving those higher stress safety margins. Figure 6-7 is overly simplified, and this mechanical design factor is a subject of continual debate. But the idea is very comforting when one is riding in an aircraft.

2. *Dimensional stability.* The product may have a functional mechanical tolerance specified that fails due to mechanical "creep" resulting from residual stress in the product. Plastic flow under stress is included in this category. The product should have sufficient static and dynamic dimensional stability to survive within the specified level of dimensional tolerances. In products whose reliability is dependent upon this primary function, this condition frequently becomes a primary failure mode. Two methods of product reliability design and control are recommended when this factor becomes a significant design factor:

A. The use of testing to failure mechanical evaluations (see Chapter 8).
B. Continuous manufacturing testing to assure that the level of designed static and mechanical strength is maintained. The continuous product manufacturing testing is commonly referred to as an ongoing reliability test (ORT).

Ongoing Reliability Test (ORT) is the continuous sampling measurement of manufactured product to assure that product reliability has been maintained.

3. *Handling damage.* The product requires a specified shock and handling damage reliability. Unfortunately, a significant portion of the product "dead-on-arrival" (DOA) failures are caused by shock and handling damage. Additional failures occur later in the product customer/consumer operation as delayed failures from the initial shipment and as failures resulting from mechanical shock applied to the product in the customer/consumer operation. A fraction of the shock and handling related failures will never be traced to the correct root cause.

This realistic view of shock and handling failures leads to several prime aspects of reliability design:

A. The remedy for improvement of shock and handling damage includes the following aspects of basic design, "fool-proof" manufacturing handling, fool-proof storage, shipping, and customer/consumer installation. This aspect is consistent with the view that "all products can be broken, and it doesn't require profound intelligence."
B. The product reliability problem related to shock and handing may require communications and instructions for care by people handling and using the product. That may be the best way to achieve the product reliability specification.
C. The design of packaging at all levels, components, subassembly, final assembly, unit test, and shipping, plus the installation aides may be as important to the control of shock and handing damage as the actual mechanical design to improve the product operating limits.
D. The basic mechanical design provides a strategic platform to plan the global control of shock and handling damage.

From the foregoing four aspects, it is apparent that the shock and handling damage requires remedy by both a mechanical design, reliability management organization, and production engineering. It is the lack of cooperative effort between these groups that causes poor timely resolution of this failure mode.

4. *Thermal design.* Thermal design is an increasingly important part of product mechanical reliability. The specified requirements are increasing in difficulty due to trends in energy conservation, lower mechanical tolerances, and broader operating environments. Again, computer analysis tools have assisted immensely in optimal thermal designs. And again, the root cause of product thermal reliability problems can be traced to unprofessional design. This conclusion is based upon the fact that the necessary design is possible to achieve, but the requirement is often not identified until after problems are observed in the product's customer/consumer use. Product reliability qualification and test history are usually an effective tool in optimizing the product thermal design.

5. *Materials control.* Materials control is essential in the design and specification of mechanical reliability. Catastrophic product failures due to materials factors are discovered most often when comparing customer/consumer failures from one supplier to another supplier. Every business has a history of materials problems similar to the following examples:

A. The pads of a printed circuit board are coated with a gold passivation, contact, and slide surface. The pads from one producer had 3 microinches of gold, which was insufficient to prevent environmental corrosion and resulted in connector contact failures. The pads from an alternate producer had 13 microinches of gold. This product exhibited no corrosion failures. A review of the specification revealed that the gold material was not even specified. The specification just required the pads not to corrode. No validation tests were performed to determine if the product met its reliability specification. We often find that even when gold-plated contacts are specified on a print, the gold-plating thickness is not specified.

B. The wires of a solenoid were loosening and creating unacceptable audible vibrations. They were product failures. The failures came from one supplier who used a natural shellac (historical material) to bond the solenoid wires in place. During the high temperature and cyclic force that accompanied high-rate customer/consumer operation, the natural shellac decomposed. An alternate product used a high-temperature urethane for the solenoid wire bonding and never observed a single wire-bonding failure. The actual problem was tested, but not identified as a potential problem, by the alternate company when it tested maximum heat dissipation at solenoid maximum rates. The company with failed solenoids did not have a reliability qualification test for this application.

C. An interior operating wear surface was failing due to extreme wear conditions 1,000 times that of designed expectations. It was found that the surface had been contaminated with a chemically active outgassing from an adhesive used to bond other parts in the enclosed mechanism. The chemically active outgassing came from an allowed adhesive, but it was not identified in qualification tests because all test units were in operation and effectively purged the product enclosure. The failures occurred later after dormant product use promoted the surface corrosion. An alternate customer/consumer did not have the problem because the operating wear surface was treated (nitrided) to assure specified wear. That treatment essentially passivated that surface from the chemically active outgassing. The solution to this problem was replacing the noncritical adhesive with a less (stated zero) active material.

6. *Contamination.*

Contamination (particulate and chemical) is a product reliability factor, particularly significant where close dimensions and tolerances are required for functional performance.

The major problem with contamination specification is standardized tests. Many tests are established to duplicate the user environment, only to discover at a later date that the environment is not represented by the tests. This is especially true when contamination is generated as chemical "gunk" from the environment. The design of filters and environmental specifications for contamination protection are fundamental to this diverse activity.

7. *Sliding wear.*

Sliding wear is a very elementary reliability property of product reliability. Whether in a rolling contact surface or in a designed sliding surface, the catastrophic failure mode and wear-out mode failures are a function of design.

Again, that topic is too immense to address for your specific product. For example, an automobile engine in 1950 would require rebuilding after an average of 50,000 miles, and by 1990 an automobile engine would require rebuilding after about 150,000 miles. In this case, the wear-out reliability growth has been increased threefold.

The three mechanical reliability factors highlighted in the preceding text are operational mechanical strength, static and dynamic dimensional control, and shock and handling damage. Upon inspection, you will discover that the reliability of these factors are indeed mutually exclusive. For example, materials that exhibit excellent dimensional control cannot absorb a great amount of energy and tend to be susceptible to shock and machine damage. Just remember that a compromise among all factors is required in the optimum design.

Redundant System Reliability

Introduction

Your product reliability specification may be met through attaining an adequate reliability design because the components used in the design have a high enough individual reliability. The predictive system reliability was calculated in the first section of this chapter. At that time, it was mentioned at the system level only a fraction of failures stem from failures of the components. The component tolerance, system environment, and operating control systems also contribute failures at the system level.

When a system reliability requirement is higher than the combined reliability of its components, the usual system level designed alternate is system functional redundancy. Spacecraft have backup (redundant) communications, computer, and power systems. Commercial aircraft have redundant electronic control systems to essentially eliminate all possibility of an aircraft control functional failure. These examples are present in systems where reliability is not an issue of cost alone but of the socially acceptable product reliability.

Fly by wire is the label given to aircraft where the traditional physical linkage between pilot and aircraft control surfaces has been replaced by electronic (wired) sensors and servers.

The use of redundant functional design has also proven of value in lower-cost products. By designing electronic storage devices that logically identify and isolate unreliable electronic storage locations, the electronic storage device can operate in a fault-tolerant manner. This is an example of many situations where it is more cost efficient to design in reliability redundancy or fault tolerance rather than design to meet an extremely large component and operating system MTBF. We use the word "system" in a generic sense, and it refers to any operating system, large or small. A system could be as large as a worldwide radar network or small as a single electronic resistor.

Redundant Design Fundamentals

Redundant design describes a system where two or more independent paths are made available to complete an input to output function.

The use of redundant design is described universally by the laws of probability and presented logically by block diagrams.

The following symbols are used in this chapter:

$$P_W = \text{probability of operating to specification}$$

$$P_{\overline{W}} = \text{probability of not working to specification}$$

$$P_W = (1 - P_{\overline{W}})$$

A system is composed of elements arranged to work together within designed conditions (e.g., Figure 6-8).

The elements presented in Figure 6-8 are connected in series. All elements of the system must be working for the system to be working. If the probabilities that all elements are working are independent, then the probability that the system is working is

$$P_W(S) = \{P_W(A)\}\{P_W(B)\}\{P_W(---)\}$$

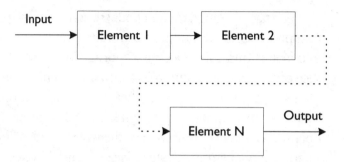

FIGURE **6-8.   All failure elements of a system in serial configuration**

This description of probability of a system composed of series elements agrees with our intuitive understandings:

1. All elements of a logical series system need to be working for the system to be working.
2. The element with the lowest probability of working (by definition the lowest reliability) will be the most probable cause of system failure.
3. The larger number of elements in a series system of the same reliability lowers the system reliability. So keep things simple.

For those familiar with mathematical description, this condition is known as a logical AND.

Although not explicitly stated, the system series probability of working was calculated in reliability prediction in the first section of this chapter. Figure 6-4 provides data for an excellent example.

Figure 6-4 displays 10 categories of components. The failure rate is given per 1,000 hours ($\times 10^{-6}$). The failure rate $\times$ 1,000 hours = failures in 1,000 hours. Since survivors at 1,000 hours (the definition of reliability) is equal to 1 − failures in 1,000 hours, a table of element probability of working (reliability) can be generated as follows:

Element	Fails in 1,000 hours	Survivors of 1,000 hours
A	0.000302	0.999698
B	0.000181	0.999819
C	0.000180	0.999820

D	0.000092	0.999908
E	0.000090	0.999910
F	0.000090	0.999910
G	0.000024	0.999976
H	0.000016	0.999984
I	0.000004	0.999996
J	0.000004	0.999996

The printed circuit board can be represented by a serial logic system described in Figure 6-8. In this case, the $P(w)$ for the system is the product of all elements of the individual categories. This agrees with our intuition of systems serial reliability.

The system elements may be connected in another way to increase the system reliability. The two series elements of Figure 6-8 may be connected as shown in Figure 6-9.

In this example, element A is replaced by element A_1 and A_2, placed in parallel. Both elements are capable of providing the system with adequate working function. An element failure can occur only if both A_1 and A_2 fail.

This "redundant" element can be described simply by considering the probability of failure (probability of not working) in each parallel branch of the element.

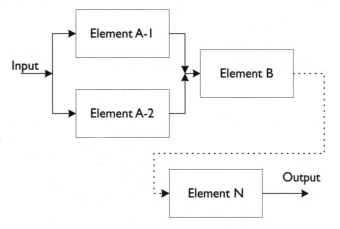

FIGURE 6-9.   A parallel (redundant element) within a system

$$P_{\overline{W}}(\text{Element}) = P_{\overline{W}}(A_1)P_{\overline{W}}(A_2)$$

This description of the probability for failure of a parallel element agrees with our intuitive understanding of the model.

1. The probability of failure in a parallel element is much lower than a series element.
2. The use of parallel or redundant element capability is the common way to maintain system capability (reliability).

For those familiar with mathematical description, this condition is known as a logical OR.

As an example, if element A of Figure 6-4 (line drivers) were designed into a redundant configuration, and then if one set of line drivers failed, another set would provide function for the system. Using the equation

$$P_{\overline{W}}(\text{Element}) = P_{\overline{W}}(A_1)P_{\overline{W}}(A_2)$$

$$9 \times 10^{-8} = (302 \times 10^{-6})(302 \times 10^{-6})$$

The reliability of element A has improved from the least reliable to the most reliable by engineering a redundant functional path in the system. It is obvious that a parallel operating element, which may be expanded to include an entire operating system, has significantly improved reliability. Many texts have been written on this subject. They quickly move into the significantly varied and complex product applications.

An Elementary Redundant Design Example

Private aircraft have excellent product reliability based upon the safety factor in mechanical design, scheduled maintenance to minimize failure, and a system of operational weather data that assures reduced risk of flying in bad weather. These aspects of flying are regulated by the FAA. The single most important factor in private aircraft reliability is pilot error. Extensive training and personal awareness is emphasized to reduce this failure. Another aspect of private aircraft reliability is an excellent example of redundant design. All single-motored aircraft may have a catastrophic failure of an

"We have 2 bathrooms in case one fails"

estimated 1 failure per 500,000 hours. This failure is defined as independent of system causality, such as running out of gas. The result would be an unplanned aircraft landing. Now, a two-motored private plane is designed to function with only one engine, yet the failure rate of each engine is not greater than that of a single engine. Therefore, the probability of two independent engines failing is

$$P_{\overline{W}}(\text{Element}) = P_{\overline{W}}(A_1)P_{\overline{W}}(A_2)$$

$$\text{FR} = (1/500,000)(1/500,000) = 1/2,500,000,000,000,000$$

Essentially, the redundant second motor has all but eliminated the probability of two engines simultaneously (and system-independently) failing during aircraft operation. This model is validated for the case of single- and two-engine aircraft.

Redundancy Design Applications

Several aspects of redundancy design and product reliability need to be considered prior to considering the optimum design. The following paragraphs discuss these aspects providing the unfamiliar professional engineer and business person with an insight to the redundant design process.

Design for Perfect Product Redundancy Function

In this design, the system always operates in a specified timely and logical manner when one path of the redundant parallel element fails. The specified "timely" and "logical" manner varies extensively depending upon the application.

1. The second, backup computer in the "fly by wire" aircraft control becomes the primary operating system after detection in monitoring a failure in the first operating system and switches to that system. The time required for this detection and switching to a redundant is insignificant when compared to the functional response of the airplane controls.
2. A hospital emergency power switches when the primary power fails. There is a delay before the emergency power is operational. This timely manner may be specified differently for various operations. The emergency power may be in parallel, with the diesel generators in operation, to a one-minute on-line redundant power capability.
3. This document is being written with a computer, which saves the written script automatically after every 100 words. The software company has specified this reliability in a timely and logical manner.
4. The public power companies and the interlocked power grid exist in a redundant power delivery mode. The economics and reliability of utilities delivering power has been excellent. However, the increased demand for reliability in electrical power has become an increasing focus of groups advocating policies that favor specific causes. The efficiencies are definitely inherent in the power grid system, and the grid is an excellent example of redundant product design.

All these examples can be considered design in terms of system functionality. Note that all specifications must meet the "timeliness" and "logical" requirements of the redundant reliability. They exist as an option to meet the reliability needs of your specific product. Reliability cost is a major factor in the optimal business decision.

Summary

Chapter 6 is directed at the selected topics of product reliability specification, physical product reliability design, and designed redundancy.

Product reliability specification provides the quantified linkage between the cost and benefit considerations of a specific product reliability. Product reliability specification is centered in prediction. The sources of data for the prediction are existing customer/consumer use product reliability data, product age-accelerated tests, materials test data, and component reliability data. All sources must be utilized to best predict a product reliability specification.

The actual format for prediction has been established in procedures, for example, of Mil Std 217 and Bellcore 332. The fundamental characteristic of prediction formats is that they rely on catastrophic component failure data as the basis for future product reliability estimates.

The actual product reliability specification goal is determined by the customer/consumer in the competitive marketplace and is achieved by optimizing the cost of product reliability elements designed into the product. This design process is primarily established through experience with specific products, but it also has an increasing basis founded in materials science, electronic, and mechanical reliability design.

Checklists of the common electronic and mechanical reliability factors were presented that describe some of the many design tools available to achieve the best reliability design for your product.

A higher level of functional redundancy design was discussed to familiarize managers and engineers with the application of this effective technique. In general, higher reliability of products is a requirement to remain competitive with your business. The choice between using higher reliability in components and the cost for redundant design requires a new product reliability expertise. The application of redundant techniques, and the impact upon business decisions, cannot be ignored in many products.

Product reliability is inherent in the design.
    —DR. LES ANDERSEN

References

1. J. M. Juran, Frank M. Gryna Jr., and R. S. Bingham Jr., *Quality Control Handbook,* 3rd ed. (New York: McGraw-Hill, 1974).
2. Armand V. Feigenbaum, *Total Quality Control,* 3rd ed. (New York: McGraw-Hill, 1983).

7

Manufacturing a Reliable Product

The manufacturing process cannot make the product more reliable than the basic design.

Introduction

Managers should read this chapter to understand the role of manufacturing control in producing a reliable product. The two subject control techniques, incoming (receiving) inspection and statistical process control, are significant factors in determining your product reliability. A description of how these tools operate in an effective, continuous manner is presented.

Engineers in general should clearly understand these manufacturing control tools. Manufacturing engineers specifically should be extremely familiar with the fundamentals of these control techniques. Development engineers should be aware of these control subjects and design the product for effective, easy manufacturing control.

Note that "control" is the key to manufacturing a reliable product. Manufacturing is primarily controlling processes to specifications in order to profitably make the specified product.

Unfortunately, the manufacturing organizations receive little credit for the vast majority of activities that are under control and an inordinate amount of attention for the rare incidents that signify lack of control. The goal is to obtain the most effective control in manufacturing your product. For the two subjects that are discussed in this chapter, the underlying premise is that lack of control in each category allows an unreasonable amount of unreliable product to be manufactured.

The two common methods for achieving control are discussed in this chapter and should be familiar to every manufacturing manager and engineer within modern businesses. The fundamental concepts are

▶ Product reliability is degraded when a supplier sends unreliable components and material into the manufacturing process. The proper control is achieved by an effective inspection and audit techniques that control the supplier product reliability.

▶ Product reliability is degraded in manufacturing when manufacturing process variables are not controlled. The proper control is maintained by an effective statistical process control (SPC) program that triggers a corrective response to abnormal process and product in the manufacturing line. The result is a higher level of product reliability.

The two control activities that affect the basic underlying factor of business economics are cost of manufacturing (yield) and cost of customer/consumer use (reliability).

The key to having a manufacturing process that has a minimum negative impact on the product's designed reliability is to evaluate the manufacturing process until an acceptable performance level is reached. Then, install adequate controls that will ensure that the manufacturing process maintains acceptable performance.

IBM has been actively involved in understanding and controlling the manufacturing process so that its degradation of the intrinsic product design reliability is minimized. For example, in IBM's TR 02.901 technical report entitled "Process Qualification—Manufacturing Insurance Policy" dated August 1991, IBM's approach to qualifying their manufacturing processes was defined. It consisted of three independent off-line evaluations conducted by their Product Test Function (an independent unit). These tests were entitled

▶ Engineering Verification Test—EVT
▶ Design Verification Test—DVT
▶ Manufacturing Verification Test—MVT

(Note: These types of evaluations will be discussed in Chapter 8.)

These tests were complemented by the following series of four independent evaluations of the processes that produce the parts that went into the test:

▶ Level I—Development Process Qualification
▶ Level II—Pilot Line Qualification
▶ Level III—Manufacturing Process Line Conditional Qualification
▶ Level IV—Production Line Qualification

Figure 7-1 shows how the three independent off-line tests and the four levels of qualifications were scheduled into the product cycle for a typical component.

To gain better understanding of the manufacturing process qualification activities that took place during these four independent qualification evaluations, let us look in detail at level III. The level III qualification consisted of three parts:

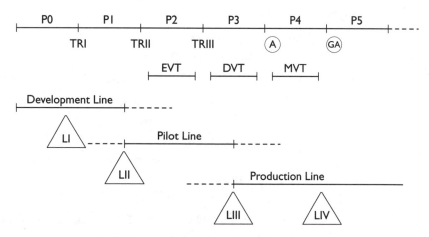

FIGURE 7-1. **Typical IBM component qualification cycle in the 1980s**

1. certifying each step in the manufacturing process;
2. processing qualification laps and stress runs; and
3. independent program evaluation.

The top line in Figure 7-1 shows the different phases that a component goes through from phase 0 (initial business proposal) through phase 5 (product deliverable to external customers/consumers). The "A" on the chart indicates the analysis point in the product's cycle and the "GA" stands for "general availability" to external customers/consumers.

Control of Incoming Material and Components

Introduction

A common cause for manufacturing unreliable product is unreliable components or outputs that enter the manufacturing process from suppliers. The goal of manufacturing is to control this incoming product reliability in an effective manner. It is for this very reason that the reliability management function (RMF) should actively participate in all supplier selections and qualification activities. The RMF serves a very special role in supplier selection that cannot be handled by any other function. This is particularly true of component suppliers. This special role is obvious by reviewing the following partial supplier reliability evaluation checklist.

1. Reliability Management
   —Is there a separate RMF?
   —What percentage of the RMF's engineers are certified reliability engineers by the American Society for Quality?
   —How is the RMF performance measured?
   —What is the reliability budget for the current year?
   —How are the various costs associated with reliability and unreliability measured?
2. Reliability Analysis
   —What is RMF's role in defining the reliability specifications that are included in the product requirement specifications that are developed by Marketing and Sales?

—What is the RMF's role in the product development cycle?

—What is the RMF's role in qualifying the manufacturing process?

—What part does the RMF play in the fault tree analysis development?

—How good is the database that is used by the RMF to make reliability projections?

—How are probabilistic risk assessments made?

—What degree of uncertainty and error is there in the reliability projections of the product that we will be buying?

—How is the environmental testing performed, and who defines the test procedures?

—How are human factors considered in the reliability projections?

—What is the gap between established product between the reliability projections and the actual reliability performance?

—What acceleration factors are used, and what level of confidence does the RMF have in these factors?

—Is continuously increasing stress testing used?

—What type of off-line test is used to ensure that the manufacturing process does not vary in a way that has a detrimental impact upon field reliability (e.g., products reliability acceptance testing, environmental stress screening, burn-in, etc.)

—How effective is the field failure reporting system?

—What involvement does the RMF have in the field return failure mode and effect analysis activities?

—What level of statistical training and competency does the RMF personnel have?

—What type of reliability training is provided to the production and development engineers? What percentage have completed the training successfully?

Experience has shown us that several major situations exist that create unreliable supplier product:

1. *New supplier product reliability problem.* A cause of product reliability failure mode may be traced to the advent of a new supplier of material and components used in manufacturing. The reliability problem stems from one to a combination of interacting factors. The supplier may be, from a business

point of view, cost effective, but the new supplier is cost effective because the cost burden of product reliability control is minimized for that item. Typically, the new supplier, when its product has been identified as a significant reliability risk, will improve reliability through an improvement plan. Of course, the additional cost of reliability improvement for compliance to specified reliability will place the new supplier in a higher cost position. In addition, a common situation is that the initial supplier's incoming test samples are selected for evaluation rather than chosen at random to enhance initial assessments of the materials and components. In general, the primary origin of unreliable product is the compromise to gain cost competitiveness by new suppliers.

Another product reliability failure mode is traced not to the deliberate inadequate reliability control at the supplier due to cost factors but to the supplier's legitimate venture into manufacturing a new material or component. A new manufacturing process and product will require some time to establish adequate control. The intuitive feeling that new products and processes possess greater reliability risk is correct. It is always less risky to purchase materials or components from a supplier once the product is established. In general, a product reliability risk exists during the transient time required to establish control over a new processes and product.

2. *Engineering changes to existing products.* Supplier products are undergoing a constant evolution primarily directed toward improving the specified product function and reducing cost. Many of these changes affect reliability. Since the environments are never completely understood, a finite possibility exists that a supplier product change will produce a significant reliability problem due to interaction within the user system. An example would be the introduction of a bearing grease that improves the lifetime of the motor but degrades the lifetime of the associated gear train within the using system.

3. *Maverick lots.*

Maverick lots are clusters of unreliable products that the manufacturer periodically produces.

For reasons such as operation interruption, work shift changes, or missed essential maintenance, a lot or batch of product misses a process step or is inadequately processed. This exceptional treatment of this lot occasionally results in a significant cluster of unreliable product.

Another common source of maverick lots is simple lack of administrative control of the supplier products. Often, rejects are mistakenly supplied instead of accepted, down-level reliability categories are supplied instead of reliability specified products, and returned failures are reshipped without reliability evaluation. Most of these activities are not malicious nor deliberate but the effect is just as dramatic.

Maverick lots are effectively reduced by manufacturing products within a managed quality system dedicated to elimination of unreliable product.

4. *"Off-specced" supplier product.* The reality of manufacturing dictates that at some time a decision will be made to manufacture product using less-than-specified incoming material. The control of this activity rests within the manufacturing administrative process. However, it should be noted that the importance of incoming inspection and control now is essential for the successful utilization of the "off-specced" incoming product. We know of suppliers who hold back components that do not meet specification and ship them later when their customers/consumers badly need the components. We were told, confidentially, by one supplier that 8 out of 10 times their customers/consumers off-spec the bad parts and use them, saving the supplier a lot of scrap and rework cost.

These are the significant contributors to reliability defects entering the manufacturing process from suppliers of incoming components to the process. A primary task for manufacturing is to identify and reduce to an acceptable level process contributions to the unreliable product.

Incoming Inspection Fundamentals

The global consideration in manufacturing is producing with the best economic efficiency of the operation, which will translate into the greatest profit. Two elements that detract from the business efficient manufacturing are products that fail to meet the specified manufacturing levels of acceptance (yield) in the manufacturing process and products that fail to perform to specified function with time (reliability) during customer/consumer use. These two elements, yield and reliability, can often be traced to a common root cause, product that does not meet the level of acceptance when entering the manufacturing process—bad incoming product.

For this book, we primarily consider the bad incoming items that will eventually result in a failure during customer/consumer use of the manufactured product. It is the responsibility of manufacturing management to determine what levels of incoming defective items are tolerable to keep an economic balance between the cost of preventing entrance of bad product into the manufacturing process and the cost of having defective incoming items impact yield and reliability. This economic balancing to achieve optimum economics during product manufacturing is the primary aspect of the dynamic management of product manufacturing.

If manufacturing is concerned about unreliable product entering their process, why not remove all unreliable product by inspecting every unit in the best possible manner before it enters the manufacturing process? This 100% incoming inspection technique is chosen by many as the best incoming inspection. It is quite effective for defect removal but does have some characteristics that may dictate an alternate method:

1. The cost of 100% inspection may make the manufactured product cost noncompetitive. You may discover that the number of items incoming to the manufacturing process would require an army of inspectors to accomplish 100% inspection. The resulting improvement in yield and reliability of your product may not economically justify the 100% inspection. The business result would be a product with a small improvement in yield and reliability beyond your competitors but in a noncompetitive cost position in the marketplace. (Note that shifting the 100% inspection back to the supplier does not significantly reduce the inspection cost.)
2. Inspection, particularly visual inspections, does not mean 100% effectiveness in identifying and removing defects. In fact, 100% visual inspection may be as low as 80% in removing defects.
3. The 100% inspection does not remove administrative error from the inspection process. For example, no matter how effective the inspection, if the rejects are mistakenly sent forward to the manufacturing process, the product reliability is lowered.

4. The inspection process in itself may be degrading the product. The extreme condition exists when the inspection test is destructive.

An alternate method of incoming inspection is to measure a sample of each lot of incoming product to ensure a level of product reliability in all product. This incoming sample inspection will significantly reduce cost and may be sufficient to control an adequate reliability in the manufactured product. The manufacturing management will balance inspection requirements for incoming items between a sample of none (0%) to 100%. The chosen level of inspection only reflects the economic balance between receiving inspection cost invested compared to the reduced cost in the resulting improved yield and reliability cost.

The crux of understanding incoming inspection is understanding the statistical relationship between the specified sample data from a lot of incoming product and the specified data of the entire lot. Sample inspection is not as simple and deterministic as the ideal relationship desired (but unachievable) presented in Figure 7-2, and it requires an understanding based upon statistical principles to be effectively utilized.

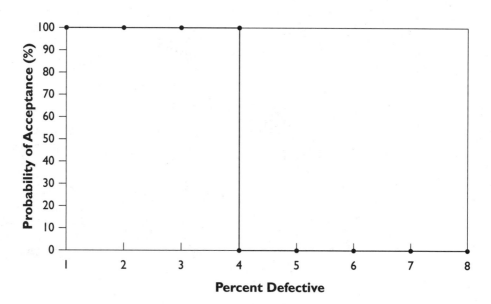

FIGURE 7-2. The ideal sampling curve

Management would prefer an ideal sampling inspection as presented in Figure 7-2. Figure 7-2 displays the relationship between the percent failures in lots of the incoming product and the probability of rejection of any lot by a sample inspection of the lot. In this example, when the lot has less than 4% defective product, the lot is always accepted. When the lot has 4% or more defective product, the lot is always rejected. (The value of 4% is arbitrarily chosen for demonstration purposes and could be any value from 0 to 100%.)

The ideal sampling inspection shown in Figure 7-2 would be as effective as a 100% inspection of incoming product at a greatly reduced cost. Unfortunately, this inspection is physically and proven mathematically impossible. However, the plot of percentage of lots accepted versus percentage defective in the inspected lot is common to all sample inspections.

Sampling Inspection Background

All incoming lot inspections involve only three physical values: the sample number (size), the number of defects in sample specified to reject the lot, and

That lot was good . . . they all fired. When does the next lot come in?

the number in the lot (size). These are the only sampling variables. Our ultimate task is to specify these three values to achieve the best inspection possible for each specific incoming inspection.

The explanation of incoming inspection fundamentals has been divided into two steps:

1. First, an example of a sample size n and acceptance number c is going to be used to generate from Poisson statistics a mathematical model of real sampling inspection called an operating characteristic curve (OC curve). This example is generated from an incoming defect level of 12%. Although this defect level is too high to represent a typical incoming inspection, it does allow a clear demonstration of OC curve generation. An example using a lower (e.g. 1%) defect level would be difficult to visually demonstrate and would invoke the immediate consideration of lot size.

2. Second, an example of incoming inspection at a reject level of 0.40% will be used to explain the use of the ANSI Z 1.4 1981, which combines the OC curve statistics of step 1 with the consideration of lot size. ANSI Z 1.4 1981 is the national standard for applying incoming sampling inspection for defects.

Generating the OC Curve

The statistical (sampling) outcomes for an incoming inspection of items can be accurately described by a model of the Poisson distribution. This description can be easily demonstrated by an example. Unless you already understand this application of the Poisson distribution, please read the following explanation to understand precisely the sample inspection technique

Let us first imagine that a lot of 500 items arrives at the back dock every day for use in manufacturing our product. Those items are sample inspected in the following manner each day:

- $n = 25$ (the random sample taken from the lot is 25)
- $c = 3$ (the lot is accepted if there are 3 or less rejects)

In this example, we are not indicating how we arrived at the sample number n and the acceptance number c. This sampling plan is specified as having an n of 25 and a c of 3.

In Chapter 5, sampling of black jelly beans was described to demonstrate the model of sampling results generated by the Poisson distribution. That model is now used directly, applying it to rejects rather than jelly beans, in our sample inspection example.

What happens if we sample inspect 25 items, chosen at random from the daily lot?

1. Our first observation is that we really never precisely know the real number of bad items in the lot. There is a statistical uncertainty involved in sampling. In our example, the real mathematical boundaries are that we picked the only 25 good ones out of the 500 units or that we picked the only 25 bad ones out of 500 units. Both have an extremely low probability of occurrence. We never know the exact number of defects, but what we can do is demonstrate by example the relationships for an assumed random reject level for the incoming product.

2. The probability for the number of sample defects observed from a lot is described exactly by the Poisson distribution. For instance, if the true lot defect level of one lot was 12% and many samples of 25 were chosen from that lot, then the probabilities of selecting samples with a specific value is given by the Poisson distribution presented in Figure 7-3.

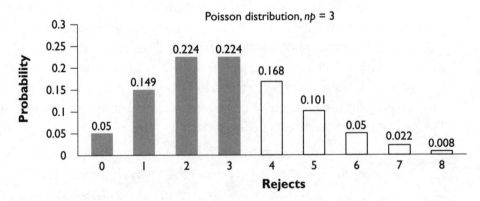

FIGURE 7-3.   **Sample defect probability distribution for n = 25, with a 12% lot defect level**

The generation of the probability distribution that determines the probability of selecting a number of defects in a sample of 25 is generated from the Poisson distribution. The equation and the input parameters are:

$$P(x) = \frac{\lambda^x}{x!}e^{-\lambda}$$

where lambda = *np*, *x* = number of rejects in the sample (in this example, 0 to 25), and lambda = *np* = 3 (in this example, 25 × 0.12).

The actual probability *P(x)* of selecting a sample with *x* defects is generated directly from the equation. Normally, calculation is not required because probability charts for *np* and *x* values are available in most statistical texts.

Figure 7-3 displays the following information:

1. The distribution of defects in the sampling inspection example demonstrates that a single sample may present data with less, equal, or more defect percentages than actual average defective percentage in the sampled lot. In our example, the average lot defective is given as 12%. However, the average defective percentage of all samples always converges to the lot average after many samples. This makes sense in that if we sampled all of the lot (100% inspection) in our example, we would precisely determine the average 12% defect level.

2. The sampling inspection does not change the actual lot defective percentage. No sampling technique can improve product.

3. The sampling distribution is determined solely by the sample number and the true lot defective. The acceptable defect level of incoming items is determined by business economics. In this case, it is acceptable to have a sampling distribution where *n* = 25 and *c* = 3. The acceptance number *c* and sample number *n* control the incoming acceptable defect level.

The Random Sample

This is a sample of the text for the definition, or these are more synonyms and usages that are commonly found in the English language.

Random Sample—A sample of given size in such a manner that all combinations of all units from which samples will be drawn have an equal or ascertainable chance of being selected as the sample.

It is extremely important to take a random sample of the lot that is submitted for inspection to get valid results. For example, 500 parts are shipped in 25 boxes, 20 parts per box. If the sample size is 25 parts, a random sample is not selecting all parts from one box at random out of the 25 and 5 parts from another box. A random sample would be made up of one part randomly collected from each box. The sample must represent the total population of the lot. Collecting data from one box could provide misleading information.

Let's take the case where an individual produces four parts per day. Over a week's time, an operator makes one box of parts. The lot consists of a week's output from 20 people. If only one box is used as a sample, only one person's work is sampled.

Another extreme would be for a single machine that can produce 100 parts per hour. After every 150 parts are processed, the tools need to be replaced or the equipment adjusted. In this case, 25 parts represent 15 minutes of machine operation. This is too short a time to evaluate that variation occurs as the tools become dull and are replaced.

Not selecting a sample that is representative of the lot is the most frequent error made in receiving inspection departments.

The OC Curve

The OC curve is a mathematical model for predicting the probability of accepting lots through sampling at specified actual defective levels in the lots.

The initial sampling example is sufficient to demonstrate the application of the Poisson statistical distribution to sampling inspection, but it included the condition that the incoming lot of items was actually 12% defective. If we already know the percentage of defective items, why would we even have to inspect it? In sampling procedures for an actual lot, God alone precisely knows the true defect percentages of incoming lots of items. However, we do know that an OC sampling distribution of a 12% defective level is acceptable to our manufacturing process.

Through statistical techniques we can circumvent that lack of knowledge of true defect percentages in lots and still create an acceptable sampling inspection.

Figure 7-4 contains five Poisson distributions that are generated by the parameters of sample size n equal to 25 and np's equal to 1 through 5. This is the mathematical model for a random sample inspection of 25 items from a large lot with assumed defect levels of 4, 8, 12, 16, and 20%.

7-4A

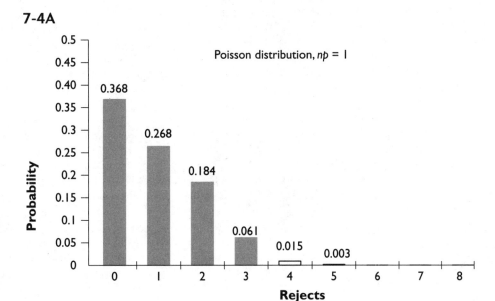

7-4B

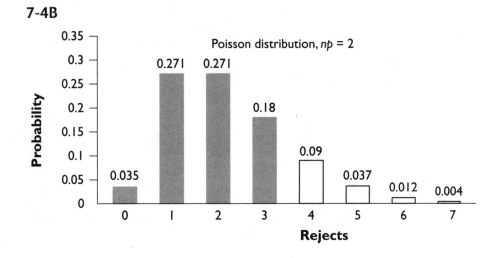

7-4C

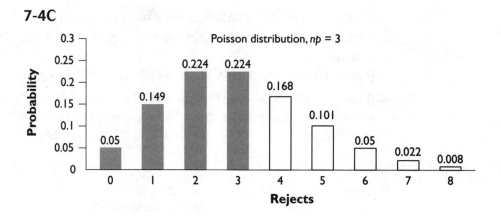

7-4D

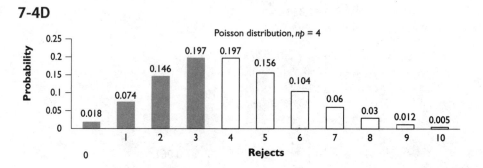

7-4E

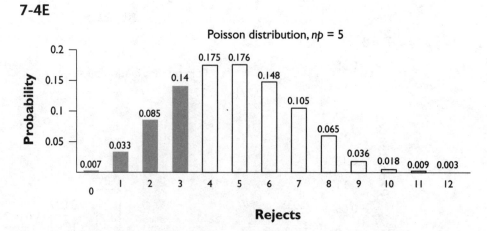

FIGURE 7-4A, B, C, D, E.   Poisson distributions for sampling **n** =25 for 4, 8, 12, 16, and 20 percentage of lot defective

Figure 7-4 is also used as a convenient display of the probabilities of accepting the lot based upon the sample plan of $n = 25$ and $c = 3$. The accept probabilities for 0 through 3 defects in a sample are displayed in black, and the reject probabilities of 4 through 25 defects in a sample are displayed in white. Take some time to clearly understand this fundamental concept.

The set of distributions shown in Figure 7-4 presents an insight into the sampling inspection process. The random sampling defect distribution is mathematically modeled exactly by Poisson statistics for every lot average defects.

1. The larger the actual lot defect percentage, the larger is the probability of sampling a higher number of defects. This is intuitively felt but now precisely determined from the statistical probability distributions.
2. There is a definite increased probability that sampling will reject lots with higher defect levels and accept lots with lower defect levels. Sampling inspection does measure the low and high defect levels in the lots.
3. Sampling can never assure zero lot defects. In fact, the Poisson equation does not allow $pn = 0$.

Figure 7-5 is constructed by plotting the information presented by all curves in Figure 7-4 as the probability of sampling lot acceptance (y axis) versus the actual percentage defective in all lots of incoming product (x axis). These are the sample variables as plotted in the ideal OC in Figure 7-2. In our

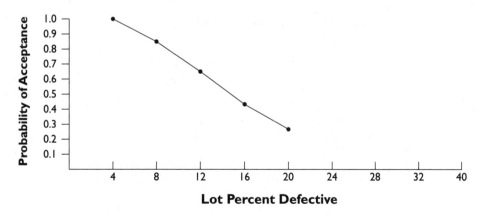

FIGURE 7-5.　The operating characteristic (OC) curve

case, we just use the decimal fraction of the probability of acceptance (decimal fraction of the black values) for each percentage defective.

The ideal sampling curve (Figure 7-2) can be practically realized only as a curve based upon a precise mathematical model creating Figure 7-5. Remember, we specified the sample inspection by the following: $n = 25$ and $c = 3$. We will randomly sample 25 items per lot and accept the lot if 3 or less (0, 1, 2, or 3) defects are found. This means also that the lot is rejected if 4 or more defects are found. The sampling parameters are used to generate Figure 7-5, conveniently presented as distributions where the numbers 0 to 3 (accepts) are shaded black and the numbers 4 and greater (rejects) are shaded white.

An OC curve is an exact mathematical model for predicting the probability distributions of accepting lots through sampling under specified conditions. *The probability of rejecting a lot with high percentage defective is greater than rejecting a lot with low percentage defective.* That agrees with our original goal. A unique OC curve describes that relationship for each set of sample conditions.

Figure 7-5 is the OC curve for a particular sampling plan. The number of defects that is allowed for accepting a lot (in our example, $= 3$) is called the acceptance number c. So for our example of a sampling plan, we have $n = 25$ and $c = 3$. Every combination of n and c produces a unique operating characteristic. All that is left to do is find an OC best suited to our incoming inspection.

Choosing an OC Curve

It is obvious that the OC curve presented in Figure 7-5 has little application because it represents inspection to a unrealistic 12% level. It is difficult to choose a proper OC. Once the OC is chosen, the sampling inspection specified by the OC is actually very simple.

Remember the principle of the OC: lots with higher defective levels have a greater probability of rejection than lower defective levels. The real problem with establishing an OC is that two unknowns exist.

▶ The exact defect levels of incoming lots, or distribution of lot level defects, is unknown. It is subject to many subjective estimations by the producer and supplier.

▶ The economic impact of the defective incoming product upon the manufacturing process can never be precisely evaluated.

The appropriate OC plan is negotiated in the best mutual interest of the producer and customer/consumer. The supplier wishes to minimize lot rejection within a specific perceived lot failure-rate distribution. The customer/consumer wishes to maximize lot rejection within a specific perceived lot failure-rate distribution.

The two dominant effects of sampling inspection considered during negotiation of the OC curve are called the producer's risk and the customer's/consumer's risk.

The **producer's risk** is the probability of rejecting the lot when the relative quality of the lot is good. In Figure 7-6, it is the case when a lot of actual 2% defect level is rejected when the actual reject level is acceptable to the customer/consumer. In this case, the indicated 2.8% defect level has a 10% (1–90%) producer's risk.

The **consumer's risk** is the probability of accepting the lot when the relative quality of the lot is poor. In Figure 7-6, it is the case when a lot of

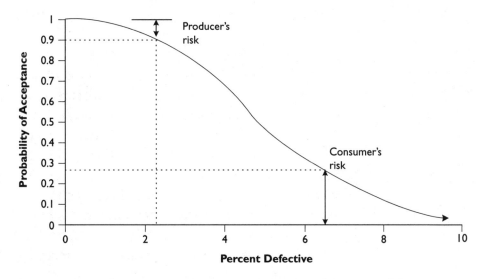

FIGURE 7-6.   Consumer's risk and producer's risk on an OC curve

actual 8% defect level is accepted when the actual defect level is not acceptable to the customer/consumer. In this case, the indicated 6.4% defect level has a 25% customer's/consumer's risk.

The statistical nature of sampling introduces producer's and customer's/consumer's risk into all incoming inspections. Producer's and customer's/consumer's risk evaluation is mainly focused upon the tails of the OC curve. There is no economic impact, beyond test efficiency, in the sampling lots that closely represent the true lot defect population. It is in your best interest to reduce your producer's and customer's/consumer's risk by choosing the best OC curve for your specific sampling inspection.

The economic significance of the OC cannot be understated. It balances reduced product cost with increased functional and reliability risk. By its very nature, nobody is satisfied with a good OC curve. The following points should be considered.

1. The OC curve is only an inspection sampling plan. It does not make the incoming items better nor does it by itself improve a poor producer-customer/consumer relationship.

2. The OC curve explicitly establishes your tolerance for defective product. Note that there usually is a significant difference between the average incoming defect level and the OC average acceptance (50) level. The incoming items can be primarily acceptable product with a few bad lots.

3. An insidious problem exists when the OC plan passes functionally acceptable product yet also passes unreliable product. If your sampling test procedure does not specifically test product reliability, you may be only optimizing your present product functionality. Stress testing and test to failure is recommended for sampling inspection.

4. The OC curve is usually established to detect bad incoming product lots. Once the defective product is detected, associated bad product can be rejected and, if needed, purged from your manufacturing operation before a serious business impact occurs. Consider whether your exposure is one of poor yield within your manufacturing operation or whether it extends to product reliability and your customer/consumer. This is key in determining your specific OC curve.

5. The sampling test procedures require a periodic review and review for new applications.

Your specific OC curve will be determined to optimize your specific incoming inspection requirements. Many books and perspectives have been presented on this subject. Several general points on OC curves should be recognized:

1. The steeper the OC curve, the greater discriminating power of your sample between different percents defective. The steepness of the curve is primarily a function of n. This corresponds to our intuition that larger samples produce greater discrimination. A 100% inspection plan has a vertical lot reject discrimination slope.
2. The shoulder at the top of the OC curve indicates how much defective product will be accepted by manufacturing. Although your average defect level may be much less, you are stating by the OC curve that you can tolerate the amount indicated by the shoulder. A zero defect acceptability requires 100% item inspection (vertical lot reject discrimination with zero defects).
3. The bottom tail of the curve shows where defective product most probably will be rejected. The producer will wish to reduce this area to an acceptable amount.
4. The disposition of rejected lots is crucial. Rejected lot disposition should be part of the OC curve agreement.

An insight to manufacturing incoming product control can be understood from the n and c parameters alone. Even the 12% OC plan used as an example may actually be used to benefit the business. The $n = 25$ and $c = 3$ are of an OC plan that indicates protection of manufacturing operation with little impact upon reliability.

Examples would be incorrect tap holes or paint matching. In this situation, the impact upon manufacturing is detection of defect product and substitution of good product during the process. But the manufacturer does not want to create a work stoppage by filling the entire manufacturing process with defective product. So a loose inspection is chosen that will reject highly defective lots with little inspection cost. If this were not so, the manufacturer would have chosen a larger sample with a smaller acceptance number. If the manufacturer wasn't worried about occasional bad lots at all, he or she would drop the entire incoming inspection.

Your exact sampling incoming inspection requirements are most likely achieved through the "cookbook" approach discussed in the next section.

Formalized Incoming Inspection Procedure

The fundamental derivation of the OC curve was done without consideration of the lot size, which is a significant factor in determining the statistically optimum sampling inspection plan.

Although the lot size function will not be mathematically derived due to the low value of this long process, a standardized method of applying incoming inspection techniques has greatly simplified the sampling inspection planning. ANSI/ASQC Z 1.4 1981 is the American National Standard for sampling inspection. MIL STD 105_ also contains the same standard for sampling inspection. ANSI/ASQC Z 1.4 1981 addresses inspection in terms of lot size, sample size, and acceptance number for attaining a desired acceptable quality level (AQL).

The AQL (acceptable quality level) is the maximum percentage defective that can be satisfactorily accepted.

The AQL standard presented in Appendix D is adequate for most incoming inspection plans.

For a normal sampling inspection, determine the sample size code letter in Appendix D1. Assume that the lot size is 500 items. The corresponding sample size code letter for normal inspection (II) is H.

Now let's turn to Appendix D2 to complete our normal sampling plan.

Let a 0.4% AQL test plan be chosen. Just go down the sample code letter column to H. Row H contains the sample size (50) for inspecting an AQL level indicated in the horizontal axis. If we choose a 0.4% AQL, circled in the Appendix D2 table, then a random sample should be accepted with 0 defects in the sample and rejected with 1 or more rejects in the sample.

The incoming inspection plan is that simple. For a 0.4% AQL, randomly sample 50 items from a 500-item lot. Then accept lots with 0 defects, and reject lots with 1 or more rejects.

The statistical process to derive the AQL standard lot, sample, and AQL relationship is complex and not given in the standards. However, some aspects of the standard are almost intuitive.

1. Note that a 0.4% defective level is relatively small for a 50-item sample. Statistically, the majority of sample inspections will have 0 defects. There is a limit to how small of a percentage of AQL can be sampled from a specific lot size. Note that Appendix D explicitly states that lot sizes of 150 or less (size code F or less) require 100% inspection to determine a 0.4% AQL.

Various schemes have been devised to circumvent the reality of losing statistical significance when attempting AQL's of 1% or lower. However, it is realistic to consider 100% inspection as a viable alternate.

2. We first derived an OC curve without considering the lot size. It is an interesting academic process to return to that derivation and calculate the resulting error. It can easily be done from Appendix D. The reason for using a 12% OC example is clear because we eliminate the preponderance of 0 values from our Poisson distributions. At low percentage defect levels, the derivation remains accurate, but the plotted results are drastically skewed toward zero.

3. Although the relationship between lot size and sample parameters n and c used for an ideal AQL plan is complex to generate, please note the following: The sample size for small lots (2 to 8 items) starts at the square root of the lot size and changes to about twice the square root of the lot size for large lots (1,201 to 3,200). This is solely mentioned for you to respond to the case where you observe sample sizes significantly different from the square root of the lot size during incoming inspection. In that case, get a professional statistician to interpret a suspect sampling plan. For instance, a sample of 10 items taken from a lot of 1,000 has questionable statistical significance.

The mathematical treatment of the statistics of incoming sampling inspection has been in use for more than 50 years with outstanding success. We are not recommending that you use a 50-year-old plan. However, the process is unchanged in its mathematical basis, it can be understood with some effort, and it should be communicated clearly to all decision-making people in your specific situation. It can be of great value to most businesses.

This book does not develop the advanced sampling inspection techniques such as repeated inspections of the same lot and methodical sample inspection optimization. If these techniques are used by your organization, the requirement and logic of their application should be documented by a competent statistical professional. However, they are all based upon the sampling model of incoming inspection presented in this section.

Controlling the Manufacturing Process

Introduction

The control of manufacturing processes is accomplished through the technique of statistical process control (SPC), which applies essentially to all manufacturing processes. Manufacturing and process control is attained by identifying and minimizing the number of processes and product steps outside specified values (process limits). These specified values are measured during the process and the final step before the product is sent to the customer/consumer. By controlling change within certain limits, the product maintains its specified functionality and reliability. The measurements made during the manufacturing process and product are only in the process steps where the measurement values predict the product's success in meeting the final functional and reliability specification. The overall yield and final test yield of a manufacturing product has a direct impact on product cost. The disposition of reject product (product that does not meet the required specified measurement values) is a manufacturing activity that is not addressed in this book.

The interest in SPC control stems from the observed fact that the higher yield (often stated as more stable) manufacturing processes produce the product with the relatively higher reliability. Products that are statistically under control allow a smaller percentage of units prone to failure to be produced by the manufacturing process. This fact, along with engineering changes that explicitly solve specific reliability problems, is the prime reason for reliability growth of a product.

The logical basis of SPC originates in mathematical concepts and applications unfamiliar to the engineers and employees working directly with manufacturing products. A large body of knowledge about SPC has been developed that avoids discussing the basic statistical concepts. These SPC "cookbook" applications have been successfully applied in many manufacturing organizations. In this chapter we will focus on the fundamental origins of SPC in order to demystify the cookbook perception that something magical exists behind the rote application of SPC.

With this basic explanation, your SPC applications are only logical extensions of basic principles. The mathematical derivations are short of completion, as this text has neither the space nor the purpose of demonstrating the exact mathematical proofs for all explicit values used in the SPC cookbook applications. We only discuss the highlights of SPC. For further discussions, any statistical professional has the ability to present a complete logical connection between the basic mathematical concepts and the generalized SPC applications.

The central purpose of this section is to present enough mathematical concepts of SPC so that you can determine if the SPC is being properly administered to your existing or proposed product manufacturing activities. The following sections of text explain the basics behind all SPC applications.

The Distribution of Measured Values

If any parameter (weight, height, resistance, temperature, etc.) is measured as values using all items within a group (set), a distribution of values for the same parameter are observed. A typical set of values could come from all of the measurements in one process step during one day. Another distribution of values also occurs when the same item is measured repeatedly. In this case, the total number of measurements is the group, and the individual measurement is the item. This observed distribution of values for all measurements uses the science of probability and statistics to assist in creating the correct decisions using information from distribution data.

2.56	2.46	2.58	2.38	2.56	2.46
2.42	2.45	2.51	2.48	2.52	2.50
2.46	2.40	2.50	2.47	2.43	2.45
2.47	1.56	2.47	2.39	2.45	2.44
2.48	2.47	2.48	2.50	2.44	2.47

FIGURE 7-7.   **Raw data of plating thickness values (mils)**

Suppose we take any common measurement on a parameter of items within a group. An example would be the plating thickness of a product in the manufacturing process. This example applies to all measuring steps of your processes and products. The plating thickness measurements are presented in Figure 7-7.

In Figure 7-7 the distribution of values is not clearly apparent from the raw data. By dividing the values into several ranges and plotting the number of values within each range, a histogram of the values is constructed that clearly presents the distribution of values obtained from these measurements.

Figure 7-8 is a histogram of the plating thickness values of Figure 7-7. The histogram presented in Figure 7-8 has several characteristics:

1. The values of the entire group have an average (mean) and also a variation (yet to be defined).
2. The one value of 1.56 doesn't appear to be part of that set of value. It seems to be an unnatural value. We feel that something is not right with that value. We could have recorded the wrong value (2.56?), really have this unexpected thin plating, or find some other reason for that unnatural value. The crux of all SPC is in this identification of unnatural values. Unnatural measurement numbers mean nothing unless the measurement results in action to correct any process or product deviations outside of natural values measured for any process (control limits).

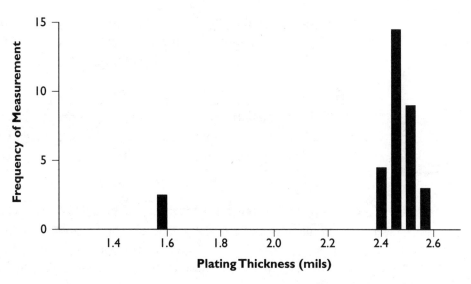

FIGURE **7-8.**   Histogram of raw plating thickness values

3. This histogram of the distribution of values applies to all such measurements of a parameter within a group of items. Since it applies to
all, we have an opportunity to invoke a common procedure (SPC).

The Mathematical Description of a Distribution

The strength of SPC is that it applies universally to groups of measurements
of all physical parameters. This generality stems directly from the causal reasons for the distribution (random events causing a probable variation to the
mean).

The variation in measurements of a physical parameter within a group
of products is caused by many small independent variations randomly occurring that affect the final variation pattern (distribution).

1. The input variations may be known or unknown.
2. The random nature of an input variable provides a good model for distributions, which approximate real measurement value behavior.
3. The total variation in the distribution can be reduced by identifying
and eliminating input variables. This is a typical manufacturing technique.

There also is a mathematical function, derived in basic probability theory, that describes the same causal relationship between the random input variables and a distribution as a function of probability.

Normal distribution is a continuous, symmetrical, bell-shaped frequency distribution of variables data that can be expressed by the Gauss distribution or Error Function.

By using the Normal Error Function, we model (assume) the distribution of measurement values from any manufacturing process or product. This technique works very well in almost all applications. We will begin the fundamental process by presenting the Gauss or normal error function (Figure 7-9).

The Gauss or normal error function does more than just represent the values of most natural processes. The equation relates the probability of a measurement value x with two parameters that define the distribution (Figure 7-10 and 7-11); the probability for each value of x is determined by the average of all x values in the distribution, $\bar{x}$ and the standard deviation of all x

$$p(x) = \frac{1}{\sigma\sqrt{2\pi}}\, e^{-(x-\bar{x})^2/2\sigma^2}$$

FIGURE 7-9.   The Gauss or Normal error function

$$\bar{x} = \frac{x_1 + x_2 + x_3 \cdots x_n}{n}$$

FIGURE 7-10.   Average value of **x** in a distribution

$$\sigma = \sqrt{\frac{\Sigma(x-\bar{x})^2}{n-1}}$$

FIGURE 7-11.   Standard Deviation of **x** in a distribution

values in the distribution, σ. The average value and standard distribution are specific to each measurement data set as seen in Figure 7-11.

The **standard deviation** (Figure 7-11) is the square root of the average of the sum of the individual measurement variations squared. Upon first glance, the standard deviation seems clumsy, but this mathematical form is required to end up with both the mean and sigma with the same dimension (*x*). The standard deviation is almost exclusively calculated by computer from the raw data so that the complexity and accounting errors are usually avoided in doing that.

Figure 7-12 is a plot of the Gauss or normal error function. It relates the probability of individual value within standard deviations (sigmas) of the

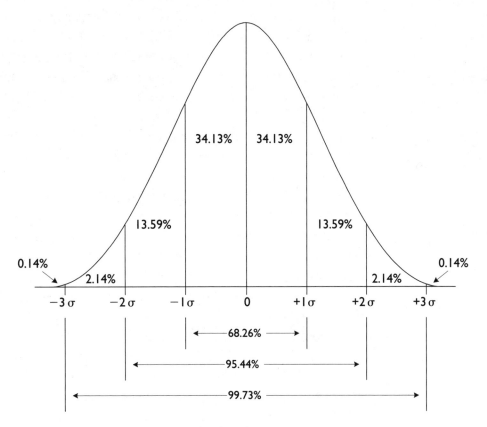

FIGURE 7-12.   The normal distribution

mean value of the distribution. It is presented in a form that uses the equation parameters $\bar{x}$ and σ, and can represent the distribution of measured values for all processes.

Figure 7-12 is the normal distribution. It has significant properties that can help us understand the behavior of our measured value distribution (SPC) technique.

1. Note that the normal distribution includes all probable values. In mathematical terms, the integral of the function is equal to 1. In practical terms, it states the obvious fact that any individual element has to be a member of the entire distribution.

2. For any individual element (x) in the set, the element (x) occurrence frequency is stated by a simple relationship; the probability of (x) occurring is precisely stated by the function probability value.

3. The relationship between occurrence frequency (probability) and sigma is presented in Figure 7-12. It is a relationship valid for all applications of the normal distribution function. It is frequently used in SPC. It can be calculated from the normal distribution function. The universal relationship, used extensively in all SPC, is that 68% of values within a normal distribution fall within 1 sigma of the average, 97% of values within a normal distribution fall within 2 sigma of the average, and 99% of values within a normal distribution fall within 3 sigma of the average.

4. Other mathematical relationships also can be calculated from the normal distribution function. An example, which we will later use, is the relationship between the range of random values and sigma values of the normal distribution function. The key point is that these relationships need only be calculated once and are constants valid for all time in all applications. Therefore, these values tend to be presented in application charts, rather than from unfamiliar mathematical equations. The charted values are a significant part of the abstract perception of SPC.

Since the normal error distribution function applies to all measurement sets, a typical example is valid for the data collected when we measured the plating thickness (Figure 7-7). Using the formulas for mean and standard deviation, we calculate the following:

$$\bar{x} = 2.440; \qquad \sigma = 0.1726$$

The distribution of values, from the raw data, are now expressed as functions that explicitly define the normal distribution.

Figure 7-13 is a mathematical model of the plating distribution using the mean and standard deviations of the actual plating measurements as parameters to determine the distribution. Note now that the mean and standard deviations are presented as plating thickness measurement values.

Sixty-eight percent of the plating thickness measurement values will probably occur within the average value −1 sigma to +1 sigma, which is between 2.227 and 2.613 mils; 97% will probably occur within the average value −2 sigma to +2 sigma, between 2.054 and 2.786 mils; and 99.7% will

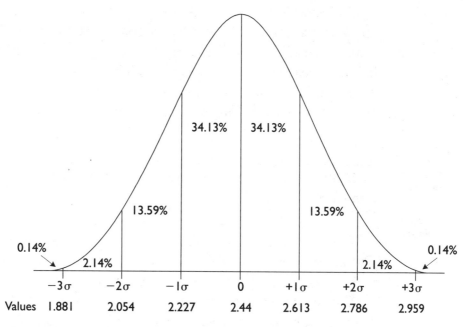

FIGURE 7-13.   A normal distribution model formed by plating measurements (mils)

probably occur within the average value −3 sigma to +3 sigma, between 1.881 and 2.959 mils.

Now, we had one reading of 1.56. The probability of that reading being part of this distribution is extremely small. (It can be calculated exactly.) We can with adequate confidence (>99%) state that that is an unnatural value to occur in that distribution. We need to investigate the reason for that "bad" value.

We have just executed every element of the SPC procedure:

1. From the raw measurement data, we have determined the natural (normal) distribution.
2. From the probabilities inherent in that normal distribution, we have determined that a measurement is unnatural or statistically extremely unlikely.
3. The unnatural measurement value will be investigated to restore the process or product to its natural state.

These three steps are statistical process control.

The elements of control limits are inherent in this activity. A control limit represents the largest value in which a measurement can vary from the distribution mean before being considered unnatural. The universal control limit has been chosen to be 3-sigma higher or lower than the distribution mean. This limit is an arbitrary choice based upon universal acceptance of a working SPC systems. Unless explicitly stated, assume all control limits to be plus or minus 3-sigma.

Isolated measurement is in statistical control if it exists within 3-sigma of the mean (average).

The three steps are so simple and logical that the most amazing aspect of SPC can be easily overlooked. The SPC process can apply to all process and product measurement steps with equal effectiveness. This makes SPC equal in manufacturing economic impact to the concept of basic mass interchangeability. The first great principle of manufacturing is making a product to a specification, and the second is controlling the process to achieve that specification with SPC.

Manufacturing Process and Product Specification

Manufacturing of a product consists of assembling elements of defined function to create, with value added, a product with defined function. This almost abstract definition is understood easily by the many examples in modern manufacturing. For instance, we take components and make a computer (product) and then use the computer as a higher-level component to make a satellite (product).

The assembly of items to make a product is the manufacturing process, the explicit goal of which is to make a functionally specified product with profit (value added). This process requires an organized procedure (steps) and specified activities at each step to effectively make a functional (and reliable) product. This organized procedure, called process flow, with its attendant measurements to specification at critical steps, is the hallmark of manufacturing.

To make a product with specific function and reliability, the process must be specified and controlled to the specified physical values at required (critical) process steps. That control to specified values is accomplished through measurements and necessary corrective action at the critical processes.

A typical sequence of applying manufacturing control, using SPC, to a process step will be presented to describe this fundamental manufacturing activity. This activity should be clearly understood by all engineers and managers.

The plating process step, whose values created our earlier distribution in this chapter, is used as a typical example.

Manufacturing Process Control Step 1 (A New Product)

Specified requirements defining the physical measurement of a process step output are initially established. In our example it is plating thickness. The physical requirement is usually based on scientific knowledge of similar products. For example, let us say that 1.5 mils of plating thickness initially is known to be the minimum plating thickness to provide adequate product function and probably 3.0 mils of plating seemed like a maximum, based upon experience, where additional plating adds no value to the product.

Process parameters are usually specified and verified during product design that tentatively produce product within the specified limits (range) required for the product. Most often the process parameter specifications are taken from manufacturing process steps already in progress. So this initial step requires clear communication and objective interpretation of data.

For this sequence of manufacturing control application, assume that a current plating machine in manufacturing has parameters (bath composition, current density, temperature, agitation, time, etc.) specified to meet the physical requirements of the product measured at that step. Let the measured values of plating in the product presented in Figure 7-7 be the output from the designed process in the development stage in the manufacturing plating machine.

The first step in manufacturing process and product control is evaluation of the product initial specified limits along with the process developed to satisfy those requirements. Figure 7-14 is a typical visual example. Note that all measured values of the process functional specification are met. Even the 1.56-mil plating measurement, which was very improbable to be part of the measurement distribution, was within the process functional specification (1.5 to 3.0 mils). Even though the process produces a plating thickness distri-

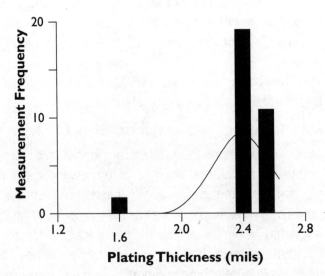

FIGURE 7-14.   The functional limits and initial process distribution of values from the plating process step

bution on the high side of the functional specification, this process step should be no trouble at all.

Manufacturing Process Control Step 2 (Adjusting to Change)

The product functional specification is frequently changed to optimize the entire manufacturing process. The yield of another process step may be increased by a smaller distribution in another step. For example, suppose the limits were reduced (tightened) to a 2.0-mil lower limit and a 2.5-mil upper limit to accommodate mechanical tolerance within the functional product. Now we have problems. Figure 7-14 displays the plating process measurements as a normal distribution. Immediately, we can estimate that the current process will result in accepting to specification only *XX*% of the product based upon the probabilities of the current plating distribution model. In order to improve acceptance within the new specification limits (yield), we will have to shift the average plating thickness value from 2.44 to 2.25 mils and establish a standard deviation at about 0.08 mils. This would assure us that 99.7% of the product meets function specification. The mathematical model, using the normal distribution, makes this change easy to define. In practical terms, we are centering the process into the functional specification and controlling variation.

Actions are directed at the controlling process parameters. In this case, plating time, plating bath temperature, current density, and plating fixtures would be major parameters that are all variables contributing to the process variation (sigma). The average would be centered at 2.25 mils and the process engineered to reduce variables such as improving temperature control, time of plating, preparation and rinse techniques, etc. The new process specification would be satisfied by adjusting the distribution as shown in Figure 7-15. Of course, this could result in an additional cost to the product, both as process rejects (yield) and as implementation and maintenance of this new process specification.

The functional change may either "tighten" or "loosen" the process output distribution of values. In a process where many variables control the final product functional specification, there are many input or control variables, never completely understood in terms of interaction with the functionality and reliability of the final product. It is no wonder that this dynamic activity

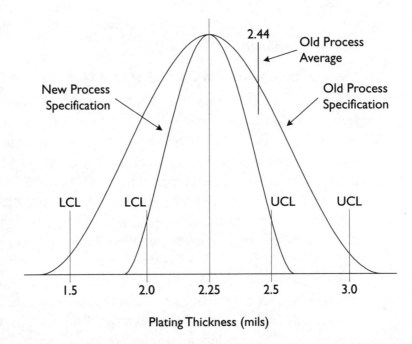

FIGURE 7-15.   **An example of adjusting to a new process functional specification**

of process and product specification and cost control is the essence of manufacturing engineering and business. This dynamic manufacturing activity accurately describes the intense adjustments made when creating a new product.

Manufacturing Process Control Step 3 (Stability Control)

The third step in manufacturing a product is the dedicated control of process outputs once the functional specifications and process output distributions have been optimized. At this point, the process yield has stabilized, and control is the primary function active in manufacturing. That element of control is supplied through SPC.

The entire reason for this extraneous discourse is to demonstrate the paramount concept that process specifications and the process specification limits are determined by final product functional and reliability specifications and manufacturing cost. That concept should never be confused with the concept of SPC itself, a tool that allows effective control to natural process and product limits. The difference between the process and product functional (reliability) limits and the SPC process and product measurement limits (presented as sigma values) must be clearly understood.

How Good Is Good?

Up to this point, we have not used the language common to manufacturing to describe the manufacturing process. Terms that are commonly used to describe the processes and products within a manufacturing activity include the following:

Process capability is the ability of a process to produce items consistently within the specified functional measurement limits.

Specified functional measurement limits are physical boundaries in which the process or product is operational.

Process capability index (called C_{pk}) is an objective measure of the process capability.

$$C_{pk} = \frac{\text{Process Specified Range}}{6\sigma}$$

The last section describes the business of manufacturing products in steps of understanding new product process capabilities and product specifications, adjusting all manufacturing process steps to achieve optimum efficiency, and maintaining control over the optimized manufacturing process.

C_{pk} is a universal and convenient way in describing how good a specific manufacturing process step is in its ability to produce specified product. As seen from the equation, it describes both the distribution of measured values and the functional requirement or specification. In almost all cases, the ability to center the process output distribution of measured values within the functional specification is assumed. There is a variety of opinion of what C_{pk} constitutes a proper or ideal manufacturing operation. An ideal goal is 1.33, but many successful operations operate under 1.00.

In general, high-yield processes, characterized as having relatively high C_{pk}, produce product with higher reliability. What has been described in this section is working with distributions of values that occur at every manufacturing process step. An efficient operation has no option but to operate in this manner. Being in control means both having measurements within the probabilities of the normal distribution and also having processes and product acceptable to the functional and reliability specification. A requirement of SPC implementation is that the process or product be in physical control. That does not mean that the process in control is operating properly within the process or product functional specification.

The SPC Cookbook Approach

The usual procedure is to provide instruction for implementation and ongoing maintenance of the SPC procedure without the burden of learning the difficult and tedious mathematical basis. This approach is adequate for the majority of SPC applications. Problems only arise when engineers, managers, and direct workers deviate from the cookbook procedures for a specific application. Then the lack of understanding of basic SPC concepts creates unwanted or harmful results. This section follows the prior sections' basic SPC fundamentals discussion as a guide.

The SPC installation is the creation of an active $\bar{X}$ and R control chart. The $\bar{X}$ and R chart is created by 3 steps:

Step 1. Collect the initial data.

▶ Select a random sample of product or process measurements continuously from a convenient time segment of a critical process. A convenient time segment is normally a working shift. A critical process is one determined to require control to produce a functional and reliable product.

▶ The selected sample size should be 4 or 5 if possible. The sample size is to be constant for all sampling.

▶ Select, measure, and record data from 30 samples to establish the $\bar{X}$ and R chart.

Step 2. Plot the $\bar{X}$ and **R** chart.

▶ Calculate the average value and range of individual values for each sample.

▶ Chart the average of the 30 $\bar{X}$s and Rs on a chart. This is the centerline ($\bar{\bar{X}}$ and $\bar{R}$) of your graphic plot. The centerline is the average measurement value and the average range of values of the samples.

▶ Calculate and chart the control limits of $\bar{X}$ based upon the $\bar{\bar{X}}$, given constants and average range.

$$\text{UCL} = \bar{\bar{X}} + A_2\bar{R}; \qquad \text{LCL} = \bar{\bar{X}} - A_2\bar{R}$$

The constant A_2 is given later.

▶ Calculate and chart the control limits of R based upon the $\bar{R}$ and given constants.

$$\text{UCL} = D_4\bar{R}; \qquad \text{LCL} = D_3\bar{R}$$

▶ The constants D_3 and D_4 are given later.

▶ Plot the initial 30 values on the chart and observe the pattern.

Figure 7-16 is an $\bar{X}$ and R chart made from typical sample data. This chart displays the distribution of value measurements in terms of the sample average and the range within each sample. The chart also displays the control limits for sample averages and ranges. Since all SPC charts use the same normal distribution, they all appear as standard, universal displays and are quickly understood by manufacturing personnel.

Step 3. Plot the ongoing samples on the $\bar{X}$ and R chart. Investigate any unnatural patterns of measurement data points. The unnatural patterns present a high probability that something has shifted the measurement from its historical distribution of values. Examples of unnatural patterns are given later.

To summarize the three simple steps:

1. Establish the process or product measurement distribution.
2. Investigate any unnatural measurement data phenomenon.
3. Return the process or product to the historical distribution.

These are the same as presented in the fundamental SPC exercise that used only measurement points and the normal distribution.

Control charts are closely related to histograms. To clarify this, think of the histogram as a snapshot and the control chart as a movie. A control chart is a histogram plotted over time (see Figure 7.17).

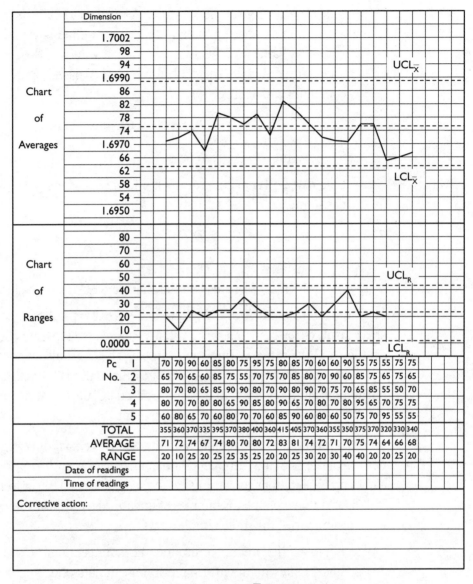

	Dimension																			
	1.7002																			
	98																			
	94														UCL$_{\overline{X}}$				
Chart	1.6990																			
	86																			
	82																			
of	78																			
	74																			
Averages	1.6970																			
	66																			
	62														LCL$_{\overline{X}}$				
	58																			
	54																			
	1.6950																			

	80																			
	70																			
Chart	60																			
	50														UCL$_R$				
of	40																			
	30																			
Ranges	20																			
	10																			
	0.0000														LCL$_R$				

Pc	1	70	70	90	60	85	80	75	95	75	80	85	70	60	60	90	55	75	55	75	75
No.	2	65	70	65	60	85	75	55	70	75	70	85	80	70	90	60	85	75	65	75	65
	3	80	70	80	65	85	90	90	80	70	90	80	90	70	75	70	65	85	55	50	70
	4	80	70	70	80	80	65	90	85	80	90	65	70	80	70	80	95	65	70	75	75
	5	60	80	65	70	60	80	70	70	60	85	90	60	80	60	50	75	70	95	55	55
TOTAL		355	360	370	335	395	370	380	400	360	415	405	370	360	355	350	375	370	320	330	340
AVERAGE		71	72	74	67	74	80	70	80	72	83	81	74	72	71	70	75	74	64	66	68
RANGE		20	10	25	20	25	25	35	25	20	20	25	30	20	30	40	40	20	20	25	20
Date of readings																					
Time of readings																					

Corrective action:

FIGURE 7-16.   Sample of a universal $\overline{X}$ and **R** chart

Figure 7-17.   Control chart/histogram relationship

Now Wait Just a Minute

When the initial example of statistical control was presented earlier in this section; we simply plotted measurement values, formed a distribution, and identified a measurement value of "unnaturally" low probability. The results are plotted in Figure 7-13, and that technique worked just fine. Now in the cookbook SPC technique, we are taking average values of small sample measurements and ranges within these small samples. What is going on?

The earlier example is an $\bar{X}$ (average) and S (sigma) normal distribution model. The later example is an $\bar{X}$ (average) and R (sample range) normal distribution model.

The earlier example of statistical control has exactly the same sensitivity and accuracy as the SPC cookbook application, which uses average and range values from small samples. The reasons for using small-sample average values and ranges are these:

1. The reason for using a small sample, rather than individual data points, is that it has slightly better generality. The distribution of averages of a large number of small samples (means) taken from a distribution of values will always approximate a normal distribution. This is true no matter what the shape of the parent distribution of measurement values. So when any measurement total distribution is actually slightly skewed, the small-sample average technique improves the discrimination of unnatural data points slightly better than directly using measurement values.

2. The use of ranges rather than sigma is only for convenience. The single small value in the plating distribution now is plotted as an unnatural range rather than an unnatural data point. But the control identification process and response for correction is the same. We could calculate and plot sigmas with the same results. It is just simpler to take the ranges. However, ranges of random samples and sigmas within a normal distribution are exactly related for each sample size within the normal distribution. The relationships, which are a function of sample size, need only be determined once. They are always listed as statistical constants to be used to accurately position the 3-sigma control limits using measurement range data. These constant ratios have been in use without change for 70 years. Some of the more important values are (and remember, they are constant forever)

Sample Size	A_2	D_3	D_4
4	0.73	0.00	2.28
5	0.58	0.00	2.11

The familiar $\bar{X}$ and R chart will produce the same process control identification of unnatural values as the basic statistical method described earlier.

The rules of SPC process control are based on observing unnatural measurement value patterns appearing on the chart. They can quickly be observed visually and trigger corrective actions directed toward the identified manufacturing process. The standardized application of SPC has proven to be an outstanding success for universal process or product control in critical manufacturing steps.

Other SPC Applications

The SPC discussed to this point focused only on measurement values used as data points within a normal distribution. Another large SPC application uses attributes data as a source of establishing control limits that identify unnatural data and trigger corrective action.

Another source of evaluation is not a measurement but whether the process or product meets a specified test. The process or product will either pass or fail the test. This is commonly referred to as the Go/no-Go test. In this technique, large samples are tested, and the attributes data are the failure percentage (or its equivalent number). If this sounds a lot like the incoming inspection plan, it should, because the statistics are based upon the Poisson distribution of sampling low percentages with large samples.

However, the p-chart is a simple method of plotting the attributes average and control limit based upon sampling attributes data.

An example of a p-chart would be the data from an automatic surface-coating detector (paint ding detector), which would inspect 100 units daily and record the event if a calibrated level of surface irregularity is detected.

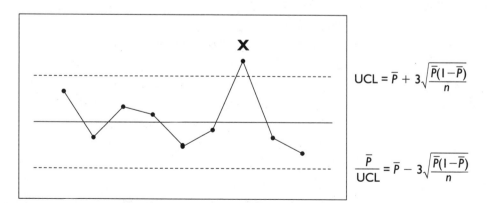

$$UCL = \bar{P} + 3\sqrt{\frac{\bar{P}(1-\bar{P})}{n}}$$

$$\frac{\bar{P}}{UCL} = \bar{P} - 3\sqrt{\frac{\bar{P}(1-\bar{P})}{n}}$$

FIGURE 7-18.   Control P-chart of attributes data

The test is a Go/no-Go. Note in this case the product was truly not rejected, but only the output was controlled to the optimum business position.

Step 1. Take 30 readings to establish a stable distribution.

Step 2. After 30 percentage values, the average percentage value is plotted on a chart.

—Determine and plot the upper control limit (UCL) and lower control limit (LCL) using these formulas:

$$\text{UCL} = \bar{p} + 3\sqrt{\frac{\bar{p}(1 - \bar{p})}{n}}; \quad \text{LCL} = \bar{p} - \sqrt{\frac{\bar{p}(1 - \bar{p})}{n}}$$

—Plot the initial 30 p values on the p-chart, and observe if the process has a stable pattern.

Step 3. Continue to plot attributes data from this process and identify unnatural patterns. When unnatural patterns exist, determine the cause for the process shift and return the process to normal.

Unnatural Patterns of Data

Several typical examples of SPC unnatural patterns are given that, when observed, trigger process investigation. The specific triggers in your SPC are well defined and can be quickly understood by a new engineer or production worker. The following $\bar{X}$ and R charts display a stable distribution with an example of a low probability event occurrence.

In Figure 7-19, a data point like the one existing in our plating data is displayed on an $\bar{X}$ and R chart. Note that the deviant data point would not drive the sample average beyond the 3-sigma limit but now is indicated in the range as a value beyond that limit. This is the example of a value existing outside of the 3-sigma control limit. This measurement point would be one of very low probability in the natural measurement values. It is probably caused by a measurement error, process break-down, or isolated random mistake. In any case, it should be investigated. If a problem exists, immediate action will return the process to its natural condition.

This is an unnatural pattern because of the low probability of two consecutive sample averages (in this case two out of three) existing close to the

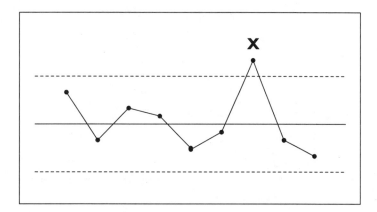

FIGURE **7-19.**   A single reading beyond control limits

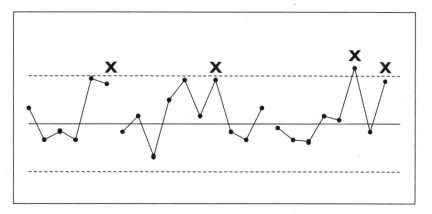

FIGURE **7-20.**   Two consecutive readings close to limit

control limit in Figure 7-20. They are both within the control limit but most probably indicate a process shift and should be investigated. An investigation is triggered into that process area to understand which control variables have changed, resulting in this unnatural pattern of measurement. If a problem exists, immediate action will return the process to its natural condition.

Eight data points on one side of the distribution average is unnatural (See Figure 7-21). This sample measurement point can be easily understood by realizing that the probability of a measurement point to be on one side of the average is 0.5; so the probability of eight measurement points consecu-

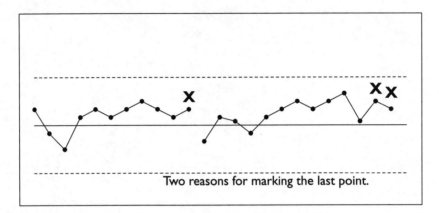

Two reasons for marking the last point.

FIGURE 7-21.   **Eight consecutive points on one side of distribution average**

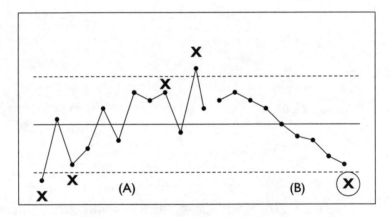

FIGURE 7-22.   **Drift of sample mean readings with time**

tively being on one side of the average is $(0.5)^8 = 0.004$, which is very low. So this pattern should be investigated so that immediate action can return the process to its natural condition. In most cases, this pattern indicates a subtle shift due to an unidentified change.

Figure 7-22 is a pattern that demonstrates drift in measurement values occurring with time. This unnatural pattern requires immediate investigation to remedy the affecting parameter. Measuring instruments, process equipment wear, and depleted effectiveness of nondirect processing (e.g., drying filters) often cause this process shift. Again, this condition should be corrected so that the process returns to its natural condition.

This unnatural pattern is effectively visualized using the chart. Notice that the data exist in two separate distributions, which is very unnatural. Investigation will pinpoint differences between people, measuring instruments, equipment, and process conditions. The binary output condition often needs to be addressed when "tightened" process control is desired.

Figures 7-19 to 7-23 are examples of SPC patterns that trigger investigation and corrective actions. These are only a few of many SPC triggers developed from determination of unnatural data points that indicate a low probability of occurring in a normal distribution. You will have specific control charts and unnatural pattern identification rules for your specific process. It is not the intent of this book to cover all applications.

However, the cookbook applications are all based on the same statistical origins and all use this reiterated method:

1. The natural distribution is determined from a significant number of data points.
2. Unnatural data points are identified due to their low probability.
3. Corrective action is applied to return the measured process or product to its natural state (when the problem is identified).

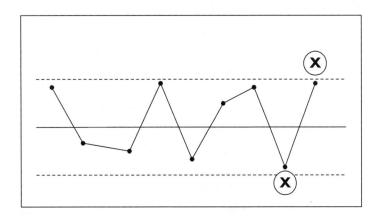

Figure 7-23.   A bimodel (two) distribution of data points

Manufacturing activity is greatly simplified by SPC. The effects of process and product specification are easily understood (we gave an example), and the SPC process in itself can be implemented with a minimum of difficulty. The unnatural pattern recognition requires little training. These reasons combine to make SPC an important universal manufacturing tool.

Summary

The fundamental development of the two most important tools, incoming inspection and statistical process control, to control manufacturing's contribution to product reliability is presented.

Incoming inspection is explained in terms of an economic decision that balances the cost of incoming-item inspection with the cost of not inspecting incoming items. The technique of the operating characteristic (OC) curve for use in obtaining the optimum sample inspection is developed in detail. The fundamental nature of the OC applications in sampling must be understood, especially if you deviate from accepted procedures. A poor understanding of the incoming sampling inspection may result in an unanticipated economic impact upon the business.

An example of statistical process control (SPC) is developed using a simplistic, but effective, model of measurement values to form a natural distribution, detect an unnatural data point, and through a responsive action correct the process back to its normal condition. This example procedure should be understood by all manufacturing engineers.

The popular application of SPC using $\bar{X}$ and R charts is explained in terms of the typical application. The underlying principles are explained as a logical convenience of the simplistic model.

An attributes SPC chart is used as an example of control charts frequently used to detect shifts in process tests. The attributes sampling procedure closely represents the Poisson mathematical model presented earlier in the chapter.

Some typical examples of SPC in action, where unnatural data patterns trigger investigation of process value changes, are given. The simplicity of this powerful technique is demonstrated.

We are not indicating that supplier control and SPC are the only manufacturing activities that need to be addressed to keep manufacturing from building unreliability into the product. Activities such as operator training, nonconforming materials control, equipment recall, and calibration system all may have a negative impact. Chapter 2 defines many other factors that may need to be addressed and controlled in manufacturing.

Understanding values as distributions is key to achieving manufacturing control.
—DR. LES ANDERSEN

8

New Product Reliability Qualification

An ounce of prevention is worth a pound of cure.

—HARRINGTON'S GRANDMOTHER

Introduction

There are a variety of tests that have been developed to determine the reliability of products or processes. The main tests include:

▶ *Environmental Stress Screening. This helps to point out weaknesses in new designs and failure in the product because of weak parts or defects in processes or other environment-related causes of defects or nonconformance.*

▶ *Reliability Development Tests. Companies undertake these tests before releasing a product to production. They usually involve a protocol to discover problems that can be solved before going to full production.*

▶ *Reliability Qualification Tests. Companies conduct this test on parts that are representative of an actual production run.*

▶ *Reliability Acceptance Tests. Companies use these tests to check production equipment to make sure no step in the production process will introduce defects. It is often undertaken after retooling or other changes have been made.*

—JAMES CORTADA AND JOHN WOODS[1]

Managers should read Chapter 8 to understand the fundamental aspects and business reasons for reliability qualification. Unfortunately, many businesses do not have product reliability qualification as a prime priority in their dynamic environment. Often, the motivation for product reliability qualification stems from fear of being bankrupted by populating their customers/consumers with unreliable product. Chapter 8 replaces fear with rational business motivation to perform reliability qualification.

Engineers should read Chapter 8 for a quick study of the reliability qualification fundamentals and the example of product reliability qualification. The broad distribution of reliability qualifications dictates that a more detailed design of reliability qualification, in addition to the material covered in Chapter 8, be used in your specific application.

Product reliability qualification is an evaluation that determines, to a degree of confidence within a relatively short period of time, the reliability of a product.

Product reliability qualification originates as a dilemma. By definition, the goal of product reliability qualification is to evaluate the product reliability prior to customer/consumer use. Before customer/consumer use, insufficient reliability data and information exist for a proper evaluation. The exact product reliability value for any product can only be obtained by measuring the time to failure for every unit under the specified use condition. The dilemma is that after customer/consumer use, the data and reliability information are of no value to the producer nor the customer/consumer.

The business response to the dilemma is a compromise between the exclusive conditions. That compromise is called the product reliability qualification. Reliability qualification always compromises data (information) accuracy and value of the resultant qualification information because it uses statistical techniques, oversimplified assumptions, imprecise test factors, and assumes working-level environmental conditions.

Various studies have been developed that compare the cost of resolving a reliability problem before manufacturing to that of resolving a reliability problem after the product is in operation. A typical cost range of fixing reliability problems, for products requiring control of reliability, will be $1\times$ before design release to manufacturing, $10\times$ in manufacturing, and $100\times$ in the field. The actual value is dependent upon specific conditions and criteria for the cost analyses. In general, if controlling reliability is a business necessity, then product qualification is justified.

Product reliability qualification is not entirely a physical test. In the majority of cases, the reliability qualification is a combination of formal physical life accelerated test data, field data on similar product, and estimated reliability parameters. This chapter focuses on the formal physical qualification tests.

Product reliability qualification will significantly reduce the risk of selling unreliable products. It will not remove all reliability failure modes from the product; but it will reduce the number of expensive customer/consumer responses to unexpected reliability problems.

The Reliability Qualification Concept

The definition of product reliability qualification has already been defined as follows: An evaluation that determines, to a degree of confidence, within a relatively short period of time, the reliability of a product. There are many good definitions of product reliability qualification, and yet it is difficult to present a single one with clear generality. However, the explanations and examples presented in this chapter will clarify the definition.

Accelerating Product Life

An **accelerated life test** subjects the product to the equivalent of a lifetime of operational conditions in an abbreviated period of time.

The key concept of product reliability qualification is to subject a sample of the projected product to a set of stress conditions, thereby approximately

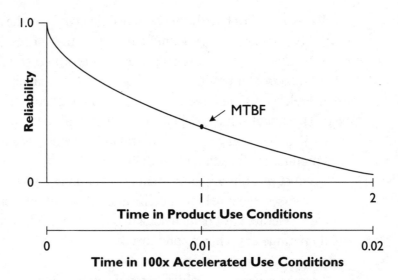

FIGURE **8-1.** **Product reliability (exponential model) and acceleration scale**

evaluating the entire product life behavior, specifically failures and functional degradation, in a relatively short period of time.

Figure 8-1 is an exponential model of product reliability that applies to all products by normalizing the MTBF to 1 on the time (*x* axis) scale. For example, the MTBF of a gear box may be 6,000 hours and a semiconductor switch may be 1,000,000 hours, but the reliability curve, normalized to MTBF, both are modeled to Figure 8-1.

Note that a second scale of MTBF/100 exists in Figure 8-1. The second scale exists to model the product reliability where a 100× factor in aging has been imposed upon the product by controlled stress techniques. Using our example, the MTBF for gear box and semiconductor product under the 100× aging factor would now be 60 and 10,000 hours, respectively. The failures still would adhere to the exponential model, only occurring at an accelerated (100×) rate. The deliberate stress evaluation is called an accelerated life test or product qualification test.

Stress factors such as temperature, mechanical stress and shock, voltage, chemical, and humidity exposure are frequently used to accelerate product aging. Whenever appropriate, these techniques are used alone or in combination to produce a lifetime of product use-condition aging within a short test period of time. One should reflect upon the fact that these factors are the same contributors to product failure modes when in intended customer/consumer use. But during qualification, these same stress factors are increased in intensity resulting in an acceptable estimate to the projected customer/consumer usage reliability in a short period of time. For instance, a car door could be open and closed in 24 hours more times than it would in a year by a typical driver.

The description of accelerated life test and conditions presented in Figure 8-1 is oversimplified. The definition of time (x axis) in actual practice may be considered time in use, time in active use, cycles to failure, ability to function once, and other specified functional criteria. The true product failures (reliability) may be a function of one or more of these indicators. This text explains and presents simple examples that contain solely the condition of customer/consumer use time in the x axis. The principles apply to all other combinations of product reliability use variables.

A Little Mathematics

The logical process of product reliability qualification is clarified significantly by understanding a relatively easy mathematical model. The model states that a confidence in the value of an entire distribution can be related to some simple sampling parameters. It can be easily demonstrated and understood by example:

Imagine that we wish to understand the time it takes for us to travel to work. The measured time is always recorded by rounding to the closest whole minute.

The first day it takes 23 minutes
▶ With our first recorded value, we stated that we wanted to know just the time to travel to work, but we find that the single 23-minute value is inadequate because it does not give us confidence in the average and variation of the time distribution to get to work. So what we really meant was we wanted to know the average time it takes to get to

work. In other words, we wanted to know the parameters of the normal distribution model.

▶ The single value is actually a sample (of 1) of all time-to-work values in a set. It can only be treated using statistical techniques. From this single value, one cannot confidently estimate the true average travel time to work. For example, the automobile may have had a flat tire during the measured single value and be a poor average value.

The second day it takes 20 minutes

▶ With the second reading, we feel more confident about our understanding of our travel time. Common sense dictates that the average travel time to work is about 20 minutes or so based upon the data. We now can calculate an average and standard deviations of our points in this set of 2. In fact, we can construct a normal distribution from the two data points.

▶ Now how confident are we that our average travel time to work is the average based on our sample measured values? Statistical theory has a simple equation that relates the probable range (limits of variation) of the average of the entire distribution (all trips to work) to the samples taken to estimate that value. It is called the confidence interval (CI) (Figure 8-2).

The confidence interval quantifies what we intuitively feel:

▶ The larger the sample, the more accurate the estimate.
▶ The less sample variation, the more accurate the estimation.

$$CI = \overline{X} \pm z_{\alpha/2}\frac{\sigma}{\sqrt{n}}$$

$\overline{X}$ = average of sample values
$z_{\alpha/2}$ = confidence that estimated value is within the calculated limits
σ = standard deviation of sample values
n = number of data points

FIGURE 8-2.   Confidence interval of average value related to sample values

▶ The more stringent our need for our estimate to be correct, the greater range of probable values required.

Note that taking more samples, increasing n, narrows the range of estimated values, everything else being equal. Based on this factor, we continue with our example.

We measure travel time to work on days 3 to 10.

The values are 19, 22, 24, 23, 20, 22, 23, and 22 minutes, respectively. From the 10 values we calculate the average sample time and standard deviation. They are $\overline{X}$ and SD = 1.62 of a normal distribution. Let us be confident that our estimated average travel time to work is probably 90% correct. A 90% confidence level for a normal distribution is 1.65. Inserting these values into the CI equation, we have the following:

$$CI = 21.8 \pm 1.65\frac{1.62}{\sqrt{10}} = 20.95 \text{ to } 22.65$$

We are 90% confident, with the 10 measurements as data, that the actual time-to-work average of all values will be between 20.95 and 22.65 minutes.

The estimate of time to work (20.95 to 22.65 minutes) was in principle correct, but we used the normal distribution to evaluate incorrectly the confidence interval. When sample sizes of less than 30 are used to calculate statistical functions, the normal distribution is too inaccurate for applications. The value of $z_{\alpha/2}$, taken from the normal distribution of probable values, should not have been used to calculate the confidence interval of 10 samples. However, the probability taken from distributions of 30 or less data points have been calculated. There is a unique distribution for each sample number, but only the common integrations at 90, 95, and 99% are required for calculations involving small sample sizes. These distributions are called student's t distributions and are given in Appendix E. The confidence interval equation remains the same, but the student's t distribution probability value is substituted in place of the normal z distribution probability.

Look at Appendix E down to row 10 and over to the column indicating a confidence of 90%. The value will be 1.81. Now let us redo the confidence interval estimate.

$$CI = \overline{X} \pm t_{\alpha/2}\frac{\sigma}{\sqrt{n}}$$

$$CI = 21.8 \pm 1.81\frac{1.62}{\sqrt{10}} = 20.7 \text{ to } 22.9 \text{ min to travel to work}$$

The correction for sample size has resulted in a slightly larger value of confidence interval. Note that in samples larger than 30, the normal z value given by the standardized normal distribution is adequate for all calculations. The following are reasons for presenting this mathematical example:

▶ It is a good idea to have all qualification plans reviewed by a competent source before deriving conclusive information. We have demonstrated that the supporting mathematics, although relatively easy, can be misapplied when one is unfamiliar with the background probability and statistics. Usually, the error will be minor and not detected. The time-to-work example is typical.

▶ We have mathematically described the qualification process variables. If we just substitute the measured values (n times) of product failure in place of measured values (n times) of travel time to work, we exactly describe product qualification. We take the measured value of failure (usually time to failure) in n samples and determine the average time to failure of the entire product set. The CI equation exactly describes the variables. The sample average is taken, the confidence required is taken, the standard deviation is calculated, and n is recorded. From this value and average failure-rate (FR) range probability (and other functions) that describe the product reliability can be calculated. Other constant relationships within the normal or student's t distributions are often implemented during the evaluation process, but the fundamental CI equation always statistically defines the process.

A Qualification Test Example

This is an example of a reliability qualification test using temperature and voltage acceleration. Intensity stress factors will demonstrate the qualification technique.

Semiconductor products have been the primary examples of using product reliability qualification tests. The qualification test will use stress (intensity) conditions to age the product a lifetime during a short (in this case 1 day) period of time. The product chosen is a semiconductor integrated circuit that has a product life of 20 thousand power on hours (KPOH).

Figure 8-3 is a reliability-rate curve of a semiconductor product with time. A basic assumption of product reliability qualification is that the use conditions FR curve and the accelerated FR curve are identical, except that the x axis has shrunken according to the acceleration factor.

Our example is qualification of a typical semiconductor product (an integrated circuit). The example will use the specific jargon of this process.

An accelerated lifetime test is performed to determine the reliability of a new integrated circuit. The two accelerating stress factors are temperature and voltage.

$$t_{eff} = A_T A_V t_{bi}$$

where

t_{eff} = effective operating time
A_T = temperature acceleration factor

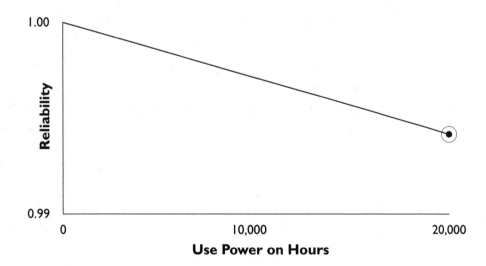

FIGURE 8-3.   Projected reliability

A_V = voltage acceleration factor

t_{bi} = time of burn-in

The temperature of an operating integrated circuit is called the junction temperature (Tj), because the junction of the semiconductor circuit is actually where the physical time acceleration with temperature occurs. The junction temperature of the operating integrated circuit can be accurately determined by the diagnostic circuit characteristics of devices in the integrated circuit. In this qualification test, the Tj of customer/consumer-designed operation is 50°C. (323 K.). The nominal use voltage of the integrated circuit is 5.0 V.

The Arrhenious and Eyring equations are used to calculate the acceleration factors with temperature and voltage. The Arrhenious and Eyring equations have been validated as suitable for use in this application.

 The **Arrhenious equation** expresses how the rate of a process increases in an exponential manner with temperature. It is named after Svant Arrhenious.

$$\text{Rate} = Ae^{-\frac{E_a}{RT}}$$

where

E_a = energy of activation

R = equation (Boltzman) constant

T = temperature

 The **Eyring equation** expresses how the rate of the process increases in an exponential manner with driving potential. It is named after Henry Eyring.

$$\text{Rate} = Ae^{-cV}$$

where

V = voltage applied to device in this case

c = constant for a given device

The activation energy for the Arrhenious equation (0.4 eV in this example) has been determined for this product. The Eyring equation constant c (2.2 in this example) has also been determined. The accelerated test temperature is within the operating range of the integrated circuit, and the constant c is only applied in a safe voltage stress range of the integrated device.

The designed operating use conditions of this device are a temperature of 323 K and 5.0 V.

Typical qualification test conditions are

temperature $= 156°C$ (429 K)
voltage $= 7.0$ V
test time $= 6$ h

The following time acceleration is calculated:

$$A_t = e^{(0.4eV/8.6\times10^{-5}eV/K)(1/323K-1/429K)}$$
$$= 36$$

The increased temperature accelerates aging by a factor of 36.

$$A_V = e^{(2.2/V)(7.0V-5.0V)}$$
$$= 81$$

The increased voltage accelerates aging by a factor of 81.
We now have all of the factors calculated for our acceleration test:

$$t_{eff} = A_T A_V t_{bi}$$
$$= (36)(81)(6 \text{ h}) = 17,494 \text{ h}$$

The qualification test aged the integrated circuit, within a period of 6 hours, the equivalent of customer/consumer operation of 17,500 hours. This high acceleration factor is not unusual for semiconductors that can operate within these temperature and voltage ranges. Typically, a lower acceleration rate is used due to the physical stress limits inherent in the product. For example, if a designed circuit signal fails to transmit at above 100°C., then an accelerated test based on that signal will be limited to about 90°C.

Figure 8-4 presents the reliability with time for the integrated circuit in specified accelerated time conditions. The qualification test will in 6 hours almost replicate that entire product life (Figure 8-3) curve. Experience has

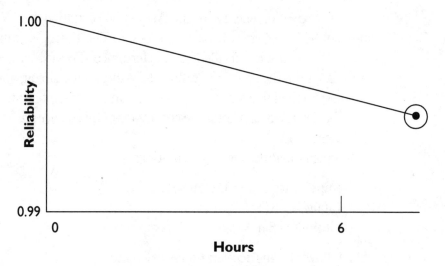

FIGURE **8-4.**   Qualification time of integrated circuit

demonstrated that qualifications can identify reliability problems and determine the lifetime reliability of new products in a short test period.

Whatever acceleration techniques chosen for the appropriate qualification test, empirical validation is required to confidently make business decisions based on qualification test results.

The Product Qualification Equation

The mathematics of a **reliability qualification test** is by definition the observed failure rate corrected to meet the conditions of (1) the statistical nature of small numbers in the samples representing the true failure rate of the entire product and (2) the acceleration factor created by qualification test conditions.

$$\mathrm{FR} = (R \times C)/[(N \times H) \times A]$$

where

FR = failure rate
R = number of test failures
C = statistical coefficient
N = number of test samples
H = hours on test
A = test acceleration factor

COEFFICIENT

Fails	60% CL	90% CL
1	2.02	3.89
2	1.55	2.66
3	1.39	2.23
4	1.31	2.00
5	1.26	1.85
6	1.22	1.76
7	1.20	1.68
8	1.18	1.62
9	1.16	1.58
10	1.15	1.54

An examination of the basic qualification equation indicates that qualifications are tests with few failures, a correct observation. This is in sharp contrast to Chapter 3, where the recommendation to use greater than 30 failure data points for FR determination was repeated. During qualification, the constraints of test time (A) and availability of testing fixtures (N) dictate that the optimum test failures be few (about 4 to 5).

The basic equation explicitly has the statistical element of confidence limit, discussed earlier, inserted directly into the calculation. This CL is a fundamental part of sampling a parent population (the product yet to be shipped). Without derivation, a coefficient is introduced into the equation and accounts for the uncertainty of determining the true failure rate of the entire product from the few failures observed in the test. As the number of samples (here a number of failures) becomes larger, the coefficients approach that of the values dictated by the z value (called z score) of the standard normal distribution. This uncertainty is a function of how confident (sure) the test results represent the real failure rate. Confidence levels of greater than 90% are rarely required in qualification.

The fundamental qualification equation is the basic FR equation with the time acceleration factor and the sampling confidence level inserted to reflect the conditions of the test.

$$\text{Failure Rate} = \frac{\text{Total Failures}}{\text{Total Operating Time}}$$

Acceleration Factors

Accelerating the life of the product (also called aging) is used to determine the product's customer/consumer use lifetime reliability during a relatively short test time. This acceleration of product use time is produced by subjecting the products to known aging environments (based on empirical data and sound science). The following are typical product aging factors (acceleration factors):

- ▶ temperature
- ▶ temperature cycling
- ▶ mechanical acceleration
- ▶ mechanical stress
- ▶ electrical stress
- ▶ reactive chemical exposure
- ▶ humidity exposure
- ▶ particulate contamination exposure

These are exactly the same factors that cause product failures, and by design, they are controlled to measure the product reliability (Chapter 5). Fewer product failures occur in time when the factors previously listed have reduced physical intensity. As mentioned in Chapter 5, the optimum reliability design is to achieve optimum profit from the product. The goal of qualification is to determine the new product reliability. Therefore, a reasoned qualification test must be generated to most effectively test the product reliability goal. This singular objective is mentioned due to the observation that a qualification goal of zero FR is often practiced. That goal is not optimum. Intensity robustness is neither a measurement of optimum design nor maximized profit.

Understanding acceleration factors is a requirement to develop effective product reliability qualification tests. In general, the acceleration factors have been empirically derived. First, they were recognized as factors that could affect product failures and wear out. They were quantified, from either use data or independent controlled test data, to obtain a value of acceleration with physical intensity. Some acceleration factors have been reduced to mathematical models based on scientific principles. The Arrhenious and Eyring equations are typical examples. Other acceleration factors are based solely on empirical evaluations. An example is vibration intensity. The acceleration factors now are used to quickly measure the future reliability of the product. The factors in general are specific to a particular product and often have measured relationships not reduced to basic physical principles. However, these acceleration factors may be more than adequate, especially if the factors are validated in the product reliability during customer/consumer use.

The product reliability qualification usually incorporates acceleration stress tests that have been utilized in design of the product. Therefore, the primary source of validated acceleration data will be your own design process. Since the specific applications of product reliability qualification tests produce unique acceleration values, the larger effort to describe the acceleration factors for specific use and scientific basis is usually a method based on the historical qualification of your product.

A brief discussion is given for the product reliability stress factors shown earlier.

Temperature

Temperature is the major factor used in accelerated life testing. An empirical relationship, derived by Arrhenious, relates aging with temperature.

$$A_T = e^{(E_a/K_B)(1/T_1 - 1/T_2)}$$

where

A_T = temperature acceleration factor
E_a = activation energy

K_B = Boltzman constant = $8.6 \times 10^{-5} eV/K$
T_1 = no minimal temperature (K)
T_2 = condition temperature (K)

The equation has only one product-specific constant, the activation energy. The constant nominalizes the choice of every activation energy dimension, and the equation produces the same acceleration factor. A general estimate is that for every 10° centigrade increase in temperature, the aging in real time increases by a factor of 2. In a product use environment, a designed increase in temperature of 10° centigrade will double the failure rate. In a qualification test, these same data are interpreted as the same failures occurring in one-half the test time due to the twofold time acceleration.

Temperature-Induced Mechanical Stress

Temperature-induced mechanical stress—the transient mechanical stress caused by the differential expansions during starting and stopping the product.

For product requiring small tolerances to operate, the strain resulting from this transient stress will cause tolerance-related operating problems. The major thrust of accelerated testing is to cause a catastrophic (physical failure) failure in a manner that can be related to the stress intensity of temperature-transient gradients. This is the basis of the ordinary temperature cycle tests. The two test variables are temperature absolute changes and rate of temperature change with time. Temperature stress tests do accurately identify design inadequacies in product start-up and shutdown. It can be used to accelerate these customer/consumer-use temperature-stress conditions. Temperature-induced mechanical stress has a more successful history in identifying reliability problems than in forming the basis for a pervasive product acceleration test for three reasons:

1. The temperature stress caused by temperature cycling is extremely product specific; therefore, universal temperature cycles are not available.

2. The upper limit and lower limit of temperature excursions may have restrictions that limit the test optimization. In electronics, the highest and lowest temperature that can be used to cycle a system is within the operating limits of the individual components. This means that the system stress test can only operate within the specified limits of the lowest tolerance (least high temperature and highest low temperature).

3. The temperature stress test is easily used for design applications to create a robust product (e.g., a product may be designed to survive a direct insertion into liquid nitrogen). However, the resulting robust design may not be related to product failures. Much effort can be wasted upon elimination of temperature stress artifacts. Field validation of temperature stress acceleration factors is absolutely a requirement if it enters into a product reliability projection.

The thermal conductivity of the product structure itself is a limiting factor in stress-intensity conditions. A rapid cycle between two temperatures will subject the product to a continuum of stress conditions based upon the product geometry and materials heat conductivity (see Figure 8-5). This phe-

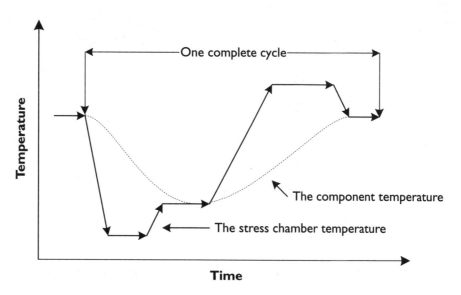

FIGURE **8-5.** **Temperature profiles during a cyclic temperature test**

nomenon causes every product and temperature stress treatment to be a unique test point, resulting in the absence of a standard technique for this stress factor.

Vibration

The ability to accelerate the product life through vibration stems from relating a time to failure (cycles) to an established amplitude and acceleration.

Figure 8-6A demonstrates how a relationship may be established between the time to failure and vibration intensity (amplitude). The relationship is generated essentially by empirical means. If the new product is an evolution of a former physical geometry, then the vibration relationship of time versus intensity does not require a complete validation. Figure 8-6B demonstrates the mechanical movement of a typical component.

The test vibrator manufacturers have an excellent education and pilot test capability that is at your disposal if you choose to investigate the vibration technique. There are several details unique to the vibration techniques:

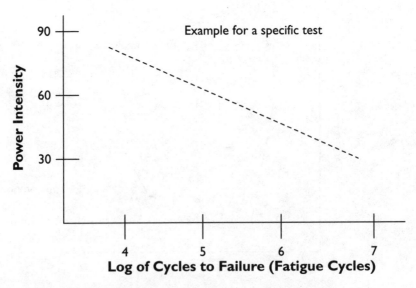

FIGURE 8-6A.   Vibrations to failure vs. power intensity

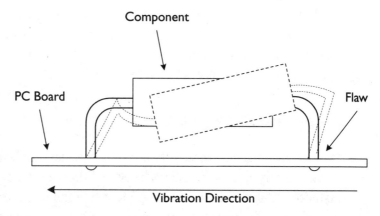

FIGURE **8-6B.   Component mechanical movement during a typical vibration test**

▶ The direction of vibration (or degrees of vibration) is a fundamental factor in identifying mechanical structures that fail during vibration. A unidirectional or even three-directional mechanical force applied to a specific product may not be as effective in identifying a mechanically weak structure as directional control that includes all direction vectors.

▶ When a particular vibration frequency is resonant with a specific known component of the product under test, the unwanted interaction between the vibrator and the product may be avoided by eliminating that particular vibration frequency from the vibrator spectrum. The activity that eliminates unwanted frequencies is called notching.

▶ The amplitude of vibration used for accelerated tests is always a topic of discussion. As a rule, vibrations are measured as intensity to failure, and 50% of lower limit of failure will not degrade the product.

Mechanical Stress

This technique is fundamentally based on the assumption that low-frequency stress applications (intensity) are related to the product's ultimate mechanical operating tolerance, fatigue and failure. As with all accelerating factors, a relationship can be developed between the intensity of the stress and the equivalent time of operating under normal use conditions. The variety of tests is endless. One example is the Timex watch tests advertised to continue operation after a variety of mechanical tests.

Mechanical Shock Tests

It is very difficult to accelerate a high-frequency application of mechanical force. Usually, unique tests are developed that determine limits of shock resistance. An example would be a 5-foot free fall into a granite block. These are correctly defined as compliance tests that cannot be accelerated. An automobile bumper capable of withstanding a 5-mph crash cannot be evaluated in a 60-mph crash.

Electrical Stress

The practice of lowering the voltage (intensity) of electrical components to achieve a higher reliability or fewer failures in time (Chapter 5) is reversed to raising the voltage of electrical components to achieve higher failures in time. The higher failures in time is correlated to the acceleration of the product's life. The semiconductor industry has developed this technique into a major method of accelerated life testing.

First, the relationship between voltage and failure rate has been determined theoretically by the Eyring equation, which has only one physical constant, c. The constant c is determined on specific products by testing at two temperatures. The Eyring equation is

$$A_V = e^{c(V_a - V_n)}$$

where

A_V = voltage acceleration factor
c = determined constant specific to a product
V_a = accelerated test voltage
V_n = no minimal use voltage

Reactive Chemical Exposure

If the product has customer/consumer failures due to environmental chemical exposures, that factor needs specification in the product and a qualification test for prediction of chemical resistance in the new product. Although standard tests are not universally available in the industry, the customer/consumer already has a test procedure installed to determine the environmental adequacy of the unique new product. The first investigation of value is to understand how the customer/consumer-reactive chemical test has been validated. The second investigation of value is to understand the empirical relationship developed that relates chemical concentration with product time to failure.

Humidity Exposure

The universal test condition for all environments is humidity. Not only does the operating environment need relative humidity (RH) specification, the test preconditioning drastically changes test results. The most direct application of product humidity testing is given in Chapter 9, where an environmental stress screen determines if an adequate humidity protection is given to each product before shipment. The testing of relative humidity resistance in a product is very difficult.

Particulate Contamination

The accelerated test in this case is a measure of product failure to high concentrations of particulate. The relationship between high concentrations of particles and accelerated times to failure is quite specious. This is particularly true when the product has few failures identified as being caused by particles. Under normal circumstances, this acceleration factor is not used in a qualification test.

The acceleration test factors themselves need an independent text to coalesce and structure the diverse data available to implement a credible, timely, and cost-efficient qualification test. *Reliability Simplified* only acquaints you with the variety of acceleration factors and the major aspects of utilizing each factor.

Planning a Product Reliability Qualification Test

The Qualification Test Request

The eternal quest of business management and engineers is to perform a product qualification with

1. The highest level of confidence
2. The shortest period of time
3. The fewest test samples
4. To an anticipated specified failure rate
5. With the most accurate prediction from the acceleration factor

It is also the characteristic of this quest that emphasis focusing upon single factors to create a product qualification planning effort that can never be clearly concluded. The following example is a qualification test that balances all of the test factors to optimize "all" input variables and produces the result of highest confidence, using the fewest number of test units, to determine reliability to an anticipated value.

The concept behind optimizing the inputs of a qualification test is to mathematically equate in all variables the change in values of each input variable with numerical output of that value. Mathematically, it is equating the differentials of all input and output. The required balance for an optimum qualification explicitly is explained for each factor and can be intuitively observed in the qualification test plan.

The qualification test plan is generated by solving the qualification test equation in terms of practical business constraints:

$$\text{FR} = (R \times C)/[(N \times H) \times A]$$

where

FR $=$ failure rate
R $=$ number of test failures
C $=$ statistical coefficient
N $=$ number of test samples

H = hours on test

A = test acceleration factor

The fundamental product reliability qualification test equation is easy to comprehend and hypothetically execute. Problems invariably arise when applying the product reliability qualification test to actual products. The following example is typical of applying common sense to create the best product reliability qualification test under the existing constraints to the basic qualification equation.

Often, the first question posed is: "How many test samples do we need for qualification?" The qualification test equation will provide the answer by determining all other variables. *In this example we are determining the number (N) of test samples to qualify a product.* The number (N) of test samples to qualify a product is what is calculated in this example. In this real example, the number of qualification units was the unknown. What is important is to recognize that the other variables are constrained to physical or statistically determined values as follows:

Constraint 1

The qualification test must confidently confirm, for the warranty period of the new product, that the reliability will track to the product's historical reliability.

The statement of the qualification goal is extremely important. Everyone must understand the scope of the test.

> ▶ Information on product
>   —Warranty period = 20,000 power on hours (this number is determined by market conditions)

Qualification general rule: The product must be time accelerated in the qualification to 40% of the projected customer/consumer usage life. While a 100% time equivalent of projected customer/consumer life is ideal, the probability of not identifying problems in the last 60% of projected customer/consumer usage life is not significant.

Constraint 2

The qualification test must use the available validated acceleration rate.

> ▶ Information on product
> — Acceleration rate = 20
>   (This relatively low acceleration rate is appropriate for this product.)
>   Constraints 1 and 2 will determine the length of test.
> — Warranty period = 20,000 hours customer/consumer operating time (COT)
> — Qualification rule = 20,000 hours (COT) × 40% = 8,000 hours (COT)
> — 8000 hours (COT)/20 × acceleration = 400 hours qualification test.

Any qualification test with less than 400 hours will decrease confidence in the final qualification test result. Qualification tests run with high unit numbers of product with short COTs are common. They are invalid qualifications because they do not represent significantly the projected product real operating time.

Constraint 3

The anticipated FR is 500 KPOH (thousand hours power on hours) MTBF or a FR of 2,000 ppm / KPOH.

> ▶ Information on product
> — MTBF = 500 KPOH

Constraint 4

The number of failures to statistically optimize the test is historically optimized at 4 or 5. We will project 5.

The statistical determination of the optimum number of failures in a qualification test can be determined by a statistician or by relative comparison with former qualification tests. It is obvious that if no failures occur during the qualification test, the test parameter of MTBF was incorrect. If the reliability of the product is much better than projected, the new improved MTBF cannot with significant confidence be calculated from the zero failure data. In any case, the advent of zero failures in a qualification test is an enjoyable reliability event.

Constraint 5

The confidence level of test conclusions must have an acceptable confidence level of 60%. In this test, the 60% CL is used to reduce the number of samples required in the test by 30%. CL in the basic equation for "5" is 1.26 for 60% and 1.85 for 90%. The 60% level of qualification test is adequate in most situations.

Determination of N (Constraint 6)

The number of product units on test in this example is the unknown quantity determined from information on the product and the basic qualification equation. In this example, the number of units required to be placed on test is determined. The number of required units will determine test lab capacity scheduling or recreate a plan to test at different requirements that would permit fewer test units. In other examples, another variable will be determined for a fixed qualification testing capacity.

$$\text{FR} = (R \times C)/[(N \times H) \times A]$$

where

FR $=$ failure rate
$R =$ number of test failures
$C =$ coefficient listed below
$N =$ number of test samples
$H =$ hours on test
$A =$ test acceleration factor

Rearranging the basic qualification equation,

$$
\begin{aligned}
N &= (R \times C)/(\text{FR} \times H \times A) \\
&= \frac{(5)(1.26)}{(2000 \times 10^{-6}/10^3 \text{ h})(400 \text{ h})(20)} \\
&= 394
\end{aligned}
$$

Within the constraints listed as input to this qualification test, the appropriate test conditions would be 394 units for 400 hours. This product has a relatively large test unit number with marginal confidence level because the acceleration factor (20) is low in the test. The acceleration factor of 17,500 in the integrated circuit test allowed a qualification of product in 6 hours. The low anticipated failure rate for the integrated circuits still requires a relatively large number to achieve confidence in the resulting FR; but the qualification test is relatively short.

This example in *Reliability Simplified* provides enough information to proceed with a product qualification test. The key to planning your individual test is to obtain all information on the product (this is often a real challenge) as shown earlier, develop a list of constraints for your product, develop the basic qualification equation, and obtain agreement on the input information and test objective before starting the test. Every variable must have a rational value.

The initial calculation of N in this example was 394. Now, realistically, you may be made aware of the fact that only 30 units are available for this product reliability test. With the assistance of a statistician, you can optimize the test by using the 30 units in equitable compromise with all other qualification factors. Maybe you will shave some confidence factor, a few hours off the warranty constraint, and use a higher product FR. This result will give the best test data using the input realistically available.

The Major Weaknesses of Product Reliability Qualification

The major trust of product reliability qualification is a goal of determining test variables and executing a valid test that is valuable to the business. In concentrating upon that goal, we minimize the actual exposures of accelerated reliability testing that occur during typical qualifications:

1. *Data source and validity.* All qualification tests are approximate projections of future product reliability. This approximate projection is adequate for business needs in most instances. Qualifications are always a compromise of accurate projection versus expedient estimates. Too often a business wants expedient values with the resulting low accuracy in reliability projection at the time of qualification, but then references the qualification data in claims not substantiated by the statistical validity of the qualification.

2. *Highly accelerated qualification tests.* A significant error in projected product reliability data occurs when we physically accelerate with such intensity that the failures become either artifacts of the test or are variables of the test rather than the use condition. An example would be subjecting a product to a mechanical shock never occurring during normal use. We mentioned earlier about trying to evaluate a 5-mph bumper ruggedness in a 60-mph crash. High values of acceleration tend to be relatively inaccurate. Significant time may be required to acquire an accurate correlation between the acceleration curve and the projected reliability.

3. *Product changes during and after qualification.* The sample size is always a problem. The qualification demands preproduction product at the product cycle time when it is least available. Product changes can lead to a serious problem if the product and the manufacturing processes are significantly changed after the qualification sample is selected.

4. *You got to go with what you got.* Insignificant numbers may be on test to statistically determine a required significance level for future failure rates (reliability). In this case, the predominant problem is that of communicating a statistical finding in a deterministic manner. The executive management wants to know if the product reliability is a problem. It does not want to hear about confidence levels and acceleration factors. Use your prior data and information to augment any perceived discrepancies in confidence levels of your constrained test. This is actually applying Baysian statistics.

These four real conditions will utilize an unanticipated amount of your time. They are not reliability science in any sense of the words but require your attention and skill to create an excellent qualification.

Summary

Product reliability qualification is the procedure that officially validates the projected product reliability claim. Although many inputs, such as existing history of similar products and generic reliability growth rates, enter the qualification activity, the emphasis in Chapter 8 is directly on the use of a stress-induced accelerated test to approximate future product reliability performance.

The qualification concept is discussed in terms of accelerating the use time of the exponential reliability model so that an evaluation of lifetime product reliability can be accomplished in a short (e.g., three-week) test time period. A mathematical section on CI is presented that relates the sample time to failure with the entire product's average time to failure in the simple terms of the normal distribution. All calculation schemes for your projected MTBF can be traced to this procedure.

A test example, using values typical of an integrated semiconductor device, is given as a procedural description of the qualification process. The time acceleration of the product ($\times$ 17,496) is an extreme case of factors combining in a test where years of validation of accelerating factors have produced an outstanding evaluation of projected reliability. The product reliability qualification equation is entered immediately to complete the fundamental concept of the qualification activities.

Acceleration factors, the controlling aspect of product reliability qualification, are briefly discussed, giving the large scope and specific nature of qualification some common basis.

A typical qualification test is planned to determine the qualification test size required to meet all of the physical constraints placed upon the qualification input variables. In every qualification, some adjustment is required to optimize the value of qualification to the business.

The major weaknesses of product reliability qualification, apart from expert skill in understanding the fundamentals, stems from interpretation of the data, use of high-acceleration factors that are not understood, product changes after the qualification, and insufficient resources to attain the desired confidence in the qualification data. These weaknesses may be considered outside the realm of product reliability science, but they are a challenge as great as the actual product reliability qualification execution.

Reference

1. James Cortada and John Woods, *McGraw-Hill Encyclopedia of Quality Terms and Concepts* (New York: McGraw-Hill, 1995).

9

Environmental Stress Screening (ESS) to Improve Product Reliability

We all age faster under stress.

Introduction

Managers should read Chapter 9 to understand environmental stress screening (ESS), a reliability technique with universal application. Managers find that the ESS technique for improving reliability is often understood and supported by the customer/consumer. The customer/consumer may even actively participate in the cost or reliability benefit analysis of ESS in your specific product. Therefore, understanding the fundamentals of ESS is very important.

Dd

This is a sample of the text for the definition, or these are more synonyms and usages that are commonly found in the English language.

Environmental Stress Screening (ESS) is subjecting new product to a time period of use and external stress that precipitates early time failures (ETFs) within the product prior to shipment to the customer/consumer.

Engineers should read Chapter 9 to understand the fundamental rationalization of ESS techniques. There are two significant reasons to perform ESS

on a product. First, product development engineers will quickly identify, from ESS, reliability problems and initiate corrective actions by obtaining data about early time failures (ETFs). Second, the product shipped to the customer/consumer after ESS has an improved reliability because of the elimination of ETFs.

The same fundamental reliability principles apply to product reliability qualification, ongoing reliability testing, and environmental stress screening. The principles of sampling characterization of an entire product set and accelerated aging apply to all three techniques. They also are three different applications that identify and eliminate failures within a product population. The intuitive concept that the product reliability can be improved by stress screening has universal recognition. If a product is operated under the appropriate stress conditions, the units that have a high probability of failure during early use time (ETFs) will also have a high probability of failing during an equivalent accelerated early use time caused by the stress operation (screening). The word *screening* is appropriate in that it indicates that potential defective product will be screened from the shipped product.

ESS is a technique that has provided major improvement in product reliability, allowing it to meet required, specified reliability goals.

The Weibull Distribution

The **Weibull distribution** plots a value in time dependent upon two parameters, the failure rate (λ) and the appropriate shape (α).

In Chapters 1 through 8, only relatively simple distributions and mathematical models are required to describe the reliability conditions and dynamics. However, we now must extend our mathematical model of product failures to include the description of the many product systems containing a significant measurable ETF region in the failure-rate (FR) curve. The key idea in ESS is to eliminate ETFs. This will be described graphically in the next sequence of figures.

A clear understanding of Figure 9-1 is critical in effectively applying the ESS technique to your product. Please review this description of exponential and Weibull FR models until this basic concept is completely understood. A significant amount of confusion exists in ESS applications, which involve the exploitation of ETF's removal modeled by a Weibull function.

Figure 9-1 presents FR (fails per time) versus time using the exponential and Weibull mathematical functions as models.

Let us review the application of the exponential model of product reliability given in Chapter 5. Recall that the universal bathtub curve presented conceptually product reliability with ETFs occurring initially during a product use lifetime. However, the ETFs presented a problem in characterizing product reliability as a commonly accepted single number. A single number, MTBF (mean time between failures), can be used to describe product reliability by using the universal application of the exponential distribution function. The conditions for using the exponential model were stated in Chapter 5. One of the conditions is inaccurate in describing most product's reliability. That condition is that the product failures occur at a constant rate and are random with time. In spite of this inaccuracy, the MTBF using the exponential distribution function has been very successful in describing product reliability. The end of obtaining a common single value of MTBF justifies the means of using a simple, yet inaccurate, exponential distribution model that disregards the ETFs.

Figure 9-1 presents this exponential FR as a single constant value for all time of product operation. The single parameter describing an exponential model is the failure rate lambda, or its reciprocal theta, the MTBF. Note that it is a constant for all operating use time.

Figure 9-1 also presents another FR curve that is initially high and becomes lower with time. Many failure rates are best described by the Weibull function, which decreases with time to lower values. Two parameters are required in the Weibull distribution: the main parameter lambda (or reciprocal theta) and the shape parameter alpha.

The mathematics of the Weibull distribution can baffle those initially applying that mathematical model to their system. Appendix B gives a very brief outline of the Weibull distribution that satisfies most engineering ap-

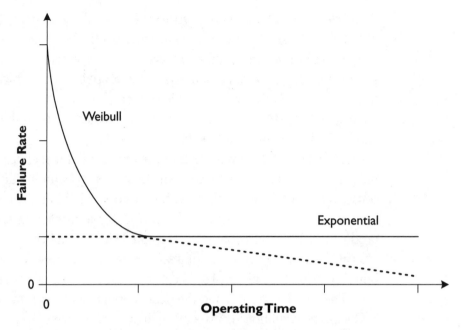

FIGURE 9-1. **Exponential and Weibull failure rate (FR) models**

plications. It is important that the two following distinctions regarding the Weibull distribution are made:

1. The probability density functions for the exponential and Weibull distributions are

$$\text{exponential: } f(t) = \lambda e^{-\lambda t}; \quad \text{Weibull: } f(t) = \lambda_1 t^{-\alpha} e^{-\lambda_1 t^{1-\alpha}/1-\alpha}$$

Note that when the Weibull $f(t)$ equation has an alpha $= 0$, the equation degenerates into an exponential $f(t)$.

2. Be very careful using various books describing the Weibull function and its uses. This book describes the Weibull function in terms of a failure rate (failures per time), and many books describe the Weibull function in terms of failures (number) alone. Although this is a simple difference, the resulting confusion has been considerable. It is sufficient for you to only un-

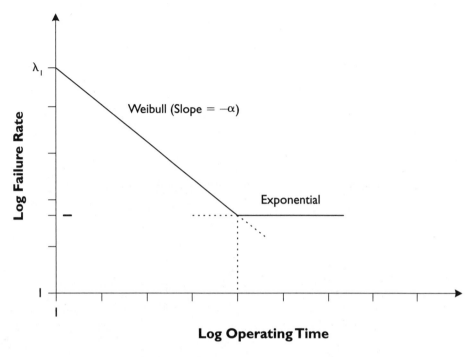

FIGURE 9-2.   The hybrid (Weibull and exponential) FR model

derstand that the Weibull shape parameter alpha can adequately represent your failure-rate data.

Figure 9-2 is a hybrid model that displays the early decrease in FR (modeled by a Weibull function), followed by a constant FR (modeled by an exponential function). Figure 9-2 has an x axis of log time and a y axis of log FR. Figure 9-2 also has time and FR scales that (1) display a crossover between Weibull and exponential model behavior and also (2) display the basic slopes and values required for representing specific data set models.

The Weibull function for failure rate is

$$\lambda(t) = \lambda_1 t^{-\alpha}$$

Taking the log of both sides of this equation,

$$\log \lambda(t) = \log \lambda_1 - \alpha \log t$$

Figure 9-2 displays, on the log-log plot, the Weibull curve with a negative alpha slope, followed by a constant flat curve exhibiting exponential FR behavior. The physical meaning of this hybrid presentation is that the ETF rate decreases in time until that rate becomes a constant caused by random failures.

The transition point is extrapolated from real data for convenience. Note that both the exponential and Weibull curves are extended, by dotted lines, beyond each others time boundaries. However, the precise crossover point in time is of little practical consequence, considering the values are changing on a log scale.

The Weibull function is described in Appendix B only in terms of FR that is utilized in this chapter. The Weibull function in itself can become an extensive subject of investigation. If you are required to understand more about the Weibull distribution, consult with a qualified mathematician or reference documents that describe Weibull function applications to your specific product.

An ESS Example

The fundamental concept of ESS is understood easily from Figure 9-2. If the product is stressed, aging it to a period of time to beyond the period of early time failures (after the transition from Weibull curve to exponential curve), then the stress-induced aging will eliminate all ETFs from the product. Several considerations apply:

- ▶ The Weibull slope alpha determines the period of time in which the ETFs significantly contribute to the total failure rate. Commonly called the time until failures stabilize.
- ▶ If alpha is 0, then the Weibull equation degenerates into an exponential equation with a constant (with time) failure rate. In this case, all failures for all operating time would be constant and random.
- ▶ The constant exponential failure rate is empirically determined.

▶ The obvious result of aging the product results in shortening the product life by an equivalent amount.

You can improve your creativity by learning about and using tools that help you see and understand the world from new perspectives.

The ESS process applied to product is also referred to as burn-in, initial operation testing, performance tested, trial operating, and a variety of similar names. The concept of eliminating the potential failures modeled by the Weibull distribution universally applies to all techniques. A similar view is to regard all product as undergoing an appropriate period of aging to improve the product reliability.

Dd

This is a sample of the text for the definition, or these are more synonyms and usages that are commonly found in the English language.

Burn-in is the common ESS practice of subjecting the new product to operation at elevated temperatures (sometimes along with other stress factors).

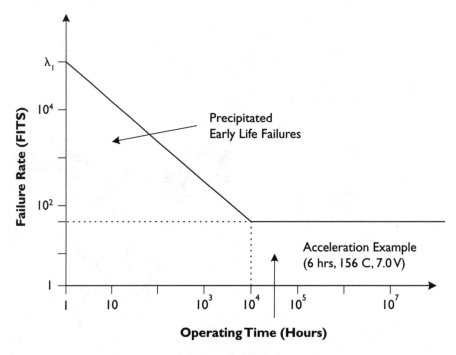

FIGURE 9-3.   A semiconductor burn-in (ESS) example

Figure 9-3 graphically represents a specific vintage of semiconductor product ESS performance with a hybrid distribution of failure rates with time.
The ELFs exist within the Weibull distribution plot.

As an example, a specific vintage undergoes an accelerated aging as described under qualification in Chapter 8. By operating the product at 156°C
for 6 hours, the product accumulates a calculated effective operating time of
17,496 hours. During this effective operating time of 17,496 hours, the ETFs
are precipitated, leaving only the random failures at the lower failure rate described by an exponential distribution.

The example presented in Figure 9-3 is only one of the many screens
and combinations of screens used to improve product reliability. Figure 9-
4 presents a list of various screen types. There is a large science evolving
around these techniques, and we are aware of a four-day seminar held just
to present only the ESS topic. The science of ESS follows the development

- Temperature
- Thermal cycle
- Thermal shock
- Vibration
- Mechanical shock
- Mechanical acceleration
- Voltage
- Current
- Humidity
- Chemicals
- Altitude
- Radiation

FIGURE 9-4.   Types of screens

of reliability stress factors, with time acceleration factors such as temperature and voltage being theoretically developed and thermal cycle and thermal shock being empirically derived. The common purpose of these stress screens is to remove defective items from the customer/consumer product.

Aging of a product by ESS is not always a correct method. If your product already has a wear out mode causing business economic impact, the ESS will only reduce the average operating lifetime of the product. Based on our earlier example of a reliability curve, burning-in incandescent lightbulbs by aging them at high voltage only reduces the average lifetime without increasing significantly the product reliability. We should not ESS incandescent lightbulbs. Conversely, semiconductor integrated circuits, with their essentially infinite life, are excellent examples where ESS contributes to a tenfold or more improvement in product reliability. The relatively outstanding reliability of semiconductor circuits can be traced substantially to the pervasive ESS technique in that product.

Although it is not immediately apparent from Figure 9-3, about 90% of total potential failures existing within this specific vintage fail and are "screened" out of the product by the ESS. The resulting improved product reliability alone is well worth the cost of burn-in.

There are four predominate reasons for employing ESS:

1. ESS is a tool to improve product reliability. The example just presented demonstrates how semiconductor product can have a tenfold improvement in reliability just by including an ESS or burn-in process prior to product shipment. In this prime example of semiconductor product, high product reliability is achieved by the common practice of burn-in. Remember that this product is in the infinite life category, with the lifetime average actually increasing by applying ESS. It is the best way of approaching the best MTBF based on the flat or exponential modeled part of the failure-rate curve.

2. ESS detects and eliminates bad product lots (mavericks) from being shipped to the customer/consumer. Some concern always has to be directed at sampling control techniques that allow, at a low probability level, maverick lots to continue to shipment in the manufacturing process. Because ESS normally stresses 100% of the product, the deviant lots will be identified before shipping damaged goods to the customer/consumer. The time period to control deviation is also shortened. That helps significantly in determining the root cause of product reliability and functional problems.

3. ESS shortens the development cycle in two ways. First, it provides a quick feedback loop for identification and corrective action required for reduction and elimination of product problems. This obvious value is especially significant to the engineering and development organization. The failure data directly generate information regarding required product improvements. Second, ESS provides an accurate measure of both the functional and the reliability performance required to specify the next product. Rather than wait for the less accurate recording schemes of customer/consumer failures, the engineers can rely on a well-controlled, accurate equivalent of information produced by ESS.

4. ESS is a monitor of product performance. The manufactured product is evaluated on a continuing basis, providing a measure of effect for engineering changes (ECs) during manufacturing, the variation in parts supplied to manufacturing, and the stability of the manufacturing process. Severe product reliability problems caused by subtle in-

teractions are rare. They are mainly used as anecdotes in product reliability lectures. However, be assured that ESS will identify most of these problems and provide an evaluation of change interactions.

These four reasons are the primary motivations for considering ESS for your product. The business management question regarding ESS is: "Is that ESS benefit worth the additional cost to the product?"

The ESS Economic Dilemma

The semiconductor integrated circuit product, used as an example of ESS, is an exception to typical ESS operation in that the application is pervasive in that product. In most applications ESS is economically feasible for a limited period of the early product distribution to consumers. The reasons for implementing ESS, expressed in the last section, are fairly clear, and the cost of implementation is no more difficult than any other manufacturing process step. A major problem occurs when the value of ESS per product item is reduced to a point where discontinuation of ESS becomes a proper business consideration. The ESS discontinuation decision, without the best insight and strategic planning, is most often an agonizing experience. We will expand upon several areas of typical frustration encountered in the discontinuation of an ESS program.

 Although there are a multitude of reasons to discontinue ESS applications on the many products, a good cross section of reasons can be generated using the motivations for ESS presented earlier in this chapter:

1. ESS is considered primarily to improve product reliability. But when reliability growth is as pronounced, the ultimate goal of product reliability may be achieved. In this case, the ESS step may become only a cost adder to the process.
2. Although 100% evaluation of product is an excellent method for ESS to identify maverick lots, the ESS may not be justified through cost-benefits analysis to be appropriate for the business. The need for effective 100% control of maverick lots varies significantly among companies.

3. The data and information provided by ESS definitely shorten the development cycle. However, the two significant sources of information needed for input to design requirements are the ESS measurements soon after initial product release for sale and the customer/consumer feedback data collected some time after initial product release. Typically, engineering only wants ESS data for a couple of months after the initial product release.

4. An ongoing monitor generates strict, pertinent product reliability information. However, the data generation through ESS may be too expensive for general use.

An excellent application in ESS will surely lead to its demise. A good example today is in the same semiconductor product, where the product is now under excellent ESS control but prompts active proposals to remove the ESS burn-in step as a cost reduction. The economic dilemma with ESS is that most indicators used to determine ESS discontinuation vary in value among the decision makers and that the decision is never without agony. The dynamic nature of critical ESS data only adds to the uncertainty. In simple terms, ESS has an inherent dilemma that, in the best interest of the organization, one should both continue and discontinue.

ESS Implementation and Discontinuation

This section has significant information regarding ESS. If you intend to use ESS on your product, definitely read and understand the following advice and observations gained from experience in actual ESS practice.

The methods of ESS are those acceleration techniques presented in Chapter 8. Considering the wide range of application of ESS, consider that any specific screening technique may be appropriate. What is presented is the ESS story universal to all ESS techniques. Familiarity with the business decisions of ESS is fiscally more important than the physical knowledge of the ESS technique. The ESS story is presented as a sequence in time from when ESS is a chosen method for product reliability control until it is discontinued. Most product organizations are affected by the ESS business process subsequently presented.

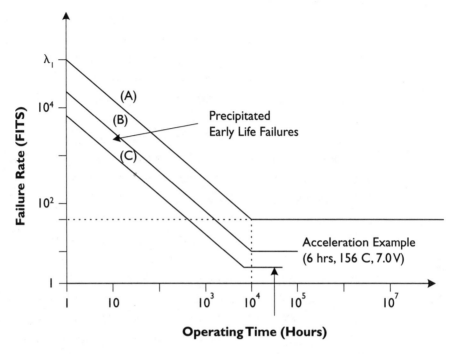

FIGURE 9-5.   **An example of hybrid FR for various vintages of a product**

Figure 9-5 is an example of hybrid (Weibull and exponential) modeled products for various vintages. Note that the first-quarter vintage has the highest initial ETF and random failures for the life of the product. The second quarter usually has a significant improvement in ETFs and also an improvement (fewer) in random failures for the life of the product. By the third quarter (in this example) the ETFs have almost disappeared, and the random failures have reached a stable low level.

Initially, the cost and benefit of ESS will be considered. ESS will be implemented to achieve a product reliability competitive in marketing the product. The prime reason may be that the new product has not stabilized due to physical manufacturing control or the product still has unidentified and unresolved problems. The management solution to produce a competitive product is to screen products for defects (ESS).

The cost-benefit analysis will use Figure 9-5 curve (A) as input. The reliability growth will be too difficult to determine, and the management really wants the impact of competitive product reliability now, when the product is new and reputations are being established. For example, the management wishes to mechanically vibrate (ESS) the product to identify and remove potential defects. The details of that process will be substantially assisted by mechanical-vibration equipment vendors confirming the intelligent decision.

Note that in the initial decision to implement ESS, subjective factors often take priority over observed product reliability data. The cost of space, capitol equipment, direct labor, overhead, and all those other elements will be clearly documented on a spread sheet and the bottom line of an ESS cost per item calculated for management. However, many conditional inputs, especially the reliability growth rate, are normally missing from this calculation. The agonizing quantification of ESS comes with discontinuation.

After gaining confidence that the new product has a reliable reputation established in the market, management will ask for some lower cost-per-unit alternates for product ESS. That request is driven by both the inability to ESS a larger volume rate of product produced with time and the lessening value of the ESS function.

Detailed explanations of the typical responses to business needs are now presented.

The Financial Analysis to Discontinue

Most often, the initial activity to optimize a continued ESS is a financial analysis. The financial analysis will provide information used to decide the fate of ESS.

How do you know when to stop using ESS to eliminate early time failures? Typically, financial analysts compare the cost of doing the ESS testing with the cost of repairing the failure if it occurred in the customer's environment. For example:

In-house cost
— It costs $5/unit for ESS = A.
— The defect rate is 1 defect/3 units in ESS = B.
— The cost of the defect found in the ESS/unit is $30 = C.

—The cost per unit = $A + (B \times C)$.

—5 + (30 x 1/3) = $15/unit.

Field cost

—The cost to repair defective unit in field is \$57/defect = D.

—Based on ESS, 1 defect was eliminated per 3 units = B.

—The failure cost to the customer/consumer is $D \times B$ = \$19.

This is an oversimplified example, but it is typical of all financial analysis. Here, the conclusion is that the ESS is justified. However, that conclusion is not correct because some of the ESS failures are not early time failures but are part of the intrinsic failures.

The example is presented in Figure 9-6. Let us assume that the ESS eliminated the early time failures, as is shown in the ESS equivalent test time. By comparing ETFs and random defects in the integrated areas under the curve, we can estimate that roughly 50% of the defects detected during ESS

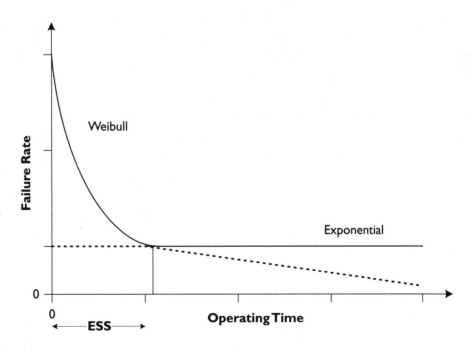

FIGURE 9-6.   The early time failures eliminated by ESS (Note that the scales are linear)

are true early life failures, and the other 50% are random failures, and as a result, the product shipped to the customer/consumer was not improved by 1 defect in 3 units, but by only 1 defect in 6 units. Thus, when we correct our assumptions used in the previous example, the ESS cost per unit remains the same, but the field cost savings is really 1 defect in 6 units, not 1 defect in 3 units. Therefore, the field cost is $9.50/unit, not $19 as was originally calculated. In this case from the economist viewpoint, ESS testing cannot be justified.

The previous example demonstrates a common error in calculations that results from the financial analyst not understanding the basic functions of Figure 9-6.

Another common error in calculation stems from not considering the impact on the customer/consumer. The costs incurred by the customer/consumer during product failures are often left out from reliability analyses. With today's competitive environment, we need to understand what it costs customers/consumers when products fail. This is necessary because customers/consumers are beginning to make their purchase decisions based on the cost of owning a product, not just the purchase price. Of course, the cost of a defect varies greatly based on the product and even on the failure mode within the product.

For example, in a car, the cost of repairing a loose screw that is causing an exhaust system to rattle is much less than the repair cost of a defective alternator. Most organizations do not take the customer/consumer-related defect cost into consideration when the product is under warranty, thinking that the entire cost of repair is being covered by the warranty. This is usually a bad assumption. The key is to understand clearly your product failures. This is just an extension of Chapter 4, learning that understanding product defects is the primary activity of product reliability.

ESS Disillusionment

The management, achieving a satisfactory level of success, will become concerned upon understanding the economic ramifications of Figures 9-5 and 9-6. If the fundamental models of reliability growth and ESS fundamentals have not been communicated to executive management by this time, the following sequence will occur:

▶ The management will quickly conclude, from Figure 9-5, reliability growth (curves A to C), that the ESS is quickly becoming a valueless cost adder. Also, why wasn't this visual factor presented at the time of ESS implementation? Remember that the reliability growth was unknown at the time of ESS implementation (but the concept should have been discussed). Also, at the time of ESS implementation, the decision to use ESS was based on intuitive reasons, because real data were not available.

▶ Figure 9-6 presents a clear input for true effectiveness of ESS. If this relationship is a surprise to the decision makers after ESS implementation, some rather unpleasant interactions occur. Often the fixed cost of ESS implementation (equipment, space, and overhead) are viewed as bad investments.

▶ The irony of the financial reassessment is that a successful ESS venture is viewed as ineffective, yet an unsuccessful ESS will continue to justify its existence. A sad, but true condition during ESS discontinuation. This is part of the ESS discontinuation dilemma. It is prudent to review the fundamental ESS process, as presented in a basic fashion in this book, with everyone prior to implementing ESS. Justifying ESS economically after successful implementation may be impossible.

What is learned from experience is that financial analysis shock, for lack of better wording, will be greatly reduced if a projection of reliability growth, ESS effectiveness, and scope of ESS is discussed in detail prior to having ESS follow its natural path to extinction without clear management.

The Secondary ESS Program

After the financial analysis to discontinue ESS has been completed and reviewed, the next logical ESS management step is to continue with lower-cost alternatives to the original 100% ESS. This logically flows from the facts that the initial fixed expenses are already realized, and at this point a complete elimination of ESS still seems to be too risky. The following two alternates to continued low-cost ESS are chosen:

▶ Using the ESS facility already in place, a plan often is devised to reduce ESS cost per unit by increased throughput with existing equipment. This is accomplished primarily by increasing the ESS time acceleration factor and independently reducing the ESS test time. This seems logical because the existing ESS equipment will then handle the increase in manufacturing volume that normally occurs concurrently with the reliability growth.

▶ Since the barrier to discontinuing ESS activity may be viewed as only a lack of data confirming the economic justification to discontinue, the 100% ESS can be replaced with a suitable sampling plan until sufficient confirmation data are available.

The implementation of these two common alternates will now be analyzed. Keep in mind that the original evaluation was focused on the economic value of ESS. The continuation of ESS by increased throughput methods and sampling plans significantly reduces the value of testing data validity and screening effectiveness. In other words, the compromise plan assures the demise of ESS in a product process, and sometimes that action will not be in the best interest of the organization. Next, we will discuss experience with ESS modified with higher acceleration factors and sampling plans.

The first effective proposal to reducing ESS cost per unit is to increase throughput by increasing the stress level of the ESS. A simple approximation is that a tenfold increase in acceleration in stress will reduce the ESS test time 10 times and result in a tenfold cost-per-unit reduction. Let us examine this proposal in detail.

Figure 9-7 presents an important characteristic regarding ESS acceleration factors. The fact that every ESS is unique prevents establishing a precise science applicable to your specific products. However, the problem of misleading data generated by ESS-induced failures (artifacts) that do not represent the actual potential ETF failures becomes an important consideration at higher-acceleration factors. By increasing ESS acceleration factors, you will be inducing more failures in good products in addition to eliminating ETFs from all products. Sometimes it is also a shock to management that ESS al-

9-7A

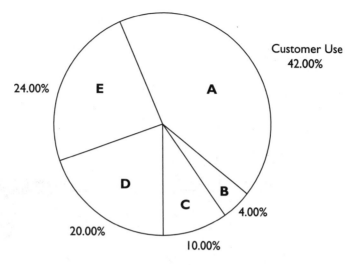

1X acceleration

9-7B

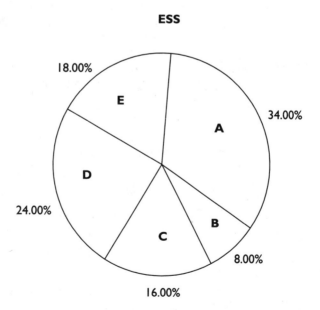

100X acceleration
Change in failure mode relative frequency

9-7C

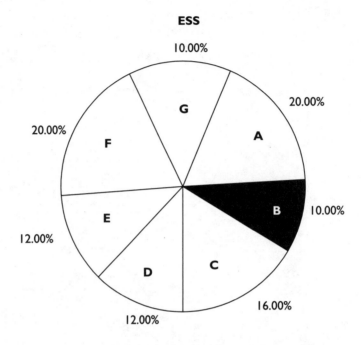

10000X acceleration
Change in failure mode relative frequency
plus ESS unduced artifacts F and G

FIGURE 9-7A, B, C.　Deviation from true predictive values with acceleration factors aging to the same customer/consumer use (10,000 hrs.) time

ways causes failure to some good product. In fact, we did not even mention this phenomenon in our prior ESS economic justification analysis. Imagine the response of an executive upon discovering that ESS is only 30% as effective as he understood and also that it creates failures in good product!

So how should we responsibly address the utilization of ESS? The mathematical model of the presented phenomenon is quite detailed and interesting. It states that the activation energy of modes and lowest level of excitation varies among the random catastrophic failures. In simpler terms, this means that new kinds of failures appear at higher stress intensities and that various failure modes observed during customer/consumer-use conditions do not increase at the same rate (time acceleration) with an increase in intensity.

The ESS that uses multiple accelerating factors makes the translation back to customer/consumer use conditions extremely difficult. The semiconductor example presented earlier had stress factors of temperature and voltage. Those stress factors applied to this specific product are anecdotal. Many years of effort have been expended to determine the relationship between stress and nominal use conditions. That relationship has been reduced to simple mathematical models and equations. But what if you used vibration, temperature cycle, and reducing atmospheric environment on your specific product? Without empirical data to support your conclusion, you cannot say with certainty how the ESS relates to ETFs or customer/consumer reliability.

ESS is very prone to generating misleading information by assuming that the data points are distributed the same among failure modes at all acceleration factor levels. Be very careful! The only true ESS is one where a specific product is confirmed to accelerate failures to a known measured observation. An ideal observation would be produced if alternate items were placed on ESS, and then the two populations (ESS and non-ESS) were evaluated during customer/consumer use. Then the true effect of ESS could be evaluated. But lacking specific data, complete communication of ESS factors is imperative.

The second common alternate method to reduce ESS cost is to institute a sampling plan. Although sampling product in ESS reduces the value of data, it does provide an excellent bridge to discontinuation because it provides continuing data during the final stages of product reliability growth. Many sampling schemes have been generated that perform well under the ESS discontinuation phase.

For example, at the IBM San Jose site, an off-line customer/consumer-simulated test and stress test facility was established. It was called the Product Measurement and Analysis (PMA) Laboratory. On a weekly basis, samples of current product ready to be shipped to the customer/consumer were selected from the shipping dock and sent to the PMA. The PMA then subjected part of the sample to an accelerated life test of 96 hours that simulated 90 days of customer/consumer operation. A smaller part of the test sample was subjected to a 22-day environmental stress test. The results of these tests were compared to a known performance model in order to detect changes in the manufacturing processes or purchased components.

Similar approaches have been used with less-complex products, like TVs. We have seen cases where a week's product was not released to the customer/consumer until the ESS test was successfully completed. If the test sample failed to meet the established acceptance criteria, the week's production was 100% screened. A typical screening action would be to burn-in the entire weeks production.

Note that the sampling ESS techniques are actually ongoing reliability tests (ORTs) that are common safeguards to manufacturing control in the business. However, the sampling technique is primarily directed toward identifying major manufacturing deviations rather than removing significant ETFs from the product. This is appropriate for a well-designed and manufactured product. It is also a preferable way of terminating ESS because the decision to stop or not stop ESS is reduced to a compromise of the long-term sampling alternate.

Remember, part of the ESS discontinuation agony is that no matter what the preferred method of ESS chosen, the feedback data are never available to indicate with certainty when the ESS procedure should be discontinued. In rodeo jargon, you have gotten onto a horse and now you can't get off. You start doing ESS out of a form of subjective desperation, you now feel very uncomfortable about the steps used to make ESS economically viable, and now you can't even quit. This is a typical problem. But preparation steps will ease the exploitation of ESS as a significant economic business tool.

1. *Understand your ESS implementation motivation.* Make a consensus list of ESS implementation motivations. Are you using ESS primarily to deliver competitive product until final manufacturing equipment is installed and process control is established? Are you using ESS for a long-term solution to provide your customer/consumer with more reliable product? Are you using ESS primarily at the customer's/consumer's request? Is ESS a primary method of product defect identification and correction? Will ESS for your new product be based primarily on old product ESS performance?

2. *Understand the mechanisms of ESS.* By definition, ESS implementations and discontinuations are difficult due to lack of compelling data. Don't aggravate that situation by inserting basic mistakes caused by not understanding ESS fundamentals. That is a goal of this chapter. Do you clearly understand the financial balance between cost of ESS and benefit to the customer/consumer? What portion of the financial

cost and benefit is good will (resulting in good reputation) implicit in the ESS implementation? Do you have a predictive model for ETF elimination effectiveness for your specific ESS? Do you have a predictive model for ESS-generated elimination of good product? Do you have a predictive model for reliability growth? Do you have an anticipated ESS effectiveness model for applied acceleration conditions? Is the model for the ESS validated? Do you plan to critically review ESS fundamentals prior to ESS implementation?

3. *Anticipate ESS discontinuation.* A successful ESS will quickly cause its own demise. If the defects that are detected are understood and prevented from recurring before too long, the cost of doing the ESS is greater than the resulting benefits. This discontinuation of ESS is in the best interest of the organization. Historically, ESS discontinuation is managed poorly based on incorrect decisions made from sparse information. If you anticipate specific data to be crucial to the ESS discontinuation decisions, obtain the data if possible, but at least communicate that requirement to all decision makers as soon as possible.

The subject of ESS, similar to the subject of product failures, is not well understood by most individuals utilizing this significant technique. The fundamentals are quite simple, yet they are not intuitive. It is a continual source of amazement that improper ESS is executed in business environments that pride themselves on business economic control. In the case of ESS, it is important to understand both the fundamental ESS operation and the business process that accompanies the ESS application. We are not so naive to think that this chapter will significantly change the ESS implementation and discontinuation process to a deliberate optimized process, but we hope that this chapter assists you in achieving a better specific business operation.

Summary

The topic of Chapter 9 is environmental stress screening (ESS) of product. The technique of ESS removes the ETFs from the reliability curve. ESS can produce a more reliable product and can produce data for fast improvement of existing and new products.

The fundamental operation of ESS is described by the Weibull distribution model. It is almost intuitive that early stress will remove the failure-prone units from the product.

A complete understanding of ESS must include the reality that ESS product failures are from ETFs, random failures, and induced specifically by ESS itself. Therefore, it is important to understand clearly the stress that is applied to all product.

The discontinuation of an ESS program creates more stress than the ESS. The prime problems of mistaken analysis, incorrect alternates to 100% ESS, and misunderstanding of ESS fundamentals are common. These topics were discussed in this chapter. These problems aggravate the inherent difficulty of ESS discontinuation.

The value of ESS has a customer/consumer satisfaction element that transcends financial analysis. In general, customers/consumers are very satisfied that a producer takes the additional step of ESS to assure the reliability of the product. That factor, in addition to a good cost-benefit analysis, will direct you toward the proper ESS discontinuation decision.

10

Product Failure Database and Field Failure Analysis

The best statistical projections in the world are not as good as real data. What happens is what counts, not what we think is going to happen.

Introduction

Managers should read Chapter 10 to determine the appropriate process of obtaining product failure information for each specific business. As stated in Chapter 4, the single most important reliability factor is to understand clearly your product's failures. In fact, the sole reason for Chapter 4 was to impress that fact upon the reader. Chapter 10 describes the methods for collecting and validating product failure data.

Engineers should understand the methods for obtaining product failure data because it ultimately validates the assumptions made regarding reliability during the development and manufacturing of the product. Specific feedback schemes of the product's field failure data collection are discussed.

The actual product failures occurring during customer use are a reality check for all product reliability assumptions and projections made during product development and manufacturing. Unfortunately, the priority of validation of product reliability assumptions is lower than the priority of producing new products on time and concern about the potentials of the new product containing reliability problems.

This superficial treatment of ongoing product reliability (failure) measurement is neither an abstract nor a trivial problem. Its detrimental results have been observed all too often to ignore:

1. A product becomes identified (tagged) with a specific reliability problem. Specific examples will not be mentioned out of fairness, but most readers can relate to at least one example. The common feature is that this bad reliability tag or reputation usually is developed over a longer period of time than one could reasonably expect to identify and correct the problem. The customer will overlook reliability problems that are quickly and responsibly corrected. Reputation is characterized as unresponsive, incompetent people making bad product. A significant portion of a bad product-reliability reputation stems from not identifying and responding to customer problems.

2. Organizations having poor feedback regarding their product failures also have poor feedback regarding product satisfaction by their customers. When losing market share due to poor reliability, it is not coincidental that often the producing organization is the last to become aware of a severe reliability problem. The organization usually is focused on product value-added and profit and not the existing customer reliability performance.

3. A bewildering array of interpretations is often made from the same product failure data. This confuses the product reliability management to the extent that only sweeping generalities are used to correct specific problems. An insidious management problem is that poorly collected data look precisely like poorly interpreted data. Under these conditions, executive management may intelligently avoid the entire product reliability subject within their businesses.

Figure 10-1 graphically presents the failure data feedback channel for all products. It is necessary to define the appropriate product failure feedback system for your specific business as a global requirement for all segments of your individual product reliability system. Product failure databases insti-

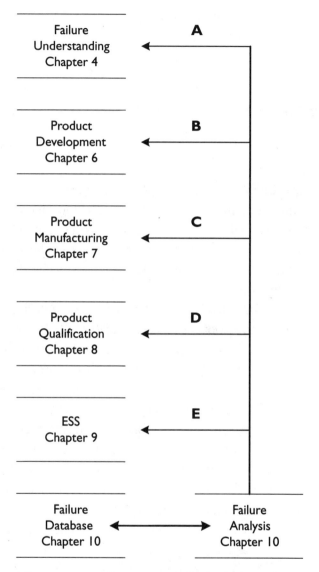

FIGURE 10-1.   The communications feedback channel

tuted to fulfill transient requirements within specific business segments or instituted as a response to critical problems are always far from optimum. The initial step of evaluating your own product failure data system starts with the critical observation of your own product's existing failure data and information.

I seldom see a field problem that someone has not already seen in house.
—H. J. HARRINGTON

The Scope of Product Failure Identification

An extremely broad scope of techniques are used to collect product failure data. This is caused by the natural broad distribution of reliability cost content (Chapter 3) and compounded by the variety of nonstandardized techniques used to achieve an appropriate, for the business, product failure database. The advent of computerization has not yet significantly reduced the high number of unique product failure database applications, but in fact it has assisted greatly in responsive data flow and timely problem resolutions within individual systems.

The most frequent inadequacy of computerized product failure data systems is that global business requirements do not take priority over isolated business segment requirements. This results in fragmented, specialized, and expensive multiple data systems where the priority is focused on the computer system capability rather than the value to the global business of the feedback data. Almost every large company, where the financial justification of product failure data collection systems is distributed, wastes huge amounts of money generating product failure feedback data specific to isolated business areas. If the information system (IS) and/or reliability management is focused within one area, due to small corporate size or organizational authority, this problem is minimized.

The many failure identification techniques also substantially vary in data content. It is globally sufficient to realize that every data element recorded regarding a product failure is (or is at one period of time) considered to be of value. Several familiar product identification and failure data gathering techniques are given to demonstrate common product failure data acquisition schemes:

1. The automobile is subject to corrective actions requiring identification of specific product. The identification process consists primarily of using existing state Department of Motor Vehicles databases for purposes of auto-

mobile licensing, environmental control, and safety. If an identification of a segment of automobile product is required, as during a safety recall for corrective action, the segment is identified and tracked to the present owners. This is an efficient and effective method. In this case a segment of product was identified and tracked, not the product failures.

2. Appliances, such as washers and dryers, are usually identified by model and serial number. In this case, the repair actions identify failed components and failure modes. Typically, a warranty registration card is available for the consumer to register for warranty benefits and information regarding product limitations and deficiencies. The small percentages of customers registering warranties still form a statistically significant database, but if the data are generated based only on recorded failures, that process can create a statistical bias. However, specific product reliability failure modes can be statistically inferred from the failure data. For example, significant failures of a specific dryer bearing would prompt a redesign and field stocking to correct the identified problem.

3. Electronic systems, especially those with fault-tolerant designs, record and characterize the failure internally for use in corrective action analysis. Large computing systems record correctable (soft error) failure rates and incorrectable operating failures (hard errors) for identification of reliability problems within the system. The system reliability may be centralized within a distributed network by automatically notifying a central location continuously about the system's reliability status. The value of continuous operation of full-time computer systems justifies the expense of creating immediate failure databases required for least interruption of the computer function.

4. Automobile tires are typical in recording product failures for a diverse, untracked consumer market. The product contains three common features:

    a. The wear-out or service "support" period is declared. For instance, a 45,000-mile tire is declared as mileage capability under specified warranty conditions.

    b. Manufacturing defects are specific failures that are not recognized as part of the tire wear-out process. These catastrophic failures do not include road hazards. The companies partition liability by failure mode.

c. Emphasis is placed on operating-use environmental conditions. In the case of tires, it would include proper alignment and absence of off-road use.

The consumer automobile tire marketplace provides a highly competitive marketplace where reliability and safety are key elements in the perceived customer value of product offerings. This product is excellent to model the reliability profit factor (RPF) presented in Chapter 2. I am sure that the business people at Michelin agree.

Again, the data collected regarding failures is an adjunct to tire service and repair activity. The advent of a tire recall for safety reasons would involve a process of public notification combined with a measure of that public notification effectiveness. For instance, in the United States, legal rules apply under the Consumer Product Safety Commission (CPSC) if it has jurisdiction for that product. The recall process is usually controlled by government regulation, and nothing would date this book quicker than specific reference to the changing recall processes. As a warning, if a recall is considered in your organization, identify and contact the proper regulatory body for guidance.

These examples are presented to demonstrate the broad scope of current product failure database activities and to provide some details that guide the fundamental operation of these activities. The existing product failure databases for identification and correction of defects are so great that these examples may not provide assistance toward establishing your own specific database.

It is not the purpose of this book to provide examples and systems of product failure databases that can apply directly to your specific product. That task is impossible. What we will do instead is expand upon the basic principles that apply to all existing product failure databases.

Constructing a New Product Reliability Failure Database

The construction of a new product reliability failure database is extremely complex and can be greatly facilitated by following the procedural steps subsequently listed. The major problem with construction of "new" databases is the compatibility and capability of the existing databased systems. Many obsolete manual data filing systems and inflexible computer databases of questionable value continue to exist due to the inability to sort, reformat, and transfer to a computerized database of the valuable "old" data and information. Outmoded databases decrease in value while creating an inertia toward establishing a valuable system. Adherence to the following steps clarifies the sorting of old data and helps establish a system of value to your business.

This process will not resolve conflicting interests among the organizations, but systematic analysis, as demonstrated next, always clarifies the path to formation of the best product failure database.

Step 1. Identify Your Reliability Failure Data Requirements

▶ *Construct a matrix of reliability database requirements.* Figure 10-2 is a matrix of the organizations desiring failure data versus the business reason that justifies their specific requirement. This figure may not be exactly suited for your situation, but the matrix has several features that could be useful in your task of constructing the database.

1. The sequence of organizations desiring the failure data is very close to the general process flow (Chapter 2) and text progression of this book. This perspective, which logically presents all business needs, removes the perceived unreasonable costs ascribed to individual organizational functions when a failure data system is being constructed.

2. The management of cost-benefit analysis is substantially swayed by history. The matrix provides a quick study of the reliability database value to the entire business based on experience.

3. The matrix (Figure 10-2) is only a first step toward construction of a database. However, the matrix is a good tool to reasonably adjust and communicate individual organizational demands and allocated costs among all organizational functions, before spending money on the actual pervasive database.

▶ *Identify all tagalong reliability and data sources.* A common practice is the utilization of existing databases to infer the information required within

	1	2	3	4	5	6	7	8	9	10
Business Management										
Product Development										
Product Manufacturing										
Customer Service										
Product Qualification										
ESS										
Sales/Marketing										
Field Product Repair										
Internal Product Repair										

1. Cost-benefit optimization
2. Customer problem response
3. Problem identification and correction
4. Problem resolution validation
5. Customer communications
6. Product qualification effectiveness
7. ESS cost-benefit analysis
8. Product reliability features
9. Replacement parts stocking
10. Manufacturing product run scheduling

FIGURE 10-2.   Matrix of reliability database requirements

an organization. For instance, warranty claims (recorded by manufacturing or customer service) will be used to represent the entire failure mode spectrum by the product reliability organization. Another example is that the field repair organization data will be used to validate the product MTBF. Note that known deficiencies will exist when abstracting inferred information from existing databases. This clever but less-than-complete method has two significant characteristics:

1. Frequently, the owner of the database discontinues operation for a legitimate business reason. Then the parasitic party is deprived of the data.

2. In times of crisis, the parasitic party, having knowingly compromised the crucial data required for problem resolution, cannot identify and correct the problem.

An actual anecdote, encountered by the author, was when a product failure was only officially declared once the root cause of the failure was determined. The product had many complex failures, many of which could not be clearly ascribed to a root cause. As a result, the amount of declared failures was significantly lower than the actual product failures. The business used this declared failure rate as a measure of MTBF. In this case, the product MTBF could be increased simply by transferring an incompetent person, one who could not determine root causes, into the group doing the failure determination!

In every case, determine what data and information are being inferred from databases from external organizations.

▶ *Understand the transient nature of product reliability failure databases.* The initial failure data from new product use is very important, but the value of data to organizations such as product design decreases rapidly within a couple of months. The recognition of transient data requirements is a major consideration. Frequently, product is initially sent in a large volume to only a few customers, and then the reliability performance is monitored by direct communications. This technique fulfills the business need but should not be considered as a reliability database requirement.

The purpose of step 1 is to identify all organizations requiring product failure data and their reasons and existing schemes to fulfill that requirement. Do not try to select the optimum data system for each organization (step 2), adjust all requirements to a global scheme (step 3), or perform a cost-benefit evaluation (step 4) until you complete step 1. Experience has demonstrated that trying to complete a business justification of a product failure database on an individual organization is hopeless without first having a clear idea of the entire business scope.

Step 2. Select a Universal Level of Detail and Communications Format

▶ *Understand level of failure detail requirements.* A problem that plagues the systematic approach to product failure data collection and distribution is that each organization to which feedback occurs has a different requirement for detail. For example, a product development organization requires that a detailed root cause analysis be performed on each for a failure, and a field repair organization requires only the failed replacement be identified in order to regulate the spare parts inventory. Natural differences occur between the financial concern of warranty-protected failures required by business accounting and the continued after-warranty failures, which may be significantly greater in number, by field repair. The purpose of this step is to analyze and prioritize organizational requirements before installing the optimum database. This prioritization should occur in a deliberate fashion by anticipating a product failure data problem before a traumatic reliability crisis occurs. Don't worry about life insurance after the death has occurred.

▶ *Understand the interaction process between each organization and the present product failure database.* Clearly understand how other existing data systems interact with the organizational failure database requirements. For the moment, don't concern yourself about the value and justification of the data itself. For example, if you have a warranty program, how is the warranty claim (failure) information gathered, formatted, and distributed? Is the warranty claim data useful in fulfilling the requirement of a specific organization (Figure 10-1)? Do you have a government-mandated product identification and complaint files that collect data of value for all organizations?

In step 1, the reference to tagalong data was not to discourage usage of nor to devaluate these data systems. Our activity in this step is to understand the validity and suitability of using these databases within a global scheme for the business.

▶ *Understand transportability and merger potential of tagalong databases.* The condition of universal access is the ideal for a reliability failure database. We have chosen a universal spread sheet with computerized access to be a standard for reliability failure database communication. If you have an ancillary (tagalong) database that is not transportable into the standard, you have a high probability that you have an ineffective system. You become data rich and information poor. Almost everyone is acquainted with reliability problems that were identified in the data but never flagged for identification and correction by the system. A significant number of data identified, but not realized problems, stem from the inability to format all existing databases into a universal format with computerized detection of reliability problems.

The goal of step 2 is to develop a data detail level and communication scheme that can optimize the business needs for all organizations. This scheme is quite controversial, and a clear presentation of the existing and proposed product reliability failure databased system is necessary to promote a balanced perspective between organizational needs and global business optimum mandates. That is precisely the value of step 2. It isolates in a detailed manner all product failure database inputs to a universal system.

In step 1 you identified all of the organizations and their requirements for reliability failure data. In step 2 you learned in detail the entire scope of interacting data sources and communication flows. You need to understand the entire corporate system of present and proposed databased systems for reliability before attempting to justify any organizational segment. Remember, the major problem with product failure database construction is specious, localized efforts to influence an optimum global system. Leave the justification to steps 3 and 4.

Step 3. Develop an Optimum Global System

 ▶ *List problems with each organization's use of a global database.* Once you have determined all product failure database participants and clearly understand ancillary data systems and shared requirements, proceed with the task of establishing a universal database.

The primary difficulty in establishing a universal database is that autonomous organizational activities toward fulfilling their individual requirements are individually supported rather than a universal shared database. The reasons are quite simple:

1. The universal database does not meet all of the perceived requirements of the individual organization.
2. The universal database information system (IS) is incompatible with the individual organization's IS.
3. The universal database is now not under the organization's control, allowing a degree of inflexibility detrimental to the organization.
4. The universal cost sharing to operate the database is too expensive or not allocated correctly.

These reasons, and similar reasons against constructing a universal database, are the origin of the observed characteristic of multiple databases.

If you have neither the authority nor the logical persuasion to consolidate the multiple databases, you can never achieve what is best for the business. A strong argument for reliability management authority (Chapter 12) stems from the need to establish a universal product failure database. Realize that this source of contention is logically derived by both individual organizations and global management.

Many severe problems can be traced to the multiple product-failure-database businesses where pervasive management is absent. Key feedback data are missing or "falls through the cracks," and as a result, severe business damage occurs. The answer is a deliberate, planned strategy with knowing participation.

▶ *Generate a tentative global product failure data format.* In simple terms, first, do your homework of identifying organizations requiring product failure data (step 1) and understand their current and proposed systems in detail (step 2); then generate a highly visible tentative universal proposal for the system.

In this book the visible proposal takes the form of a computerized spread sheet capable of being electronically transported into the universal system chosen by the corporate information system.

Figure 10-3 demonstrates the working format of a system that is proposed to satisfy all requirements for the business in communicating feedback of product failure data. The spreadsheet should be so user-friendly that only deliberate coding should prevent a clear understanding of the data.

There are several features of the database that need explanation:

1. During repair actions the prime goal is to return the system to specified functional operation. This results in a significant number of system subassemblies and components being replaced during the repair action without a clear diagnostic identification of the failed unit. An extreme example is that many repair actions may occur on a machine that is susceptible to an adjacent high-current welding operation. Until the root cause of the problem (welder) is identified, many good components will be entered into the product failure database. As listed in the spreadsheet in Figure 10-3, this category of failure (actually good product) is listed as not-analyzed-yet (NAY), or, if analyzed and found to be within functional specification, it is listed as no-trouble-

			Firenzo Product Failure Database					
Ref	Entry	P/N-EC	Day Code	Fail Date	Status	Service Area	Contact
677	6/10/97	576201-00	5/10/97	6/9/97	NAY	VAS-4	EDD
678	6/10/97	576196-01	1/6/97	6/9/97		East	
679	6/11/97	576201-00	5/10/97	6/6/97	E-Frame	East	LNI
680	6/11/97	576196-01	10/15/96	9/9/97		VAS-1	LLD
681	6/11/97	234234-00	7/1/94	5/30/97	NTF	East	LNI
682	6/11/97	576196-01	1/1/97	6/9/97	S-plug	VAS-1	LLD
683	6/11/97	576201-00	1/1/97	6/10/97	E-Frame	VAS-4	
684	6/11/97	576196-00	10/15/96	5/30/97	NAY (Ret)	Mid	
685	6/11/97	576196-00	12/6/96	6/9/97		VAS-4	EDD
686	6/11/97	576196-01	5/15/97	6/10/97	DOA	VAS-4	EDD

NAY = Not Analyzed Yet
NTF = No-Trouble-Found
DOA = Dead on Arrival
  FE = Field Engineer identification of the failure
  FA = In-depth failure analysis
   * = The area within the assembly that the failure occurred

FIGURE 10-3. **Example of the proposed universal product failure database format**

found (NTF). In complex systems, NAY and NTF are your largest category of product failures.

For example, I was having problems with my car's electrical system. The warning light was on all the time. The repair shop first replaced the regulator, and that did not correct the problem. They then replaced the alternator, but the light still would not go out. The shop then cleaned the battery and the battery terminals, and that corrected the problem. They left the new parts in the car because it would cost a lot to replace the old parts that may have been defective anyway. Probably both of the replaced parts will test no-trouble-found.

The business decisions regarding NTF failures are not a topic of database construction but have significant financial impact. Various schemes have been implemented to reduce the financial burden of NTF failures. In life-preserving products, the option is to destroy NTFs to reduce risk to the customer. In non-life-preserving products, the products are salvaged through a scheme of retesting to the functional specification and classifying the products as equivalent to new (ETN).

You should be aware of this segment (NAY and NTF) of product failures. A challenge to database implementation is to implement the data system without getting involved in the controversial business resolution of NAYs and NTFs.

2. The failure-analyzed components are listed by both product identification number and type of failure. This assumes both a product identification process and a failure analysis process within the product failure data system. These both cost money to implement and require a proper cost-benefit analysis in the best interest of the business. As stated in the last step, a major variable in the product failure database specification will be level of detail among organizations. The reason that the step 3 proposal is tentative, at this point, is because the cost-benefit analysis in step 4 has not occurred. During step 3, only create a database that reflects the desired level of detail. The cost considerations for the global system are to be considered in step 4 by the proper authority.

3. The identified failures are coded according to a failure analysis scheme. Note that there are two categories of failure identity. The first (FE) is that cursory opinion of the failure by the field engineer repairing the system, and the second (FA) is the in-depth analysis by the field failure analysis (FFA) organization. There is nothing wrong with using these two inputs simultaneously. Both FE and FA data can be beneficially utilized in the information feedback loop. Ultimately, the quality of failure data depends on the individual determining the failure mode in both cases. Coding enhances electronic data formatting, confidentiality of data, and categorization of failure modes. However, it does reduce communications of key observations, oversimplifies the failure descriptions, and suppresses the identification of new

failure modes. The quality of data is a major problem in product failure databases.

4. Figure 10-3 is void of an information-gathering scheme necessary for the effective use of the product failure data system by each organization. Typically, the database will have pages of data without any information generated by an intelligent sort and conclusion from the data. We spoke of being data rich and information poor. We spoke of "missing" key information, only to observe it after a crisis. Although it is not your responsibility in constructing a database information process for each using organization (it is their problem), you should be aware of this glaring deficiency within this proposed, and indeed all, large data systems. With 10 or less using organizations, it may be wise to outline for each a scheme in which to extract key information from the database, not just screens and paper of unending details. Often special reports are generated from the field failure database to meet the specific need of each organization that uses the database.

The last four items were selected as the major observed operational difficulties using product failure databases. They are effects created within organizations that have to be addressed and are as important as the physical failures themselves. The large scope of product failure database applications portends that you may not have any of these organizational considerations. However, identify your list of barriers to effective data system implementation. This will facilitate your discussions in the following step.

Step 4. Obtain Universal Approval of the Global Optimum Product Failure Database

 ▶ *Justify and obtain the business authority to merge existing systems, if any, of product failure data collection and dissemination into a universal global system.* The following is a summary of business organizational interactions that are encountered by all establishing product failure databases. The quotes are only mental hooks by which to remember each category of response.

1. "You don't understand what we need here!" Business authority perceives product failure data systems as a probabilistic ancillary cost. Even

when forced by governmental regulatory edict, business wisdom dictates a minimum allocation of resource toward items such as product failure database systems. Yet individual organizations claim inefficiency and potential business disasters if specific requirements are not met. A "smart" compromise is to "empower" the organizations to establish what is best for the business. So using modern management techniques, we avoid addressing the problem of ineffectual, fragmented, and expensive systems. We need a strong reliability management structure (Chapter 12).

2. "Who records the failure data?" Although each organization desires an excellent meaningful product failure database, individually they have no authority to control the input to meet their individual needs. For example, the development organization may want to understand the product failure use environment, but the service representative only records the part number of the failed unit for the purpose of spare parts stocking. But the service representative is not being paid to record and enter into a database the failure environment. We now are concluding the truth of product failure data systems. Databases that are financially supported produce data of value that may or may not be a favorable business arrangement. But an element of participation and control, a fundamental part of management, exists. "Free" data, used in critical business management, is usually worthless and often detrimental.

The following alternatives must be proposed to organizations within your business. Participate in the global database operation or financially support the data gathering efforts on an individual basis. The use of free tagalong data usually is not a prudent choice. The clever use of existing databases is less than optimum management.

3. "Our management information system (MIS) won't support all of your requirements." Clearly understand your global product failure database and the ability of the IS group to meet your requirements. Items such as the form of the data input, transportability and compatibility of the data, and the confidentiality requirements are key to the data system's ease of operation. An aggravating situation occurs when a system upon implementation is compromised by the IS capability. And it occurs after the IS representatives state that that problem would not occur. It is best to determine the experience of the IS people, and, if possible, get a second opinion.

From experience, these three (and your own) implementation problems exist in every product failure database installation. It is sad to say that the planned effectiveness of the global product failure database is often compromised to the extent of significantly reducing the value of the data.

Step 4 is directed at justification and authoritative implementation of the global product failure database. The difficulties are presented not to discourage your efforts, but to assist you in achieving a higher level of success. This process of constructing and implementing an optimum product failure database in itself is of significant value to your company. Ignoring the gap between your existing operation and an optimum operation is bad business.

▶ *Communicate the process of global database implementation.* The key to successful implementation of an optimum product failure database is persistence. A persistent documented effort will accomplish the following:

1. Provide your business with the best management information regarding your product failures at the customer/consumer.
2. Provide individual organizations with a defined link to the global business requirements and strategy.
3. Establish yourself and your organization as a center of competence regarding this business activity.
4. Provide rational positions for working relationships among all participating organizations.
5. Provide a conduit for assistance in specific business problems. For example, maybe the service representation should record the serial number and date of manufacture in addition to the failed product part number.

Reputations and centers of authority are established by demonstrating your capable work, business sense, and mutual respect over a significant period of time. This is only mentioned because this task is often viewed incorrectly as a project rather than a continuing effort.

Conclusions Regarding Constructing a Product Failure Database

This is an extremely complex activity. Unless it is accomplished in a step-by-step manner, the activity will end in hopeless chaos. The subject matter is boring to read but is extremely important to individuals engaged in installing the appropriate product failure database within the company.

If you extract the steps (1 to 4) and the bullets from the text, they produce an audit procedure that applies to all companies. The result of the audit will be a determination of your need for a product failure data system and your precise response to that need. The deficiencies identify the gap that exists in your current business.

It is recommended that anyone contemplating working with product failure databases reread this information. Not only is the topic one of business importance, but the product failure database process installation characteristics are too important to learn from personal experience. It is better to achieve familiarity by reading the text.

Product Field Failure Analysis

Why do we want to understand the precise nature of our product failures? The simple reason is that the precise data are of value to the person in the communication feedback loop (Figure 10-1) in order for them to do their assigned tasks. A hierarchy of precise failure knowledge helps to define the broad scope of product field failure analysis:

1. *No failure information.* In this category, failed product is replaced to maintain customer functional ability, and the failed product is scrapped without any recorded information. The only information of importance to the producer and customer is that sufficient replacement product is available. This category includes the vast amount of anticipated wear-out product, such as light bulbs, garbage cans, and even shoes. Our waste disposal sites are filled with unexplained failures.

2. *Specific failure information.* In this category we include all of the specific feedback requirements embedded into the product failure database. Figure 10-4 is a summary of common business requirements for precise failure data. This is another perspective of the product failure database discussed in the last section. Note that almost all requirements are transient in nature. Even the manufacturing requirement is

I	Marketing	Unique failures Reliability growth
2	Development	Unforeseen failures Competitive Specifications Environmental effects Warranty targets
3	Manufacturing	Quality problems Process validation
4	Reliability	Dormant problems ESS information Qualification validation
5	Purchasing	Component reliability Source variations
6	Customer Service	Repair parts stocking Procedures

FIGURE 10-4. **Typical precise failure data required by organizations**

reduced to an ongoing reliability test (ORT) confirmation, if continued at all.

3. *Regulatory compliance.* For products affecting life-preserving functions, governmental regulations require an identification and often continued tracking of product, along with precise failure details and potential failure conditions. Public safety improvement has been accomplished primarily by this precise failure analysis method. The prime examples of tainted-food recalls by identification number and airplane crash investigations are widespread news items. They are part of product field failure analysis.

Figure 10-4 is used as a strategic guide to precise failure or detail level data requirements. Product failure identification and corrective actions are a fundamental part of regulatory compliance. Specific failure information or the need for no information has to be determined in the best interest of your business. Some guidelines assist in providing the best strategy:

1. The best field failure analysis is done by the organization most interested in the failure data. Product development is best qualified, based on physical examination of product failures, to determine if its engineering change really fixed a product problem. Reliability assurance is best qualified, upon physical examination of product failures, to determine if its qualification was valid. Manufacturing is best qualified, upon physical examination of product failures, to determine the product reliability degradation causes by the manufacturing operation.

2. A significant problem is the logistics involved in delivery of the failed product to an FFA activity. At the product failure (customer) site, a procedure must be established to return the failed item to the FFA department. Already, you must abandon the ideal FFA performed by the most interested organization and replace it with a workable centralized FFA area.

3. The conditions under which the failure occurred is often as important to product reliability as the failure itself. A burned product may be caused by faulty product design or by a fire in the customer's building. A strategic problem is the procedure for inputting failure condition data and the competency level of that data.

4. What FFA determinations get entry into the product failure database? This is a problem. In order to reduce complexity and assist in computer data analysis, coded product failure databases are preferred (Figure 10-3). However, the coded information may not truly reflect the FFA conclusion. For instance, a burned component due to over stressing may be coded without indication of the root cause of performance under a specific use condition. Since the only code available is "burned component," the root cause of the problem, "use sensitivity," is never mentioned. Therefore, the FFA database misrepresents the failure identity and the proper corrective action does not occur. This is a common problem where the organization interested in the specific FFA data resides in a remote location. Many misguided computerized conclusions that result in corrective actions have originated with poor communication from FFA organizations.

In most cases, the requirement for FFA is transitory. The FFA activity is remote from organizations interested in the FFA data. In both instances, the solution to optimizing the feedback of FFA information is the personal contact between the FFA and interested organization. This solution to optimize FFA effectiveness also extends into permanent FFA organizations. It seems incredible, and we know of at least two cases where FFA did uncover a new failure mode and entered that information into the system, yet no corrective action toward the responsible party occurred. Then a major field reliability problem is identified: the FFA organization should not just update the database but should also be sure that the area that can correct the problem has agreed to implement corrective action. Just keep in mind this exposure when evaluating your FFA requirement.

An Example of a Reliability FFA

In this chapter, we do not attempt to create a template for your specific field failure database and failure analysis requirements. In fact, such an effort substantially limits the value of the presented template to a few cases within the extreme scope of applications. Instead, what is presented is the basic rational and common difficulties encountered in most field failure database and analysis applications.

The following example is given of a restricted, yet excellent field analysis report that is typically available in the literature. However, as we will repeat in the summary below, its true value is in its excellent adherence to good fundamental principles, not to its use as a template.

Figure 10-5 is presented as Figure 3-5 in Lloyd and Lipow's book *Reliability: Management, Methods, and Mathematics*.[1] It is an excellent book and is recommended for use as a reliability reference. The figure presents an excellent example of a good failure analysis report, consistent with our presentation of fundamentals within this text:

1. The failure description is clearly stated, easily understood by even those not familiar with the physical product.

1.	General	Failure Report No. <u>LA 00498</u>	[Fig. 3.1] Attach.
	Facility <u>ABC</u>	Reliability Act. Req.No. <u>167</u>	[Fig. 3.3]
	Location <u>L.A.</u>	Date of Analysis <u>10 Feb. 196_</u>	
	Page <u>1</u> of <u>1</u>		

1. General

   Facility _____ABC_____   Failure Report No. __LA 00498__   [Fig. 3.1] Attach.

   Location ___L.A.___   Reliability Act. Req.No. __167__   [Fig. 3.3]

   Page __1__ of __1__   Date of Analysis ___10 Feb. 196___

2. Item Identification   Manufacturer _____ABC_____

   Name __Case-Loaded__   Part Number ___1274 LV___

   Serial No. ___S102.21___   Type or Model ___Minerva A___

3. History

   No previous analysis

4. Analysis Methods and Techniques

   Visual examination

5. Results, Conclusions, and Actions

   The problem of solvent leakage from Thrust Termination ports was investigated. The cause of the leakage was determined to be improper fit and improper potting of the Thrust Termination port flaps. The T.T. port flaps have been redesigned and all leaks discovered during the air test will be potted with a mixture of 60% activator "W" and 40% "C.7." The redesigned T.T. port flaps will be available March 5, 196_, and S.O.P. 179 has been revised to incorporate the new procedure.

6. Signature of Analyst ___R.L. Higgins___   Date __16 February 1997__

FIGURE **10-5.   Example of a Failure Analysis Report (FAR)**

2. The method of failure analysis is clearly stated.
3. The cause (identity) of the failure is clearly defined.
4. The proposed fix (correction) was clearly defined.
5. The follow-through implementation date and documented correction (S.O.P. 179) was clearly stated.

Let us closely examine the FAR of the fictional (maybe) Mr. Higgins. Several aspects of this activity significantly contributed to his excellent work:

1. Communication problems do not exist because Mr. Higgins alone is inferred to precisely know the failure description, the failure cause, and the details of the failure correction.
2. The failure description (solvent leakage) was clearly apparent and not weakly inferred from stress testing.
3. The use of free-style FAA reporting allowed Mr. Higgins to efficiently and effectively report details. He was not restricted to coding and limitations of a computer spread sheet.
4. The use of a disciplined FFA within the rocket deployment business does not have the elements of cost-benefit justification common to most commercial businesses.

This excellent example of a field failure analysis is presented to support the following situations encountered in researching literature for information regarding product failure data systems and field failure analysis:

1. The referenced example is dated. Note that the FFA is from the 1960s. Advances in computers have significantly changed data reporting systems. This is especially true in the fast-changing corporate intent systems applications.
2. The example is directed at a zero failure level (100% reliability) appropriate for the rocket propulsion business. The business cost-benefit aspect, important to many organizations, is missing.
3. The data structure and field failure analysis detail requirements are not an issue in the example. In most commercial situations, they are key considerations.
4. The requirement for centralized authority to implement product field failure databases and field failure analysis is missing from this semi-military system with a life-sustaining or zero failure aspect.

This example is given to demonstrate that most excellent references to product field failure database and field failure analysis will lack essential inputs when applied to your specific situation. You will have to return to the principles explained in this chapter and generate a system best for your unique application.

Summary

Product field failure database and failure analysis capability has extreme variation in size between companies. It is primarily dependent on the business perception of the failure data value, but also its extreme variation may be due to the proper capability not growing in time with the company.

This chapter provides a framework for the reader to identify the proper scope of product reliability database and failure analysis within the company, develop the economics for business and internal company consideration, and provide the appropriate communications feedback channel.

The fundamental difference between excellent failure analysis and database systems and those inadequate to serve the business needs, is that the excellent failure analysis and databases are always carefully planned and executed with open communication. Inadequate systems are created by responding to business needs for product reliability problem resolution using available data and information at the time of crisis. The message is that planning always is best for the business, whether or not the planned system fulfills its objective.

11

The Customer/Consumer

The reliability engineer projects reliability; the customer/consumer measures it. Quality closes the sale. Reliability brings the customer/consumer back to buy again.

Introduction

Managers should read this chapter to develop a clear understanding of the producer-customer/consumer relationship. The four customer/consumer-related activities required for good business are listed:

1. *Defining your customer/consumer set.* Your customer/consumer set may be very difficult to define. This is particularly true for product reliability. For example, who is your customer/consumer, when your product is sold through value-added retailers (VARs) or embedded as a subcontracted component within a larger system?

2. *Understanding customer/consumer needs.* It is relatively easy to specify a product based upon customer/consumer needs at the point of sale. Understanding customer/consumer reliability needs is very difficult for the following reasons:
   —Product reliability is often a secondary factor from the customer's/ consumer's standpoint during the purchase cycle, in favor of such

primary factors as operating performance, cost, initial quality, and usability. Reliability becomes the primary consideration when the customer/consumer starts to use the product.

—Product reliability need may not be understood by the customer/consumer. Many customers/consumers search for adequate product reliability after an earlier traumatic experience caused by not understanding their product reliability requirement.

—Customers/consumers set natural attributes. Some product reliabilities affect few customers/consumers (e.g., aircraft), and some affect many customers/consumers (e.g., telephones). It is naturally more difficult to identify the reliability requirements of the huge telephone market compared with the closed aircraft market. In every case, the new product design reliability requirement should be a relative sample of the customers/consumers.

3. *Educating the customer/consumer.* It is in your best business interest to educate the customer/consumer regarding your product reliability. In a competitive market, this infers that the customer/consumer gains appropriate knowledge of the product's reliability. Product reliability claims based on manipulated data sets are frequently used to influence the market. A comfortable, nonthreatening method must be used to educate the customer/consumer regarding the true meaning and business consequences of competitive product reliability claims.

4. *Customer/consumer reliability communication.* This subject requires some planned activity, insight, and prudent control to optimize your business.

These four topics are quite independent in practice; but all are significant to your business effectiveness. They are complicated, but far from abstract. Each topic should have a deliberate, planned management activity that will result in a satisfied customer/consumer. This creates a satisfying business profit.

Engineers should read this chapter because they will probably be the individuals executing the four activities, and the success of customer/consumer relationships will actually depend upon their continuing evaluation, education, and communication. If, as an engineer, you are not communicating with your customer/consumer, then you lack insight into the purpose of your activity.

A **customer** is any individual or organization that receives an output from another person or organization.

A **consumer** is the individual or organization that is the final purchaser of a product, service, or commodity. (For example: The customer of a can of soup from Campbell Soup Company is Safeway Stores. If you buy the same can of soup from Safeway to feed your family, your family is the consumer.) A consumer is someone's customer, but the individual or organization that consumes your organization's output may not be your organization's customer.

As individuals or organizations interested in reliability, we have to understand the needs and expectations of both our customer and the consumer of our products and services. Too often organizations are buffered from the consumer of their output by other organizations (e.g., distributors, stores, other manufacturers, value-added retailers, etc.). In the long run, the success of any organization is more related to the consumers of its output than by its customers. It is for this reason that the reliability process must have a realistic understanding of both the organization's customers and the consumers of the organization's output.

Overview

Always remember that the customer/consumer is the reason that you are in business. Customers/consumers provide everyone's salaries. A competitive environment in the marketplace is created by too much product availability compared to customer/consumer demands.

The measure of success created by the customer/consumer-driven competitive market can be gauged by the efforts and success of those avoiding competition in pricing products and services. Monopolies and socialized industries have led to poor product and service values. The trend of this decade is for governments to privatize industries in order to regain the effectiveness and efficiency of the private industry counterparts.

In addition, we must consider the impact of the information age. Business opportunities exist for external groups to provide expert information regarding the performance of products and services. *Consumer Reports*, which focuses on the functionality and reliability of products, is an excellent example of this expert evaluation and information trend. If you don't control the product reliability evaluation and information at your customer/consumer interface, an external business will gladly control that activity.

Part of the trend in the 1990s is the awareness that the customer/consumer is the final judge of a product or service. Even government programs are being viewed as services purchased by the taxpayer. The trend is toward allowing the customer/consumer (taxpayers) access to data that will offer them an understanding of what is being purchased with the tax dollar. As a customer/consumer, wouldn't that be great? The central point of this paragraph is to alert you to a future where customers/consumers will control your business using intelligent information that will be used to assist in the purchase decision.

There is a strong bond between the external customer and reliability management. The reliability professional serves as the ombudsman for the customer within the organization. This partnership begins when marketing is defining the product requirements and continues long after manufacturing has processed the last production item.

Unlike quality which needs to meet customer's/consumer's requirements at only one point in time (acceptance), reliability needs to fulfill the customer's/ consumer's needs and expectations each time the customer/consumer uses the product or service. This means that quality products are relatively easy to deliver to the external customer/consumer. It is reliability that provides the real challenge, and very few organizations stand behind the reliability of their products for the total product life cycle. Most organizations stand behind the quality of their output. A case in point is that whenever you buy a car, the dealership will ensure that you are satisfied with the car's quality. Car reliability, on the other hand, is another thing. Car reliability is guaranteed for 30,000 miles on most cars, although the life expectancy of the car is in excess of 150,000 miles. That is five times longer than auto manufacturers will stand behind the reliability of their products. One of the very few organizations that is proud of its product reliability is Craftsman Tools, which provides a lifetime warranty on their product.

Because of the commitment that the reliability organization has to the customer/consumer, there is an important need for continuous dialogue to take place between the reliability organization and the external customer/consumer. This communication is used to

▶ Verify the accuracy of the reliability projections.
▶ Develop an understanding of competitive reliability.
▶ Obtain feedback on acceptability of the product's reliability.
▶ Identify problems that present opportunities for improving the product's reliability.
▶ Verify maintainability projections.
▶ Collect component failure-rate data to be used in future projections.
▶ Project customer/consumer reliability requirements for future products.

Defining a Customer/Consumer Set

Why We Want to Identify the Customer/Consumer

The reason for identifying the customer/consumer set is extremely basic. Managing the understanding of customer/consumer needs, educating the customer/consumer, and establishing appropriate communications are critical to creating a business profit. As a result, defining the customer/consumer is the first step toward meeting business objectives of optimized profit. Remember that the needs of the customer may differ from the needs of the consumer. (For example: The customer may be a distributor who needs to have

20 dozen Model 105 steak knives that cost no more than $2.00 per knife in the warehouse by November 1 to cover orders that he will be getting for Christmas. The consumer needs a very sharp knife that will stay sharp for many years without resharpening it.)

The motivation for including identification of the customer/consumer in this chapter is that ineffective customer/consumer business activities frequently have a root cause in poor customer/consumer identification procedures. For example: Air conditioner reliability specifications did not consider that the product would be used in Alaska; as a result, product return and warranty expense is unacceptably high at our retail outlets, identification of customers/consumers is required to understand the product reliability in terms of specified environmental use conditions. The failed units alone do not furnish enough information for corrective action to be taken.

Ultimately, optimum business relationships with the customer/consumer fundamentally require a precise personal understanding of the customer/consumer rather than an abstract concept. This is expressed as: What it really is rather than what we think it is.

Figure 11-1 presents a flowchart description of many of the sales channels used in business to deliver the products to the customer/consumer. The

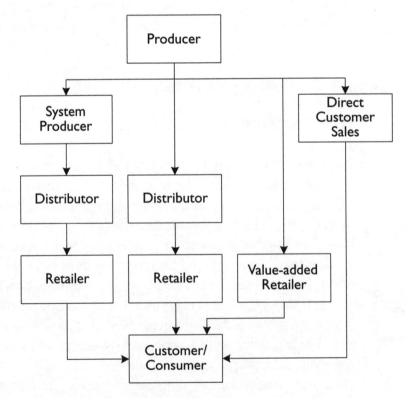

FIGURE 11-1. **Typical product sales channel**

great variation in sales channels presents the greatest difficulty in properly managing the customer/consumer set identification. Not only are the customers/consumers naturally difficult to identify within a single sales channel arrangement, but the practice of using multiple channels, in a seemingly arbitrary manner, makes the task of customer/consumer identification very difficult.

The lack of understanding customer/consumer needs is in focus during supplier–customer/consumer problem periods. Two questions should be asked:

1. Supplier, do you have a list of the customer/consumer requirements and how you and the competition satisfy those requirements? Is that list explicitly updated on a meaningful periodic basis?
2. Customer/consumer, can you present a concise history of identification and communication of this problem?

If you have been part of these supplier–customer/consumer problem resolution efforts, you can appreciate that the response to these predetermined questions will provide a sad but true evaluation of the supplier–customer/consumer relationship.

The reason for the lack of recognition of precise customer/consumer needs and concise problem definitions does not originate in the lack of good will. The reasons originate in the inability of the supplier and customer/consumer to distinguish problems that can be handled routinely in the relationship from those that require special handling. The need to understand the customer/consumer is ignored on a routine basis. Understanding the customer's/consumer's needs and problems is crucial during special problem resolution efforts.

The periodic assessment of customer/consumer needs varies substantially among all products and services. Market survey activity is concentrated on the market potential. The customer/consumer service activities for sales and service provide a broad feedback of customer/consumer satisfaction. However, these activities are distinctly different from the assessment of product/service reliability of the future needs of the customer/consumer.

Defining Customer/Consumer Needs and Expectations

Once the potential customers and consumers have been defined, the organization needs to define the customers/consumers needs and expectations for the potential product that the organization is considering providing. The primary responsibility for developing these requirements in most organizations rests with the marketing organization. This does not relieve the reliability organization from ensuring that the reliability requirements truly reflect the needs of all the customers/consumers in the sales channel and the final customer/consumer. It is also very important that the distinction between needs and expectations is well defined for each requirement. There is a big difference between needs and expectations. The customers/consumers usually specify their needs but measure an organization upon how well it satisfies their expectations. Usually, expectations require more skill and thought to satisfy than needs (e.g., car owners need a car that will get them from point A to point B. Their expectation is that the car will get them from point A to point B without stopping in a garage to get it repaired). The consumer will tell the auto dealer that the car must have an AM/FM radio and the dealer will take the order. However, ask the dealer to put in writing that the radio will not break down but once in 10,000 hours of operation and you won't get a car. The customers/consumers usually define their needs but seldom define their expectations. The customers'/consumers' reliability requirements are usually embedded in their expectations. To do this, in most cases, you will need to probe deep into the customer's/consumer's thoughts to define the true reliability expectations.

Usually, customer/consumer need is defined before the product is designed. It then can take years before the product is consumed. This means that the reliability specification cannot reflect the current consumer's need but must project how this need and competitor's products will change while the product is being designed, manufactured, and delivered to the consumer. Often these projected values are too conservative. It is for this reason that the reliability requirement must be continuously reevaluated and updated if necessary.

Measuring Customer/Consumer Reliability Satisfaction

Many organizations believe they have a successful product when its reliability performance in the customer/consumer environment is equal to or better than the reliability specification. Meeting the reliability specification only proves that the product design and the production process are capable of providing an output that meets the reliability requirements. It does not mean that the output is capable of satisfying the customer/consumer. Remember these reliability rules.

▶ Meeting reliability specifications that are unacceptable to the customer/consumer is unacceptable.

▶ Not meeting reliability specifications that are acceptable to the customer/consumer is unacceptable.

▶ Meeting reliability specifications that are acceptable to the customer/consumer for only part of the product life cycle is unacceptable.

▶ Meeting customer/consumer reliability expectations for the life of the product is what is expected by the organization and the customer/consumer.

To ensure that the reliability process is meeting expectations, a measurement system needs to be set up to

▶ Measure the product reliability performance in the customer/consumer environment throughout the product's life cycle.

▶ Measure the changing customer/consumer expectations throughout the product's life cycle.

▶ Measure how different vintages of product are performing in the customer/consumer environment.

It is important to note that there are two very different types of measurement systems required to provide the required data.

▶ Product performance reliability measurement system

▶ Customer/consumer reliability expectation measurement system (a sales and marketing function)

Product Performance Reliability Measurement System

Establishing a product performance reliability measurement system is theoretically very easy to do. All that the organization needs to do is determine when the customer/consumer starts to use the product and then record each time a failure occurs. In real life, this is not as simple as it sounds. There are two main things that detract from acquiring the needed data:

▶ The cost of the product. If the product is very inexpensive, the customer/consumer has a tendency not to report a failure because it is easier to dispose of the defective item and purchase a new one than it is to fix the present item.

▶ The number of interfaces between the producer and the customer/consumer in the sales chain.

The distance an organization is from the customer/consumer in the sales chain has a major impact upon the organization's ability to collect information related to its product's reliability in the customer's/consumer's environment. If there are a number of distribution-type organizations that buffer the supplier from the final customer/consumer, it often becomes very difficult to determine when the customer/consumer purchases the product. This is the reason why many products have time-limit warranties that require the purchaser to fill out a form and return it to the producer. In other cases where suppliers are buffered from the customer/consumer by another organization, the final product that the customer/consumer purchases may be made up of many other components and value-added content other than the product that the supplier provided to its customer.

Example: A connector supplier provides parts that go into a circuit card that is sold to another manufacturer that produces computers. The output from the computer manufacturer then is sent to the distributor and finally delivered to a customer/consumer through an outlet store. The customer/consumer buys a computer, not a connector. The feedback on the connector's performance from the connector's supplier's customer/consumer is often quality-related data (no reliability data) because the board manufacturer is exercising the connector for a very short period of time. In this case, the connector's supplier must make use of the data that are collected by its customers/consumers (the computer manufacturer) to define the connector's reliability.

To add additional complexity to this situation, there often is more than one supplier for the same part number. When a failure occurs in the customer's/consumer's environment, it is impossible to determine which supplier's part failed unless it is returned for failure analysis.

It is sometimes difficult to determine when a failure occurs in the customer/consumer environment because the customer/consumer may not bring back the defective item to the organization's repair center. Failures that are repaired by neighborhood repair centers are often not reported back to the producer of the item. To make this situation even more complex, the neighborhood repair center may not use the same make component that was in the original product when it repairs the defective unit, so there is no spare parts usage data.

It is often difficult to determine whether or not the item is defective unless you understand how the customer/consumer was using the product when it failed. It is also important to determine if the replaced component is truly defective. In order to verify that the unit is defective, parts need to be subjected to a failure analysis. We are surprised at the high quantity of no-trouble-found returned components that are detected during the failure analysis process. Often the failure analysis process will also point out how the components were misused in the customer's/consumer's environment. For example, a high percentage of the Reebok shoes that had an air pump installed in them were defective because the customer/consumer pierced the bladder with a sharp object (a pin or a knife, for example).

It is easy to see that collecting field reliability performance data can be difficult to do and that many of these measurement systems provide data that are very conservative. As a result, many organizations rely on customer/consumer complaints to determine when they are having problems rather than trying to solve the measurement problem. This type of reactive approach to reliability is very dangerous. It is based on the assumption that no news is good news. In reality, no news may mean that the customer/consumer has given up on the organization and is looking for a new supplier. It is very important that the organization establishes a reliability performance reporting system even if it is inaccurate, because the reported trends provide valuable data. In some cases these reporting systems are required by your customer/consumer or the government. For example, the FDA, in many cases, requires a compliance reporting and correction system.

Customer/Consumer Reliability Performance Expectation Measurement System

Customer/consumer satisfaction and expectation measurements are normally obtained by surveys and focus groups with customers/consumers. These contacts are normally made on regularly scheduled interviews where a group of the organization's customers/consumers are contacted plus a sample of the organization's competitor's customers/consumers. (Example: A survey of 50 of the organization's customers/consumers and 50 of the competitor's customers/consumers is conducted every 3 months. If it is possible, a different group of customers/consumers is used each time.) The purpose of these contacts is to determine if the reliability performance specifications are correct and to define how much safety factor there is between the products' present reliability performance and the customer's/consumer's expectations. The information collected from your competitor's customers/consumers also provides the organization with input on how to improve its products to capture a larger share of the market. It is very important that the customer/consumer contacts are performed by people who have been specifically trained in how to interview customers/consumers and who have an excellent understanding of the product.

Customer/consumer satisfaction and expectation contacts are usually conducted by sales and marketing or quality assurance functions within most organizations. The reliability department should work with the function that is assigned this responsibility to ensure that the appropriate reliability data are collected and reported back to the reliability group.

Many organizations collect data from consumers and make it available to the general public. The following is a summary of the U.S. national customers satisfaction survey:

INDUSTRIES RATED IN ORDER OF THEIR CUSTOMER'S SATISFACTION

1 Beverages: Soft Drinks
2 Parcel Delivery and Express Mail

3 Food Processing
4 Household Appliances
5 Consumer Electronics: TV and VCR
6 Telecommunications: Long-distance telephone service
7 Personal Care and Cleaning Products
8 Automobiles, Vans, and Light Trucks
9 Beverages: Beer
10 Apparel: Sportswear, Underwear
11 Apparel: Athletic Shoes
12 Gasoline
13 Telecommunications: Local telephone service
14 Tobacco: Cigarettes
15 Solid-Waste Disposal
16 Department and Discount Stores
17 Insurance: Personal, Property, Homeowners, and Automobile
18 Supermarkets
19 Electric Service
20 Commercial Banks
21 Insurance: Life
22 Motion Pictures
23 U.S. Postal Service: Mail Delivery and Counter Services
24 Personal Computers
25 Hotels
26 Hospitals
27 Broadcasting/TV (Network News)
28 Restaurants: Fast Food, Pizza, Carryout
29 Airlines: Scheduled
30 Publishing/Newspapers
31 Local Police
32 Internal Revenue Service

THE TOP 20 COMPANIES BASED ON THEIR CUSTOMERS' SATISFACTION RATINGS

1 H.J. Heinz
2 Hershey Foods
3 Cadillac
4 Coca-Cola
5 UPS
6 Pillsbury
7 Mercedes-Benz NA

 8 PepsiCo
 9 Cadbury Schweppes
10 Federal Express
11 Mars
12 General Mills
13 Dole Food
14 RJR Nabisco
15 Kellogg
16 Kraft Foods
17 Whirlpool
18 Dial
19 Procter & Gamble
20 Zenith Electronics

Source: American Consumer Satisfaction Index published jointly by American Society for Quality and University of Michigan in Fortune Magazine dated February 3, 1997, pg. 108.

Reliability Education for Customers/Consumers

One of the major problems that every reliability department faces is developing a common understanding related to how reliability is measured and reported between the organization and the potential customer/consumer. Unfortunately, many competitors measure their output's reliability in different ways. In addition, different customers/consumers have different interpretations of what reliability is and how it should be measured. In order to provide the consumer with the capabilities to make the best-value selection for themselves, they need to be provided with compatible data and understand what the data means. A simple reliability statement could be worded as follows: Our mean time to failure is 20,000 hours. This type of statement cannot be used to compare competitors unless the customer/consumer understands what the key modifiers are. For example:

▶ Is the 20,000 hours power-on hours, elapsed time hours, or usage hours?
▶ What are the preventive maintenance requirements to meet the 20,000 hours' performance?
▶ What constitutes a failure? If the cycle is repeated and works the second time, is the failure in the first cycle considered a defect?
▶ Is operator error counted as a failure?

This subject is discussed in Chapter 4.

It is very important that the reliability department identifies key decision makers in the customer's/consumer's organization and is sure that the reliability projections and reporting systems are compatible with the customer's/consumer's definition of reliability. The key decision makers within an organization usually include marketing and sales, purchasing, product engineering, and reliability engineering. We recommend that the reliability department maintain a list of key contacts for each major customer/consumer that the reliability department has worked with to be sure that there is a common agreement on what considerations are included in the reliability requirements. This often involves educating functions that do not have a thorough understanding of reliability concepts.

We find that organizations often review their competitor's reliability claims and then redefine how they measure their product's reliability so they can advertise reliability figures that are better than the competitor's figures, when in truth, their product's actual performance may be much worse. (For example: The first computer company projects a MTBF of 2,000 hours that includes software problems. The second computer company projects a MTBF of 3,000 hours but does not include software problems in their definition of a failure.)

Providing reliability data to the consumer presents an even more difficult problem. The situation is most complex if the product is consumed by the general public. If this is the case, it is impossible to provide the related information to the masses short of an all-out public awareness campaign, which would be very costly. The only reasonable way to provide comparison reliability data to the general public is through the use of an independent performance evaluation organization like *Consumer Reports*. The other approach is to have an industry standard prepared for the product type that defines an agreed-to reliability measurement and reporting system for the specific products. This type of approach is becoming much more practical as the International Organization for Standardization in Geneva, Switzerland, becomes more influential around the world. In the past, national voluntary standards met the needs of most organizations. Today, the situation has changed as most organizations face competition from the far reaches of the world. If you have a customer/consumer today, you can be sure that there is someone out there looking at that customer/consumer with the objective of taking him or her away from you. The effective use of voluntary international reliability standards provides consumers with the comparative data they need to make their purchase decisions.

Responsiveness to Customer/Consumer Problems

All organizations must have an effective way of capturing customer/consumer complaints and problems and must react quickly to correct these situations. Research has proven that less than 10% of customers/consumers who are not satisfied with an output complain about the problem, but 80% of the dissatisfied people tell a minimum of 8 other people about the poor product, and 10% tell more than 20 other people. Keeping this in mind, each time a customer/consumer complaint is identified, it should be amplified 10 times because that complaint represents 9 other dissatisfied customers/consumers who make up this silent majority. These are 9 other customers/consumers who will not buy your organization's output again if they can find another organization to do business with.

All customer/consumer complaints should be pulled together in a central database where they are tracked to ensure that both corrective and preventive action is taken. It is very important that the complaints are answered rapidly. The best approach is to empower the first person who identifies a complaint to resolve the problem before he or she undertakes another activity. Data indicate that if a customer/consumer feels that the supplier quickly reacts to his or her problem, the supplier has a 90% chance of selling another item to the customer/consumer. On the other hand, if the customer/consumer feels that the supplier is not responsive to the complaint, there is only a 30% chance the customer/consumer will purchase another item from the supplier.

Product Recall

Product recall is the act of notifying customers/consumers that they have products that should be returned due to potential reliability supplier problems.

All of the reliability performance data, complaint data, and customer/consumer satisfaction and expectation data should be contained in a common database that the reliability department is continuously monitoring and massaging. The reliability department should pay particular attention to the action taken to correct the performance problems to ensure that the action taken is both corrective and preventive. In addition, the reliability department should closely monitor the data and corrective action to identify reliability problems that should be removed from the field by reworking the items that have already been delivered to the customer/consumer (product recall).

One of the reliability department's critical but undesirable tasks is the instigation of a product recall activity. The product recall decision represents the organization's realization of its social obligation to the general public to remove an actual or potential discrepant output from the customer's/consumer's environment and to protect the organization's reputation. Often product recalls are used when a potential safety problem exists or when the projected field failure rate is so high that it will have a significant impact on the customer/consumer and on the organization's reputation.

In order to minimize the impact that a product recall activity has on the organization and the customer/consumer, a product recall procedure should be carefully planned and documented even if it is never used. The objective of the recall procedure is to define how the potential discrepant items can be removed from the customer's/consumer's environment as rapidly as possible while minimizing the disturbance to the customer/consumer. This procedure should also ensure that all side effects of the change have been taken into consideration and that data are available that quantifies to a high degree of confidence that the change will have a positive impact upon the product performance and eliminate the identified problem. To obtain this degree of assurance, the reliability department should be an active member of the recall team. As a member of the recall team, the reliability representative should pay particular attention to the repair procedures, the design experiment that verifies that the change will have a positive impact upon the item's total performance, and any problems that occurred during the implementation of change into the manufacturing process. The reliability representative should also be responsible to quantify the impact of the change on the field population's reliability. Only after this quantified data indicate that the recall will meet its intended objectives should the recall procedure be released to the field.

Summary

Sales, marketing, quality assurance, and manufacturing usually focus on the customer with the objective of providing a very high level of customer satisfaction. The reliability department must look beyond the customer to understand and measure the product's performance and impact as it is being used by the consumer. This reliability focus requires that a new partnership is developed that lasts long after the last product is shipped to a customer/consumer.

During this chapter we explored the difficulties and needs related to capturing reliability data in the customer's/consumer's environment. Admittedly, this is not an easy task, and it requires a great deal of cooperation between the supplier, customer, and consumer, but the results are well worth the effort. It is only through a comprehensive understanding of the product's performance in the customer's/consumer's environment that real reliability improvement opportunities can be defined. We are not suggesting that the customer/consumer serve as your product evaluation area. Quite the contrary. Problems that are detected in the customer/consumer environment represent inadequacies in the organization's marketing, engineering, manufacturing and reliability procedures. Of course, in reality, the customer/consumer is the final judge of the product and the organization that produces that product.

The first rule in building a customer/consumer partnership is to ensure you know both the customer's/consumer's needs and expectations and understand the difference between these two factors.

The second rule is that when you fail to meet the customer's/consumer's needs or expectations, you should react swiftly to solve the problem and give the customer/consumer something extra to make up for the inconvenience you caused.

"If we are not customer driven, our products will not be either."
—H. James Harrington

12

Product Reliability Management Structure

Reliable products and services don't repeatedly happen by accident. They are the result of a well-managed reliability system.

Introduction

Managers should read this chapter to assist in clearly defining the role of reliability management within their organizations. It is essential to your entire product reliability effort to have top management's support and understanding of the reliability methodology in order for them to delegate the reliability activities correctly. One of top management's most critical responsibilities is to define the mission of each function within the organization. Imbedded within these mission statements must be the function's reliability direction. In addition, managers in the organization need to understand their role in assuring that the customer's/consumer's reliability expectations are fulfilled and the reliability processes within the organization mesh together to create the desired results. Product reliability requires continuous management attention to be an effective and efficient business function. Chapter 12 provides assistance in articulating these requirements.

Engineers should read this chapter to learn about the organizational role of product reliability in their organization and how their activities mesh into the total reliability system.

In this chapter we will look at four very important elements related to establishing an effective reliability management system:

▶ Upper management's support and direction of the reliability system.
▶ How the reliability management function relates to other parts of the organization. (The reliability management function's external relationships.)
▶ The reliability management function's internal operations.
▶ The reliability responsibilities of the other functions.

Upper Management Support and Direction of the Reliability System

Upper management must actively support the reliability system by releasing a series of reliability directives that will be used to direct the organization's reliability system, establishing a series of reviews for each major program that verifies compliance to these directives.

Organizational Reliability Policy Statement

The first thing that upper management needs to do is to define what the objectives are for their reliability system. This is accomplished by top management preparing and releasing a "reliability policy statement." This policy statement should be well communicated and understood in all functions.

The following is a typical Reliability Policy Statement:

The customers/consumers of our products will perceive our product's reliability as being significantly better than that of our competitor's product. All of our new products' reliability performance at first customer/consumer ship will be better than the present reliability performance of the product it replaces. When failures occur in the field, a minimum of 98% of them will be repaired within four working hours of the time we are notified.

Dave Farrell
President
RMS, Inc.

Key functions that need to be part of developing this policy statement and the upcoming objectives are

1. Marketing
2. R&D
3. Product engineering
4. Manufacturing engineering
5. Quality engineering
6. Reliability engineering
7. Purchasing
8. Manufacturing
9. After-sales service

In many cases qualitative reliability objectives are defined for product type, and in many organizations, the qualitative objectives cover all products because reliability is often an evolving process rather than a revolutionary process. Reliability objectives should address the following points:

1. Customer/consumer expectations—responsible organization: marketing
2. Competitive evaluation—responsible organization: R&D
3. Replacement products—responsible organization: product engineering
4. Life-cycle cost—responsible organization: product engineering
5. Maintainability—responsible organization: after-sales service
6. Controllability—responsible organization: manufacturing engineering
7. Confidence—responsible organization: reliability engineering

 ## Customer/Consumer Expectations

This objective is normally developed by the marketing organization. The customer/consumer expectation level should be set at a point where the or-

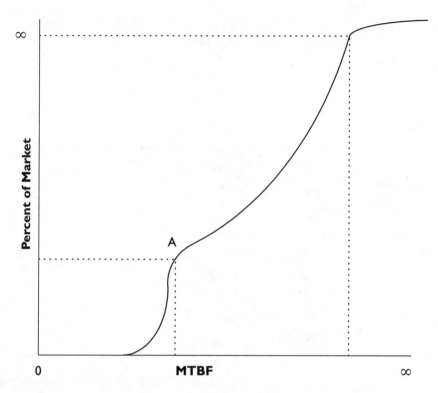

FIGURE 12-1.   Market shares versus MTBF

ganization can capture a targeted portion of the market share over the predicted product cycle (see Figure 12-1) based upon meeting the reliability performance.

You will note that the percentage of market changes drastically at the beginning of the curve in Figure 12-1. This curve is constructed based on past expectations and knowledge of the customer/consumer, based on direct contact with the customer/consumer and market studies. For most products, the general population of potential customers/consumers has already established a minimum acceptable reliability performance level that they expect. As a result, improvements in mean time between failures at the starting point of the curve do not result in an increased number of potential customers/consumers because the product has not reached this minimum reliability performance threshold level. You will note that there is very little increase in the number of potential customers/consumers at the end of the curve because the product's reliability is exceeding customer/consumer expectations, and exceeding these expectations even further does not attract additional customers/consumers although it does have a major impact on getting them to come back and buy from you again. For example, if you have a credit card that is replaced every year, extending its life expectancy from 2 to 10 years provides little additional value to the customer/consumer as a life expectancy of 2 years already exceeds their requirements. For most products, the customer/consumer expectation value will be set someplace between point A and point B on the curve. Based on the percentage of the potential market that the organization is trying to capture, the customer's/consumer's reliability expectation will be defined. A typical customer/consumer reliability expectation objective will state: The reliability specification and the product's performance must meet the requirements of 75% of our potential market place when the first product is shipped to an external customer/consumer.

Competitive Evaluation

Competitive products often turn out to be the primary driver for most reliability programs as competitive technology often drives reliability trends in most products. As a result, the organization has to have an excellent understanding and extended reliability database for all major competitive products. The data related to the way competitive products are presently performing are usually acquired by the use of reverse engineering techniques, comparative shopping techniques, or by data provided from independent test centers. (Appendix F provides information on reverse engineering techniques.) The problem with this type of data is that it is usually historical-type data, and the reliability specification is a future projection. As a result, the data collected related to how the competitor's product is performing need to be enhanced with information related to new products and methodologies that the competitor is planning to release during the next two product cycles. This is accomplished through the use of a data research project directed at defining what their development engineering department is working on. This data research project may sound like industrial spying, but it is not performing anything illegal. The data research project collects information that

Typical sources for the data research project

has been released to the general public, and we are surprised at how much important information slips out. Typical places that this type of data can be found are

- ▶ Newspapers
- ▶ Magazines
- ▶ Patents
- ▶ Resource papers

▶ Conference talks   ▶ Professional meetings

▶ Organization tours   ▶ Annual reports

▶ Industrial analysis

Another good place to get technology-related data is by understanding the related development work that the government has under way and from the development work that is going on in universities around the world. The hard work begins once the data are collected. To obtain a picture of competitors' future products and a projection of their reliability is a lot like putting together the bits and pieces of a puzzle. Using your competitors' present data and the knowledge gained from the research data, the competitive future reliability performance should be a projection (see Figure 12-2).

Figure 12-2 represents a product type that has a 3-year cycle from concept to first customer/consumer ship (FCS) and a 5-year product cycle. You can observe from this graph that the competitor C is projected to have a reliability breakthrough in the projected period. The first question that needs to be asked is how accurate are the projections? The next question is should our reliability specification be based upon the competitor's performance at (1) FCS, (2) halfway through the product cycle (2.5 years), or (3) at the end of the cycle? A typical competitor reliability policy statement would read: All new product reliability specifications must be better than the projected reliability for all the competitors' similar products at the midpoint in the products' production life cycle.

Your product's reliability must be better than your competitors' to keep from losing your customers/consumers.

Replacement Products

Product reliability often improves as the product progresses through its production life cycle due to failure analysis (FA) and corrective action taken as a result of failures in the customer's/consumer's and manufacturing environment (see Figure 12-3).

In Figure 12-3, the current product met its reliability specification (performance level A) at first customer/consumer ship but continued to get better due to an effective customer/consumer performance reporting system and related corrective action. In Figure 12-3, we see that the replacement product

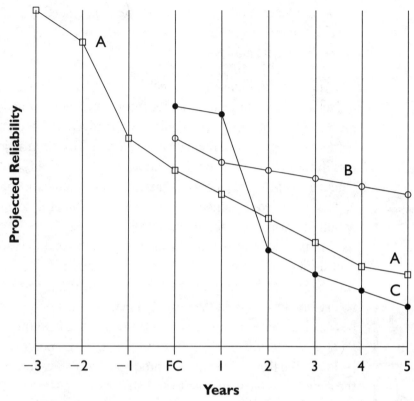

FIGURE 12-2.   **Competitive reliability analysis for three organizations**

for the current product is scheduled to be shipped to its first customers/consumers 5 years after the current product was shipped to its first customers/consumers. It is important to note at the 5-year point in time, the current product has significantly improved to an MTBF equal point B. If the replacement product used the same reliability specification as the current product, it could be shipped at a reliability performance level equal to point A, which is much worse than the actual performance of the current product. It is for this reason that the reliability of replacement products should not be based on the

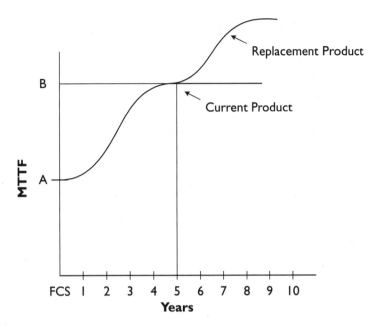

FIGURE 12-3.   MTBF performance by years after first customer/consumer ship

present products' reliability specification but should be based on the projected actual performance of the current product when the replacement product is shipped to the first customer/consumer. Realistically, management is often inadequate in assuring the most reliable replacement product and parts. Note that this drives a continuous improvement cycle because the replacement product goes through an initial problem resolution and corrective cycle that results in significant reliability performance improvements. For example, one of IBM's corporate instructions states: "Before we announce a new product, our product must be better in terms of quality and availability than the product it replaces or our competitors' products."

Just think about how well cars would be performing today if the Big Three of the United States and the Big Three of Japan set the same requirements for their new models. We estimate if they were using this criterion in setting their reliability requirements over the last 20 years, the present models' life-cycle repair costs would be less than 30% of what they are.

Life-Cycle Cost

A product's reliability life-cycle cost is divided into three distinct sections after the product enters the production phase:

1. Product control cost
2. Warranty period cost
3. After-warranty cost

The product control phase is a constant cost that is incurred to ensure that abnormal variation does not slip through the production process and impact the product's performance in the field. Items that are included in this cost are

▶ Off-line testing
▶ ESS
▶ Burn-in
▶ In-process controls
▶ Supplier audits

To simplify the warranty period and the after-warranty period discussion, we will assume in Figure 12-4 that the product as delivered is functioning at the flat of the bathtub curve. (See Figure 12-4.)

Note that the total failure-related cost in this example includes the warranty cost in the first year. Even then, the supplier covers the repair cost during the first year (x); the total cost related to failures in the first year is double the warranty cost that is paid for by the supplier ($2x$). The additional costs are the cost the customer/consumer needs to cover related to his or her expenses of taking the product to the repair area and other expenses that the customer/consumer incurs related to the repair. In this case, the customer's/consumer's failure-related cost over a 5-year period is 90% of the total failure cost, and the supplier only pays for 10% of the total cost. It is for this reason that suppliers of products need to calculate what the total repair cost is of the products that they deliver. For many products, the customer's/consumer's failure cost during the product life cycle exceeds the purchase price. To keep the cost of owning a product more in line with the purchase price, the organization needs either to reduce the repair cost or to improve the reliability,

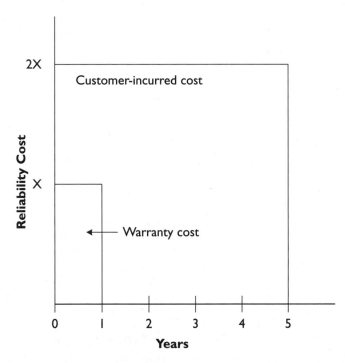

FIGURE 12-4. Total cost for a product during a 5-year product life-cycle

thereby decreasing the product life-cycle cost. We believe that the second approach is the most desirable. A typical statement that would address this issue would read: "The total life-cycle repair cost for the product should not exceed the purchase price when the customer's/consumer's incurred costs are included in the total life-cycle cost."

Maintainability

This category includes two items: the cost of preventive maintenance and the cost to repair a failure.

The cost of preventive maintenance is governed by the end of the bathtub curve. (See Figure 12-5.)

Preventive maintenance is usually scheduled to take place just prior to the components reaching point A in Figure 12-5. If the cycle time from the

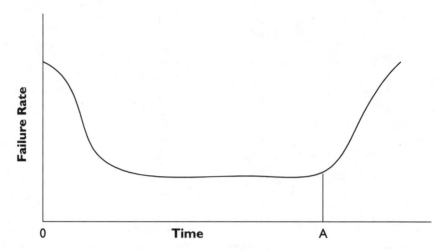

FIGURE **12-5.   Life-cycle bathtub curve**

start of the bathtub curve to point A (start of the wear-out point) is relatively close together, then preventive maintenance will be high. Through the proper selection in use of components, the wear-out point can be significantly improved, greatly increasing the intervals between scheduled preventive maintenance, thereby greatly reducing the cost of owning the item. For example, Cadillac has improved its design and components to the point that its duration between scheduled tune-ups is 100,000 miles. This represents a 300 to 400% reduction in tune-up preventive maintenance cost.

The other type of preventive maintenance is the use of relatively inexpensive replaceable materials like oil, grease, or coolants that are used to prolong the life of other more expensive parts of the product. These preventive or scheduled repairs also represent major costs to the customer/consumer that add up over the life of the product. For example, Ford Motors recommends that the oil be changed every 5,000 miles. If the car life cycle is 150,000 miles, the oil will be changed 30 times. At an average cost of $50.00 per oil change, the total paid to the garage would be $1,500.00. Add to this the value of the time lost by the customer/consumer of about 4 hours per oil change at $12.50 per hour ($1,500.00 over the course life-cycle), and the total cost of oil maintenance is $3,000.00. This is 17% of the cost of an $18,000 car just to do part of the regular maintenance required by Ford.

Here again is an opportunity to decrease maintenance cost by increasing the wear properties of the oil or the parts it lubricates.

The other maintainability factor is the cost to repair a failure when one occurs. This factor can be subdivided into three smaller parts: labor cost, parts cost, and customer/consumer personal cost.

The average labor cost is related to the time required to fix the defective item. Repair cycle time is highly dependent upon the product design, supporting test diagnostics, repair equipment, and the replacement parts philosophy. As a result, the cost to repair a failure must be a major design consideration. The designer needs to understand how the service personnel will analyze the symptoms to define a true failure mechanism. Then careful consideration needs to be given to balancing the repair labor cost compared to the parts replacement cost. The concept of pluggable unit replacement in place of component replacement used in a personal computer is a good example. This reduces the time required to repair the product and allows lower-skilled technicians to do the repair, reducing the repair cost but increasing the replacement cost.

One of the assignments often given to the reliability department is replacement parts analysis. This analysis evaluates how much time is required to identify a defective unit and repair it. This type of analysis often leads to major changes to the product design, the diagnostics repair programs, repair equipment, and the replacement strategy.

Here again the customer/consumer has a major personal cost related to delivering the car to a garage and picking it up. Typically, the customer/consumer has to make arrangements with someone to pick him or her up at the garage when the car is dropped off and make similar arrangements when the car is picked up. This can represent a loss of 4 productive hours plus the travel expenses. If the repair cycle lasts for more than 1 day, a replacement rental car may also be required. Although we used a car as an example, the same type of analysis can and should be prepared for any type of product.

A typical reliability statement related to this issue would read: "The product must be designed in a way that will minimize the combined cost of labor and parts. The average repair cycle time should be less than 1 hour." It is important to note that "repair while you wait" approaches reduce the customer's/consumer's personal costs.

Controllability

If we had a perfect world, we would always deliver products that were as good as they were designed to be. Unfortunately, we do not live in this type of environment. Equipment drifts with time. People get sick and are replaced with less-skilled employees. Sometimes, suppliers provide us with components that do not meet all of our requirements. We get behind schedule, and we relax our diligence. The list of things that could degrade the product-designed reliability performance is almost endless. Controllability addresses how the production processes will be controlled to minimize the impact that abnormal variation can have on the product. Typical ways that these concerns are addressed are

▶ Process qualification
▶ Supplier audits and qualification
▶ Statistical process control
▶ Off-line stress testing
▶ In-process audits
▶ Operator certification

 A typical controllability statement would read: "All of our processes must be qualified before first customer ship, and all critical subprocesses must have a $C_{pk} = 1.4$ or more. In addition, ongoing off-line stress test of products will be conducted throughout the product's production cycle to identify reliability trends." Whenever an out-of-control condition is identified within the manufacturing process, the process will be shut down until the root cause of the shift is defined and corrective action has been implemented.

 As far back as the early 1980s, IBM San Jose manufacturing process qualification required that all operations meet a C_{pk} of 1.4 or more before the product is shipped to IBM external customers (IBM's Technical Report TR 02.901 dated August 1981).

Confidence

This refers to the confidence level related to the reliability projections at FCS. The reliability management function (RMF) should be responsible for calculating the projected reliability of the product based upon available data (component, unit, and final product test). The sample size, duration of testing, and related cost will vary greatly depending upon the degree of assurance (confidence) that is required by upper management that the estimate is correct. A typical statement would read: "At first customer/consumer ship, the organization should have at least an 85% confidence that the average product will meet its reliability specified requirements during the first 3 months of usage."

The role of reliability management as presented, within an organization, is a logical consequence of seeking the optimum business practice. A critical conclusion is that the importance of reliability management must have the support of higher management to effectively operate as a valuable partner within the business organization. Having top management release a series of reliability statements like the ones shown is one of the best ways top management can demonstrate the importance of reliability.

The Reliability System

The reliability system is complex because it involves many different activities and responsibilities that take place throughout the product life-cycle. Some of these activities should only be performed by the RMF; others should never be performed by RMF.

The following is a list of activities and responsibilities that are key parts of the reliability system. After each item in the list, the activity or responsibility will be classified into one of the following categories.

1. Should be done by RMF.
2. Could be done by another function, but RMF must be involved in the plan as well as analyze the results.
3. Should be done by another function.

Activity or Responsibility	Category
Reliability Management Function Mission	
Reliability evaluations	I
Reliability apportionment	I

Design review for reliability   1
Design control   2
Reliability knowledge source   1
Mathematical and statistical services for reliability problems   1
Reliability education and training   1
Internal coordination of reliability activities   1
Advise upper management on reliability-related issues   1
Define the reliability business case   1
Review designs for reliability   1
Conduct reliability indoctrination programs   1

Product Development Activity

Specification, materials, and processing reviews   1
Test planning execution and analysis of reliability   1
Define customer/consumer reliability requirements   2
Statistical reliability projections   1
Product design   3
Taking a position on the capabilities of the product to meet
   external reliability performance specifications   1
Approve new product reliability requirements   1
Define component assembly unit and product stress testing   2
Conduct product reverse engineering studies   2
Study customer/consumer specifications in detail   2
Assist in determination of environmental conditions   2
Conduct system-reliability study   1
Perform reliability predictions   2
Apportion reliability between subsystems   1
Review subsystem specification for reliability content   1
Plan failure and operating-time reporting systems   2
Identify critical parts and characteristics   2
Conduct systems qualification tests   2
Perform reliability demonstration tests   1
Study effect of maintenance on reliability   2
Study effect of field storage and handling conditions on reliability   2

Product Manufacturing Activity

Vendor controls   2
Component supplier qualification   1
Reliability and failure reporting system   1
Manufacturing process design   3
Manufacturing process qualification   2

Evaluate design and manufacturing process changes to determine the impact on reliability	1
Define manufacturing process acceptance testing	3
Define manufacturing process control test procedures	3
ESS testing expertise	1
Prepare overall quality plan	2
Prepare production test plan	3
Prepare inspection and test procedures	3
Design, construct, purchase, maintain test equipment	3
Survey vendors for quality capability	2
Visit vendors routinely	2
Monitor vendor-reliability programs	1
Inspect and test purchased and fabricated parts	3
Inspect assemblies	3
Test units, subsystems, systems	3

Ongoing Product, Customer, and Consumer Activity

Failure analysis of field return parts	1
Field performance analysis	2
Maintainability analysis	1
Maintain component reliability database	1
Customer/consumer complaint handling	2
Track field problem corrective action	2
Maintain the reliability central database	1
Monitor test areas	2
Collect and analyze field data	1
Follow up to correct manufacturing problems	2
Determine spares quantities	2
Report to customer/consumer on reliability	1

The totality of specialized knowledge needed for each and all of the many interrelated components within a complex system tends to transcend the capabilities of small organizations. Consequently, just as the systems have grown in technical complexity, so also have the organizations grown.

—DAVID LLOYD AND MYRON LIPOW[1]

In Juran's *Quality Control Handbook*,[2] he recommends the organizational structure defined in Figure 12-6.

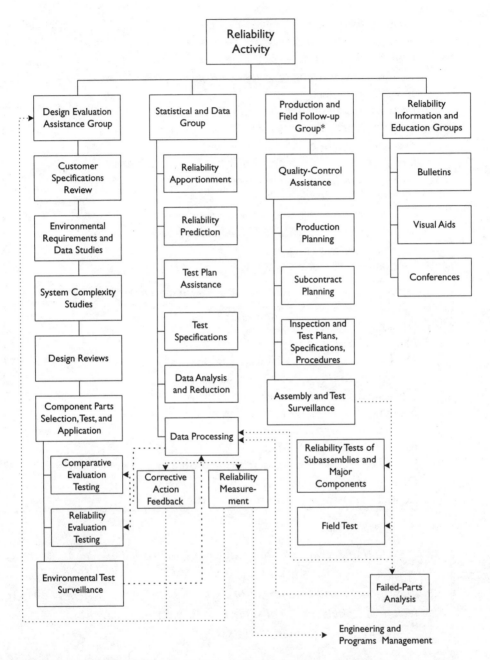

FIGURE 12-6.   Functional organization of a reliability activity
*Note: This group can be the same group as assigned to design-evaluation assistance on a normal program.

Reliability Management Function's Personnel

The RMF is a very unique group of personnel that has been provided with the special training and background required to perform the required reliability assessments. Your reliability personnel should have most, if not all, of the following background and be able to effectively use it.

1. Systems engineering analysis
2. Statistical probability theory
3. Operational analysis
4. Design and analysis of experiments, both physical and statistical
5. Project management
6. Data collection analysis and reporting
7. Accelerated test planning and execution
8. Environmental testing
9. Manufacturing operations
10. Statistical process control
11. Component design
12. Testing, planning, and execution of complex systems
13. Programming and software development and analysis
14. Failure analysis
15. Reverse engineering
16. Failure mode and effect analysis
17. Maintainability analysis
18. Physics of failure
19. Reliability growth analysis and curves

The technical guidance for the reliability system should come from a subgroup of the RMF called reliability engineering.

Reliability Engineering is the branch of engineering devoted to improving product performance. It includes a set of practices that focus on accurately predicting when and under what circumstances products or processes might fail or not deliver acceptable outputs. Using that information, companies can improve product designs and set operating limits for equipment. They also

work with others to develop fail-safe and backup procedures and build redundancies into a product if this is cost effective and/or demanded by customers/consumers. Best practices include procedures for delivering feedback to design engineers working on product improvements.

—JAMES CORTADA AND JOHN WOODS[3]

Reliability Engineering's Body of Knowledge

Reliability engineering is a professional discipline unto itself. The American Society for Quality has defined the body of knowledge as comprising eight separate areas. (See I through VIII.)

  I. Reliability Management
    A. Planning and Resource Management
      1. Common terms and definitions
      2. Benefits of reliability in programs, products, processes, and services
      3. Responsibilities of the reliability organization in the team environment
      4. Interrelationship of quality and reliability
      5. Unit of measure of reliability for nonrepairable systems
      6. Unit of measure of reliability for repairable systems
      7. Training programs
        a. Needs assessment
        b. Training plan
    B. Operations Management
      1. Elements of a reliability program
      2. Relationship between reliability and product life cycle
      3. Reliability growth
      4. Reliability plans and integrated schedules
      5. Various costs associated with reliability and unreliability
  II. Probability and Statistical Tools
    A. Basic Concepts
      1. Population and sample
      2. Basic probability concepts
      3. Random variables

      4. Discrete and continuous probability distributions

      5. Assumptions made in the analysis of reliability data

      6. Mistakes in applying statistics to reliability problems

      7. The "bathtub curve" and its limitations

      8. Theory and use of control charts

      9. Terminology

     10. Probability plots

     11. Pareto concept

  B. Statistical Inference

      1. Point and interval estimates of parameters

      2. Statistical tolerance intervals

      3. Statistical prediction intervals

      4. Confidence intervals

      5. Hypothesis testing

      6. Characteristics of estimators

      7. Probabilistic simulation tools (i.e., Monte Carlo, GASP, war games)

  C. Design of Experiments

      1. Sample size determination for discrimination of differences

      2. Randomization needs and methods

      3. Experimental design characteristics

      4. Correlation and regression analysis

      5. Analysis of variance

      6. Full and fractional factorial designs

      7. Evolutionary operation

III. Modeling and Prediction

  A. Data Sources

      1. Sources of reliability data for common applications

      2. Part count and part stress predictions

  B. Modeling

      1. Reliability models

      2. Fault tree analysis (FTA)

      3. Block diagrams

      4. Probabilistic risk assessment (PRA)

      5. Time-dependent modeling (i.e., standby)

320 **Reliability Simplified**

C. Reliability Predictions
1. Purposes of reliability predictions
2. Uncertainty and error in reliability predictions
3. Reliability predictions for nonrepairable devices
4. Subsystem reliability apportionment

IV. Data Collection and Analysis and Corrective Action
A. Collection
1. Collecting and evaluating field and in-house data
2. Appropriate data to be collected
3. Control measures for data collection
4. Computerized data collection and storage
5. Censored and incomplete data sets

B. Failure Reporting and Corrective and Preventive Action
1. Critical elements of a continuous improvement process, including preventive action
2. Critical elements of a failure reporting, analysis, and corrective action system (FRACAS)
3. Management of a FRACAS
4. Classification categories of corrective action for failures

C. Tools
1. Root-cause analysis
2. Trend analysis

V. Reliability Tools in Design and Development
A. Developing Customer Needs and Specifications
1. Quality function deployment (QFD)
2. Design evaluation

B. Design Techniques
1. Reliability critical items and critical environments list
2. Stress-strength analysis
3. Failure mode effects analysis (FMEA) and criticality analysis
a. Hardware
b. Process
c. Functional
d. Software
4. Failure mechanisms versus modes

      5. Tolerance and worst-case analyses

      6. Robust-design approaches for products and processes

      7. Consideration of human factors

  C. Parts Control and Management

      1. Parts application and specification

      2. Methods of selection, control, and integration of parts and materials into the reliability process

      3. Benefits of parts standardization

      4. Derating methods and principles

  D. Management Techniques

      1. Concurrent engineering

      2. Purpose and use of FMEAs

      3. Benefits and difficulties of performing FMEAs and FTAs

VI. Maintainability and Availability

  A. Management

      1. Preventive maintenance strategy and optimal parts replacement

      2. Reliability, maintainability, and availability trade-offs

      3. Establishment of maintainability and availability program

      4. Reliability centered maintenance (RCM)

  B. Analyses

      1. Maintainability allocation

      2. Maintenance time distributions

      3. Testability

VII. Reliability Testing

  A. Predevelopment Planning

      1. Elements of a reliability test plan

      2. Types and applications of reliability testing

      3. Consideration of human factors

  B. Development Testing

      1. Combined environments for reliability testing

      2. Accelerated life tests

      3. Step-stress and continuously increasing stress testing

      4. Qualitative and quantitative analysis of accelerated tests

      5. Test, analyze, and fix method of reliability improvement

C. Product Testing
   1. Product reliability acceptance testing (PRAT)
   2. Environmental stress screening (ESS)
   3. Burn-in testing
VIII. **Product Safety and Liability**
   A. Assessment
      1. Analysis of safety issues
      2. Analysis of customer feedback and field data to identify potential safety issues
      3. Risk assessment
   B. Planning and Management
      1. Reliability engineer's role in situations of safety and product liability
      2. Ethical issues for a reliability engineer
      3. System safety program plan including applicable regulatory requirements
      4. Elimination of potential defects

All of your reliability engineers should be tested to be sure they can meet these requirements. If your product engineers perform the reliability engineer's role, they need to be certified by ASZC by taking the reliability engineers exam. Most product engineers will fail this exam unless they are given special training. How many of your engineers, who are doing reliability type assignments, are certified? We recommend that you do not do business with any organization whose answer is none. Does your engineering training process cover all the areas required in the reliability engineer's body of knowledge? If not, maybe it is time to upgrade your training package.

The Reliability Management Function's External Relationships

The RMF are established to help execute the reliability statements. We will present only the management requirements unique to the reliability function. It is a list of activities and characteristics recognized by the rest (external to the RMF) of the business that defines the reliability function's role, accountabilities, and responsibilities. This is a description of "what" the RMF is.

The RMF provides three major activities: a center of reliability technical competence, a center of authority, and expertise on business optimization.

1. *The RMF as a center of technical competence.* The RMF is a recognized center of product reliability competence. The common narrow view is to define the RMF as the formal organization or person authorized and responsible for a company function. Let us view the RMF in a broader perspective. Let its size vary from one individual performing all the requisite RMFs to large segments of the formal organization, performing all the requisite product reliability. In every case, the RMF functions as a center of competence. Some of the distinguishing features are

   a. The reliability management function's competence is a clear understanding of reliability principles, both fundamentally based in science and experienced in applications.

   b. The reliability management function's competence is an ability to evaluate and apply reliability tools and skills. In other words, the product reliability manager is an excellent interacting professional. The product reliability manager is part of the larger professional community that determines the selection of techniques and appropriate resources to be applied for optimizing the reliability of your specific product.

   c. It has a clear understanding of the product requirement for a reliability specification. The center of competence in your product reliability is most often recognized by this characteristic. This is the reason that the RMF plays a key role in design reviews.

Reliability design review is an essential activity; it is not a duplication of the effort of the design engineer. The designer's mind tends to be oriented towards new designs and configurations and he is not "probability conscious" As we have mentioned in the introduction, a design which is feasible is not necessarily reliable.

—DAVID LLOYD AND MYRON LIPOW[1]

d. It understands the requirements for and provides reliability related training for all other segments of the business organization.

These features define "what" an RMF uniquely controls within an organization.

2. *The RMF as a center of authority.* The Reliability Management Function is the center of authority for decisions related to the reliability of the product. Authority, in this definition, means that the reliability management has the freedom and is the prime arbitrator in reliability decisions and disputes, speaking for the corporate organization. Some of the distinguishing features are

   a. The RMF's authority is demonstrated by being the prime communicator of product reliability information to the customer/consumer. The customer/consumer works directly with this authority to obtain a clear, single, helpful set of reliability information to support the customer's/consumer's business. A major customer/consumer requirement during product reliability problem resolutions is to have single intelligent human contact from the supplier to provide advice, guidance, and procedure. The reliability authority is recognized universally by customers/consumers as the communications link. The key benefit in having a trained reliability professional serve in this role is that the information is not filtered and that the customer/consumer perceives the supplier as being more technically competent.

   b. The RMF produces the expert input to executive management regarding product reliability activities. Particularly in product reliability, where the language may be unfamiliar to executive management, a single authoritative individual or group is required to furnish an unbiased appraisal of product reliability status to executive management.

   c. The RMF has the final approval for all product reliability activities. These activities would include approval of product reliability specifications, requirements for ESS, competitive product reliability evaluations, etc.

3. *The RMF as a business partner.* The RMF is the center of reliability business optimization for the business. The objective of your business should be to optimize long-term profits, and that is the prime objective for reliability management. The RMF should participate in the profit objectives of your business. The reliability costs and benefits are understood best by the RMF.

The burden of the proof is on the reliability group. They must convince management of their effectivity and the long-range savings in money.
—DAVID LLOYD AND MYRON LIPOW[1]

a. The product reliability system and its control is an important part of the cost-benefit analysis required as part of any business plan. The control of product reliability costs is extremely important, because in many organizations these costs are considered discretionary, like picnics and free coffee. It is the RMF that presents a rational value of product reliability and justifies a prudent business level of financial resource and return on investment in product reliability activity.

b. The product reliability system evaluates the competition's product reliability and the reliability price factor (RPF) (Chapter 3).

c. The product reliability planning process results in optimized business operations. Very similar to the bottom line input to management presented in the first characteristic, a strategic plan must be evolved that efficiently satisfies the reliability needs of the business.

All of these reliability management functions and characteristics are neatly presented in the following checklist (see Figure 12-7):

Figure 12-7 is a checklist of the RMF's external characteristics. It includes the key Reliability Management Function's characteristics. Take five minutes and create a similar checklist for your specific organization. Your list does not initially have to be entirely accurate; because the continuous process of defining the organization's RMF will optimize the way the organization performs. Just delete inappropriate required characteristics and add your specific required characteristics. Many potential turf battles can be avoided by a crisp, deliberate discussion of the RMF with your peers.

❏ Expert and experienced in product reliability

❏ Works well with reliability tools

❏ Understands the product reliability specification

❏ Provides reliability training

❏ Communicates with the customer or consumer regarding product reliability

❏ Reliability authority for executive management

❏ Organization center of reliability competence

❏ Understands business reliability cost and benefit

❏ Understands competitive product reliability

❏ Plans an optimized product reliability function

FIGURE 12-7.   Checklist of the Reliability Management Function's characteristics

Each item in Figure 12-7 points to a work product that should be exclusively controlled by the RMF. This external description defines the role and mission of the reliability management function.

Reliability Management Function's Internal Operation

Assuming that your company already has a defined product reliability structure (Figure 12-7 or equivalent), another unique list of internal characteristics describes the operation of a corporate reliability management function. These characteristics must be managed effectively to achieve the best corporate business results:

1. Communication
   a. The effectiveness of product reliability information and conclusions results from a clear, systematic communication with all affected parties. The channels of communication must be established

that allow information to flow on a timely and business priority basis. It is the responsibility of the RMF to establish and maintain these communication channels.

b. The scheduled generation of product reliability test data and the periodic conclusive review of product field failure data must be accessible by the total organization to effectively generate an appropriate business response. It is the responsibility of the RMF to clearly maintain these specific communication activities.

c. The internal requirements and priorities of the business must be communicated in real time to all members of the product reliability team. All work should be coordinated and the product reliability team must closely track the business priorities to optimize work effectiveness. This continuous awareness is a key internal requirement for product reliability.

2. Test capability

a. The product reliability expertise is measured by the establishment of meaningful formal testing procedures that generate the basis of product performance predictions. The RMF has the internal responsibility for creation and maintenance of product reliability test procedures.

b. The physical test capability is a significant business investment and commitment to a reliable product that requires a strategic and ongoing business plan furnished by the RMF. Examples are temperature cycle chambers, burn-in chambers, altitude test chambers, electronic functional test instruments, unique mechanical test fixtures, and other physical testing instruments.

c. Out-of-house reliability testing facilities are commonly used to efficiently support the product reliability evaluations. The identifying skill required to execute out-of-house reliability tests and documented testing procedures is the responsibility of the RMF.

3. Professional identification

a. Nothing demonstrates product reliability competence quicker than presenting a formal menu of capabilities, clearly documented test procedures, and histories of successful evaluation completion. Without a deliberate effort to maintain the capability menu, the test procedures, and the summarized history, the RMF will be evaluated as less competent than it actually has demonstrated. Improvement is simply doing a better job in presenting the product reliability evaluation capabilities.

b. The reliability management functions are often labeled as secondary contributors to the business. That label is enhanced by the adversary relationship that may occur in the natural business proceedings. It is especially important to recognize the need for special emphasis in nurturing the concepts of the importance of product reliability and the importance of the individual worker. External professional organizations provide an excellent source of objective information on the importance of product reliability. The special emphasis on the importance of product reliability may also be improved by casual gatherings of topic discussions at pizza time.

c. If you don't already have one, try to appoint a Mr. or Ms. Reliability. A walking representation of the RMF does wonders in promoting the concept of functional product reliability competence and expertise. In observing various RMFs, the presence of a champion changes the attitude among product reliability evaluation customers/consumers from "product reliability is something we have to do," to "product reliability is something we should do." The champion is an asset for everyone in the business. The person who first defines the entire RMF requirements according to this chapter often becomes the organization's reliability champion.

Communication, test capability, and professional identification are not considered external work products of a product reliability area, but they are the basic internal ingredients requiring management attention equal in importance to the work recognized by mission identification. Your specific list of internal management requirements may slightly differ, and it is well worth the effort to list the unique internal requirements for your organization.

Diffused Reliability Management Function

This chapter presents a detailed description of the reliability management function's direction that clearly defines the business value and advantages of an independent, responsible, and contributing RMF. This organization can only be managed effectively as a corporate entity.

The chapter avoids the problems of forming an RMF by defining the rationale and goals in terms of a completed organization. Realistically, readers of this book must first understand their present organizational structure, its products, its customers, and its problems in establishing and integrating into the business an RMF. You will also need to be able to clearly define and articulate the process of an RMF creation to approving higher management. Chapter 13 directly supports this activity.

Typically, a new company that grows from a few individuals in a laboratory to a 5,000-employee company with a gross revenue of $1 billion per year in 10 years will have a key growth problem with the establishment of an RMF system. Unless an independent RMF was created by governmental regulation, competitive pressure, or business trauma, the product reliability activity will not be consolidated due to lack of urgency and planning. This scenario is very common and can be used as an example for the Chapter 12 presentation.

Executive management in these organizations often ask: "Why is our reliability program costing so much and getting such poor results?" The answer is that the RMF is diffused and suboptimized. In these times of team participation and superficial flexibility of assignments, how well a reliability management system is integrated into most organizations suffers for two prime reasons:

1. The RMF does not have consolidated and synergistic expertise. It requires unique technical expertise beyond people management skills. Instant product reliability experts exist only in the imagination.

2. The RMF is adversely affected by changing applied resources. Product reliability effectiveness critically depends upon a continued operation. In product reliability, it is better to have fewer resources over time than to apply many resources reactively to problems. It is desirable to have a committed set of reliability experts designated by management who continuously function as the reliability center of competence for the organization. Often this is not the case because the dollars required to support the reliability system are distributed into many different functions.

Speak now or forever hold your peace."
—Everyman

A major reason for lack of early establishment of reliability programs lies in the budgetary practices of military agencies and industrial companies.
—J. M. Juran[2]

Executive management often ignore reliability expertise requirements and change product reliability resources. This is the root cause of many of the reliability management problems. Executive management would never consider eliminating the accounting department and assigning their responsibilities to the groups that are spending the money due to the unique capability of the accountants. Reliability activities (management) also have unique competencies that are difficult, if not impossible, to distribute throughout the entire company. The key activity is for the reliability champion to articulate a reasonable business case to executive management for the existence of a consolidated RMF.

The major cause of an ineffective RMF is a diffused product reliability operation. A diffused product reliability operation is counterproductive and a real operating problem for the RMF. This diffused condition usually evolves as a result of the individual functions within the organization trying to react to the growing reliability concerns of the external customer. The prime cause of RMF problems is trying to use skills distributed throughout the entire organization.

The first task is to identify the current product reliability activities within the organization. Probably, your RMF is diffused all over your organization and can be identified only by first establishing the "what" and "where" of your RMF today, then next identifying the "who," wherever they may be, and, to one's surprise, some won't have product reliability in their job descriptions! However, you must discover all product reliability related activity for presenting to executive management a persuasive business case for supporting an RMF.

The identification of existing product reliability related activity is greatly assisted by using the checklist in Figure 12-9 (or you can use your specific checklist) of the reliability management function's characteristics representing the current external description of product reliability. Taking that same checklist, let us find where the reliability management function's characteristics of the current organization exist today.

The list creates an organized method for analyzing the current status. The following paragraphs are typical.

Expert and Experienced in Product Reliability

An expert, experienced in component temperature and humidity testing, is in the manufacturing engineering organization. When product reliability temperature and humidity testing is required, that person is contacted for either in house testing, on our old T&H chamber, or contacting an outside vendor. The T&H work is of low priority to the purchasing work and that person does not do test monitoring equipment.

Works Well with Reliability Tools

Manufacturing would like to evaluate environmental stress screening of the new product. Because a recognized reliability engineer was not available, product engineering assigned an engineer to complete a feasibility assessment of the ESS. Actually, there is another reliability engineer with experience in ESS in quality assurance busy on another assignment.

Understands the Product Reliability Specification

The MTBF for the new product was generated by the operations (business) and marketing organizations. After all, it is a business and marketing compromise. Even when the projected MTBF information reaches the RMF, no validation nor any action occurs.

Prime Authority on Reliability Information

Quality has been assigned as the authority on all reliability subjects. After all, reliability is just quality over time. As a result, all of the quality engineers were provided with a good book on reliability where they can look up the answers. As a result, the quality function never really felt committed to managing the reliability program and became a rubber stamp during the design review cycle. They do not have the time to develop and maintain an effective field performance and failure analysis database.

Provides Reliability Training

Training for reliability has been left in the hands of the training function. They have never had a request for reliability training from anywhere in the organization.

Communicates with the Customer Regarding Product Reliability

A typical example is that a specific product program manager is appointed to handle the product recall, due to inadequate reliability. The product program manager is new to the customer communication channel and unfamiliar with the customer and the field support processes.

Reliability Authority for Executive Management

A development or manufacturing individual who has superficial knowledge related to the reliability methodology is selected to interpret reliability data and explain conclusions to upper management. As a result, management is provided with interpretations that are at best biased, and often misleading.

Organization Center of Reliability Competence

The design reviews are not previewed nor approved by a center of competence but addressed by the closest individual involved with the development activity. This is a clear sign of a diffused RMF.

Generates Product Reliability Cost-Benefit Analysis

Product reliability is funded unilaterally by the residue of budgeted overhead. This RMF's characteristic cannot often be traced to an individual or even a group; it is just missing in the business process.

Understands Competitive Product Reliability

For example, the competitive business aspects of product reliability are formally disregarded. The competitive reliability business aspect may have been considered, but the activity is not recorded. The research & development organization looks at competitive product to see if it gives them any good ideas.

Plans an Optimized Reliability Management Function

If the reliability management function's activity is already diffused throughout the organization, chances are that the optimization of that function is explicitly missing. Details such as head count, space planning, outside help, level of qualification, regulatory requirement, training, work flow, etc., the essentials of the RMF, are missing in the business organization.

The value to yourself and your company by clearly identifying the diffuse reliability function throughout your company is to provide an accurate assessment for cost-benefit analysis to executive management for a change to a centralized RMF.

Internal Considerations for Reliability Management Function

In the last section we focused on the most important problem in preventing an effective RMF capability, the diffuse product reliability activity. An excellent way to initiate RMF formation is to consider the important operational characteristics of an effective RMF. To achieve general application, we are going to assume that we have an RMF the size of a department. Also, let us assume that a continuous improvement plan is in place. The same three identifying functions—competence, authority, and business participation—are used to outline this section in a consistent manner. This assists in providing material for executive management unique to product reliability requirements.

Using an ideal consolidated RMF structure, how can we improve the performance of the organization? Start by assembling a list of existing factors that contribute to performance, then prepare and prioritize a performance improvement plan. Your specific list will be different according to your need. We cannot prioritize your performance improvement plan because it requires specific evaluations of your unique factors. A key point to remember is that this is continuous process improvement in action and the process applies to every organization.

Summary

Chapter 12 defines the role of the reliability management function. A major task for all optimum business is creating the best RMF for the organization. This chapter provides the enduring RMF's characteristics that add value to the business. The RMF is not a quick study nor an application of MBA business optimization techniques. It is the deliberate planning of a global activity designed to optimize your business profit.

The three major sections of upper management support, external RMF's relationships, and internal unique reliability management requirements are emphasized because, from experience, they remain the crucial components of the RMF.

The ideal RMF contains these characteristics and principles of business management. In this chapter you were provided with a view of how reliability management should exist within the organization.

The following is a complete list of typical reliability policy statements that were generated in this chapter. This makes up the reliability principles that every organization should be based upon.

Reliability Policy Statement—The customers/consumers of our products will perceive our product's reliability as being significantly better than that of our competitor's product. All of our new products' reliability performance at first customer/consumer ship will be better than the present reliability performance of the product it replaces. When failures occur in the field, a minimum of 98% of them will be repaired within four working hours of the time we are notified.

Customer/Consumer Expectations—The reliability specification and the product's performance must meet the requirements of 75% of our potential market place when the first product is shipped to an external customer/consumer.

Competitive Evaluation—All new product reliability specifications must be better than the projected reliability for all the competitors' similar products at the midpoint in the products' production life-cycle.

Replacement Products—Before we announce a new product, our product must be better in terms of quality and availability than the product it replaces or our competitors' products.

Life-Cycle Cost—The total life-cycle repair cost for the product should not exceed the purchase price when the customer's/consumer's incurred costs are included in the total life-cycle cost.

Maintainability—The product must be designed in a way that will minimize the combined cost of labor and parts. The average repair cycle time should be less than 1 hour. It is important to note that "repair while you wait" approaches reduce the customer's/consumer's personal costs.

Controllability—All of our processes must be qualified before first customer ship, and all critical subprocesses must have a $C_{pk} = 1.4$ or more. In addition, ongoing of-line stress test of products will be conducted throughout the product's production cycle to identify reliability trends. Whenever an out-of-control condition is identified within the manufacturing process, the process will be shut down until the root cause of the shift is defined and corrective action has been implemented.

Confidence—At first customer ship, the organization should have at least an 85% confidence that the average product will meet its reliability specified requirements during the first 3 months of usage.

References

1. David K. Lloyd and Myron Lipow, *Reality: Management, Methods, and Mathematics* (ASQC Quality Press, 1984).
2. J. M. Juran, Frank M. Gryna Jr., and R. S. Bingham Jr., *Quality Control Handbook,* 3rd ed. (New York: McGraw-Hill, 1974).
3. James Cortada and John Woods, *McGraw-Hill Encyclopedia of Quality Terms and Concepts* (New York: McGraw-Hill, 1995).

13

If It Can Go Wrong, It Will Go Wrong

It is far easier to talk about managing your reliability system than it is to do it.

Introduction

After a combined experience of more than 85 years, we have seen many good reliability programs produce unacceptable results. In this chapter, we will point out some of the common reliability related errors that organizations make that get them into severe reputation-ruining positions.

Managers, especially those engaged in establishing a reliability management function (RMF), should read this chapter to learn the details of common errors that other managers have made related to their reliability system. Difficulties may be avoided by awareness of these problems and the solutions experienced by similar organizations.

Engineers should read this chapter to learn the fundamental dynamics of RMF and the associated definition of problems. This knowledge will greatly assist engineers in articulating the organizational requirements for increasing their effectiveness. It will also help to minimize those long working weekends that we all have put in when a consumer has a reliability problem.

337

Problems and Solutions

This section is added to communicate to the reader information regarding what he or she may encounter while developing an RMF within an organization. What we have done so far is create information that represents two conclusive bodies of knowledge:

1. A determination of exactly where our present RMF exists within our organization.
2. A description of the elements used by the RMF for continuous productivity improvements.

The following are roadblocks to establishing an effective RMF:

▶ You will find that change toward an ideal system, even though justified by logical considerations, will be opposed by organizations that have the reliability activities integrated within different departments diffused throughout the organization. In fact, you will be amazed at how efficiently the diffused reliability organization resists change.

▶ The ideal system includes important human traits, such as the champion, that are not appropriate in considering the RMF's external performance.

▶ Often the change from a diffused to a centralized RMF occurs only during a severe business trauma. The value of logical, carefully prepared plans during this time of crisis cannot be measured, but the impact upon the immediate decisions is significant.

▶ An organization that has reliability responsibilities diffused among a number of departments will find it is difficult, if not impossible, to develop a consensus among the relative departments related to the responsibilities of the RMF. This resistance usually results from the individual manager's unwillingness to surrender resources and to be evaluated by a second party. We have observed instances where organizations had a dire need to consolidate their reliability activities; but the primary activity of determining that need (making out the lists) was not possible within the totally depleted diffused product reliability resource.

A significant understanding of the RMF is realized when a reliability management function is defined, present product reliability operation is defined, and an ideal self-supporting reliability management function is defined according to the lists proposed in this chapter.

We will now discuss some of the problems you may encounter in forming a reliability management function. These problems will occur whether you presently are in a diffused RMF condition, an RMF created by business trauma, or a natural performance improvement cycle within a business optimized RMF. These problems frequently occur:

Problem 1. The reliability personnel are inadequately trained.
Many of the people who are designing products, making performance projection, and analyzing impact on performance of changes to the design and manufacturing processes have no or very little formal reliability training. They do their best with the meager knowledge that they have, but that is not enough to reduce the risk of shipping unacceptable product. Management cannot let this critical problem go unsolved.

Solution: Both general and activity-specific training needs to be developed and implemented. This book is written to provide information regarding specific aspects of product reliability. For technical requirements, including regulatory elements, each individual requires certification of reliability test capability and a clear training strategy for future test capability. Cross-training is very important to retain reliability test capability redundancy within the RMF. The adequacy of the training of the reliability management function's personnel should be verified by having the engineering management team undergo and successfully complete ASQ's reliability engineer's certification exam.

Problem 2. Reliability personnel are perceived to be second-class citizens. When the reliability management function's understanding and test expertise is diffused throughout all organizations, it is common for the product reliability area to become a service center for physical tests only. In that process, the RMF loses its identity and work control. Individual departments often define and request tests to be performed by the RMF without explaining why the tests are

needed and how the results are to be used. This leads to minimal RMF personal involvement in designing the test and analyzing the data. Without this involvement, test results are not optimized, and the RMF personnel function more as technicians than engineers. The feeling of being an unintelligent function naturally develops.

Solution: Some of the tools available to combat this condition are
— Personnel rotation
— Reliability work (plan) explanation
— Adherence to departmental mission
— Area recognition

The product reliability managers should maintain open and frequent communication with the executive team and their interfacing department managers that highlights the contributions made by the RMF.

Problem 3. The organization has outgrown product reliability capability. This problem happens more often than not in expanding organizations. The business starts with one person, part-time, fulfilling all reliability requirements while working in the Quality department. With growth, the product reliability expertise is identified physically among the product development engineers and a statistician is added. Note that we have already established a diffused RMF system. As the organization grows, management soon determines that it is more efficient to apply the tools of product reliability (Chapters 5 to 9) in a formal manner, and a physical product reliability test area is designated. The RMF is now a diffused mixture of experts and professional operations. Then a trauma such as a recall or withdrawn product offering occurs. This trauma precipitates a formal RMF with a direct communications link with executive management.

This is the same story of an unplanned RMF typical for a significant portion of products today. The new international quality standards (ISO 9000) and specific standards (e.g., CRF 820 for FDA) have contributed toward planning of reliability management functions. However, note that the diffused RMF and the trauma for change to an ideal organization are normal, and ISO 9000 does not require that the reliability activities are centralized into a single area.

Solution: The reliability system should be well documented and define the organization's existing procedures. As an organization develops and the internal reliability activities expand, executive management should analyze how to effectively meet the requirements defined in this chapter. Typically, this is accomplished by establishing a cross-functional team to analyze and flow chart the current reliability processes and recommend procedural changes that will make them more efficient and effective.

The solution is to plan, plan, and plan. The three analysis lists suggested in this chapter are optimum for planning the containment strategy of your product reliability requirements.

Problem 4. The reliability management function is naive. This problem originates with the simple but incorrect guideline that states that higher reliability is always better for the business. Optimum reliability is the goal to be achieved for the business. Incorrect product reliability testing and unreasonable business positions often only alienate other elements of the organization without any possible benefit.

The naive higher reliability only concept loses its innocence when a product recall introduces the business concepts of size of defect population, total cost of replacement, and reliability-business trade-off considerations.

Solution: Provide the RMF with education in the economics of product reliability, not the involvement of confrontational noncompromising arguments without quantified data and information.

Problem 5. The reliability management function is isolated. Often during dormant periods the RMF is not informed about the business, and in active periods it is too busy to listen.

Solution: To minimize this communication gap, the RMF should gather product reliability-related information and present it to the department members on a regular basis.

Problem 6. Lack of current external product failure information. Ask any member of the RMF what is the status of recent product failures. In general, they do not know. Yet this information is of key importance in rationally understanding work objectives and personal contributions to the organization.

Solution: Take a formal outline, as presented in Chapter 10, and explicitly inform, on a fixed periodic basis, product reliability personnel about the product failures at the customer. After all, the reliability organization's work is predicated as a reaction to that product failure information. We also recommend that members of the RMF make field visits to the external customer's location or to the organization's service departments to observe first hand the problems that the customer/consumer is having with the product. The results of these visits should be documented and shared with other members of the RMF.

Problem 7. Lack of an emergency communications channel. During times of intense, acute activity, communications often are lacking because everyone is busy. Very similar to earthquake preparedness, the key is to prepare communications channels before the emergency situation occurs.

This emergency communications channel can take many forms. Once we saw a white-board taped to a manager's office window. Every time he was made aware of significant information, he wrote that information immediately on the white-board with a marking pencil. Everyone in the area was informed of ongoing product recall activities. It was so simple and effective.

Solution: The solution to this problem takes on many forms and is highly dependent on the communications system that is used during your normal work situation. Frequently, daily update meetings are held to ensure that pertinent information is shared with all involved parties. In organizations with E-mail capabilities, this system is an effective way of sharing up-to-date information. In smaller organizations, a single bulletin board proves to be effective. The important thing is that the organization should consider, before an emergency occurs, the importance of a rapid, effective communications system and determine its operation prior to emergency circumstances.

Summary

This chapter is presented to assist readers in establishing or reorganizing a reliability management function. Experience has shown that deliberate analyses assist in understanding where your goal, your present status, and key elements are of an ideal RMF.

An RMF is not just the proper understanding and implementation of the physical information presented in this book. The reality of a typical RMF is much more difficult:

1. You will not be able to selectively change most elements of your current RMF without a great degree of difficulty. The prime reason is that the RMF does not control its own activity.
2. Authority and business partnerships are often not included in the RMF. The prime reason is that the RMF is "stuck" in a diffused mode and will not change until traumatic conditions exist.
3. Allocated resources in reliability are often insufficient to promote the RMF explained in Chapter 12. A long-term business justification and communication with executive management are required.

The information provided within this chapter is based on an actual experience of the two authors. The advice to structure your analysis of an RMF with the lists provided is golden. It seems to work effortlessly in a broad distribution of conditions. Also, the characteristics and problems presented truly represent many of the usual problems encountered today. Managing product reliability functions is challenging in general and very difficult under actual conditions.

Reliable products attract consumers like flowers attract bees. They just can't get enough of them.

APPENDIX A

Glossary

AQL (Acceptable Quality Level)—The maximum percentage defective that can be satisfactorily accepted.

Accelerated Life Test—Subjecting the product to the equivalent of a lifetime of operational conditions in an abbreviated period of time.

Arrhenious Equation—Expresses how the rate of a process increases in an exponential manner with temperature. It is named after Svant Arrhenious.

Bathtub Curve—A graph of an item's failure rate versus time. It shows how the failure rate decreases during the item's early life to its intrinsic failure rate level and remains at that level until the item starts to wear out and its end-of-life failure rate begins to increase. It got its name because it looks like the dissected view of a bathtub.

Bernoulli Distribution—Specifies that the probability $p(x)$ is related to the occurrence of x only for the values of $x = 0$ and $x = 1$. Equation 1 represents the simplest case of where a result is not certain but has two probable outcomes. This is the primary building block of probability. The following equation represents the Bernoulli distribution: $p(x) = p^x(1-p)^{1-x}$ $x = 0,1$.

Block Diagram—A chart that shows the operation, interrelationships, and interdependencies of components in a system. Boxes, or blocks (hence the name), represent the components; connecting lines between the blocks represent interfaces.

Burn-in—Subjecting the new product to operation at elevated temperatures (sometimes along with other stress factors).

Functional Block Diagrams—Illustrates the flow of a system's subsystems and outputs and how all relate to each other.

Reliability Block Diagrams—Illustrates factors that influence reliability of systems, processes, or items.

Consumer—An individual, group of individuals, or organization that is the final user of a product, service, or commodity (e.g., the customer of a can of soup from Campbell Soup Company is Safeway Stores. If you buy the same can of soup from Safeway to feed your family, your family is the consumer). A consumer is someone's customer but the individual or organization that consumes your organization's output may not be your organization's customer.

Consumer's Risk—The probability of accepting the lot when the relative quality of the lot is poor.

Contamination—A foreign substance that should not be in or on an item (unclear, impure). A product reliability factor, particularly significant where close dimensions and tolerances are required for functional performance. It is usually in the form of particulates or chemicals.

Customer—An individual, group of individuals, or organization that receives an output from another person or organization.

Design Verification—An evaluation of the product design to determine if it is capable of meeting the design requirements.

Design Verification Test—An evaluation to ensure that the design is complete, that the product meets final functional specification and external customer needs, and that the product can be manufactured and serviced effectively.

Distributions—The accumulation of measured observations that have been made about a particular dimension and displayed as a diagram showing the range of observations and the frequencies of the different values that occurred.

Engineering Validation Test—An evaluation of development-level hardware that contains pilot line components to determine if the product can perform to its design objectives and reliability requirements.

Environmental Stress Screening (ESS)—Subjecting new product to a time period of use and external stress that precipitates early time failures within the product prior to shipment by the external customer.

Exponential Distribution—The mathematical model that universally quantifies product reliability. The greatest benefit of using the exponential distribution to quantify product reliability is that everyone requiring product reliability information uses a mutually understood number to plan their future work activity. The exponential distribution equation is:

$$p(x) = e^{-x/\theta}$$

External Customer—A person or organization that receives a product, a service, or information but is not part of the total organization supplying it.

Eyring Equation—Expresses how the rate of the process increases in an exponential manner with driving potential. Named after Henry Eyring.

Failure Root Cause—This is the primary physical or environmental condition within a system that logically initiates a path to system failure.

Fault Tree Analysis (FTA)—A tree diagram that shows failures and/or defects in increasing levels of detail. It helps to narrow the root causes and focus on prevention.

Flow Chart—A graphical presentation of all the activities in a process. Relying on a technique used in software design, inputs, process, outputs, and decisions are represented in blocks and other symbols. It is one of the most widely used quality tools because it is an easy way to document the flow of activities in a process.

Fly by Wire—The label given to aircraft where the traditional physical linkage between pilot and aircraft control surfaces has been replaced by electronic (wired) sensors and servos.

Gaussian or Normal Distribution—The most widely used distribution. It is useful because it closely represents the natural distribution of variation in values when many small random effects interact to influence the measured outcome. The following equation generates the Gaussian or normal distribution.

$$p(x) = \frac{1}{\sigma\sqrt{2\pi}} e^{-(1/2)[(x-\mu)^2/\sigma^2]}$$

Internal Customer—A person, group of people, organization, or process within the total organization that receives output for another person or process with the same total organization.

Isolated Measurement—A single independent isolated measurement point.

Item—Any output. It includes processes, products, parts, assemblies, services, equipment, and computer programs.

Knowledge—Understanding acquired through the combination of education, training, and experience.

Manufacturing Process Certification—An evaluation of a new manufacturing process to determine when an acceptable level of confidence has been reached that the operation and/or equipment is producing products to the requirements when the documentation is followed. Typically, this will require that the process capability be a minimum of plus or minus 4.0 sigma.

Manufacturing Process Validation—An evaluation of the manufacturing and its supporting processes to ensure that they don't degrade the product design to an unacceptable level.

Manufacturing Product Qualification—An evaluation to ensure that the product or item meets the design specification.

Manufacturing Verification Test—An evaluation of a large quantity of products manufactured on the production line that will be used to ship products to customers. The purpose of the test is to see if the product can be produced in volume and still continue to meet expectation during the first 30 days of operation.

Maverick Lots—Clusters of unreliable supplier products that the customer periodically receives.

Mean Time between Failures—The average time to failure of a repairable product plus the average time to repair or replace the product (return function to system). In this book, MTBF is mean time before failure assuming only operating product time.

Normal Distribution—A continuous, symmetrical, bell-shaped frequency distribution of variables data that can be expressed by the Gauss distribution or Error Function.

OC Curve—A mathematical model for predicting the probability of accepting lots through sampling at specified actual defective levels in the lots.

Ongoing Reliability Test (ORT)—The continuous sample evaluating of manufactured product to assure that product reliability has been maintained.

Organization—Any group of people who, due to the management structure, are assigned to work together. (Example: A department, a function, a corporation, a team, a hospital, a government, or a university.)

Poisson Distribution—A discrete probability distribution of values, $p(x)$, obtained in randomly selecting a sample of n items from source with a fixed value of x.

The application of this distribution to sampling of product to detect failures levels is extremely important. This describes the binary distribution at conditions of high n and low p.

$$P(x) = \frac{\lambda^x}{x!}e^{-\lambda}$$

$\lambda = np$ (lambda)
x = number of successes in a sequence of n trials
n = fixed number of single trials

Process Capability—The ability of a process to produce items consistently within the specified functional measurement limits.

Process Capability Index (C_{pk})—An objective measure of the process capability. C_{pk} is a universal and convenient way in describing how good a specific manufacturing process step is in its ability to produce specified product.

Producer's Risk—The probability of rejecting the lot when the relative quality of the lot is good.

Product—Any output from a process, activity, or task. It can be hardware, software, or service.

Product Failure Rate—The ratio of failed items to the initial amount of items (in time) or the ratio of failed items to the surviving amount of items (in time).

Product Recall—The act of notifying customers/consumers that they have products that should be returned due to potential supplier problems.

Product Reliability Cost Content—The percentage of the product cost explicitly expended toward lowering the product failure rate during usage.

Product Reliability Qualification—A relatively short evaluation that determines, to a degree of confidence, the reliability of a product.

Product Reliability Specification—The reliability requirements that define the maximum interruptions to the item's performance that the average consumer will be subjected to.

Quality Product—Items that conform to the specification at a specific point in time.

Random Sample—The selection of items in such a manner that all combinations of all units from which samples will be drawn have an equal or ascertainable chance of being selected as the sample.

Redundant Design—A system with two or more independent paths that are made available to transform an input into an output.

Reliability—The probability of an item to perform its required function under specific conditions for a specified period of time.

Reliability Qualification Test—An evaluation where the observed failure rate corrected to meet the conditions of (1) the statistical nature of the small numbers in the samples representing the true failure rate of the entire product and (2) the acceleration factor created by qualification test conditions.

Sliding Wear—This is a very elementary reliability property of product reliability.

Specified Functional Measurement Limits—Physical boundaries in which the process or product is operational.

Standard Deviation—The square root of the average of the sum of the individual measurement variations squared.

Temperature-Induced Mechanical Stress—The transient mechanical stress caused by the differential expansions during changes in the temperature of the item being stressed or the environment that the item is in.

Tortured Data—Data have been manipulated to obtain a predetermined answer. This is a label derived from the comment "If you torture data enough, it will say exactly what you wish."

Total Organization—A complete entity that is made up of smaller organizations (e.g., a corporation, company, hospital, government, or university).

Weibull Distribution—A plot of value in time dependent on two parameters: the failure rate (λ) and the appropriate shape (α).

The Weibull Reliability Distribution

The Weibull reliability distribution is a mathematical model used to represent product reliability (and failure) under the following conditions:

1. A finite set of products starts at time zero.
2. The failed product is not replaced (only survivors and failures).
3. The failure rate varies with time (power-on hours). (As modeled by the Weibull shape parameter alpha.)
4. All products in a set have the same FR(t).
5. The product use environment does not affect the FR.

The only difference between the Weibull distribution and the exponential distribution is that the Weibull distribution has a parameter to account for changes of the FR in time, while the exponential distribution can only model a constant FR.

The Weibull reliability distribution is flexible in representing actual product failure behavior with time. Complexity is added to the Weibull distribution function to provide that flexibility. That complexity places the Weibull reliability distribution beyond the scope of this book.

The Weibull functions are

A. The failure rate is $\lambda(t) = \lambda_1 t^{-\alpha}$, $\quad \alpha < 1, t > 0$. $\lambda(t)$ in a Weibull distribution is dependent upon the initial failure rate λ_1. This is a required value of the Weibull equation. The shape parameter α is a variable adjusted to represent the actual change in the FR modeled by the Weibull equation. When $\alpha = 0$, the Weibull equation degenerates to an exponential equation with a constant failure rate.

B. The survivors with time of any operating set of product in a Weibull distribution are

$$S(t) = e^{-(\lambda_1 t^{1-\alpha}/1-\alpha)}$$

The survivor function, by definition the product reliability, is now given for a Weibull distribution that includes variation of failure rate λ with time. When $\alpha = 0$, the equation represents the exponential function.

C. The failures with time of any set of operating product in a Weibull distribution are $F(t) = 1 - S(t)$.

D. The number of failures per unit time of the survivors. In the case of the Weibull distribution, it is explicitly the failure rate at the time of the calculation (FR now varies with time) times the surviving product.

$$f(t) = \lambda_1 t^{-\alpha} e^{-[(\lambda_1 t^{1-\alpha})/(1-\alpha)]}$$

This is also called the probability density function. This function becomes complicated due to the shape parameter alpha.

Example

This example assumes that the required failure rate and Weibull slope parameter have been correctly determined. The procedure is to select the proper Weibull function necessary to determine any specific inquiry, then calculate the resulting information.

A company produces electronic devices in which the FR has been determined to be initially at 38×10^{-3} failures/KPOH with an α of 0.7. Of the 12,000 units that were shipped last month, how many will fail between their second and third years?

Note that the request is quite complex. However, one path of resolution for the answer to the request is to calculate the survivors after two years and subtract from that value the calculated survivors after three years. The result will be, as requested, the failures during the two- to three-year period.

$$S(2) = e^{-[(38 \times 10^{-3})(17.4^{0.3})/0.3]}$$
$$= 0.743$$

or $12,000 \times 0.743$ units $= 8,920$ units survive until the second year.

$$S(3) = e^{-[(38 \times 10^{-3})(26.1^{0.3})/0.3]}$$
$$= 0.714$$

or $12,000 \times 0.714$ units $= 8,560$ units survive until the third year.

$S(2) - S(3) = 8,920$ units $- 8,560$ units $= 360$ units fail between the second and third years.

Note that the mathematics (and the actual failure pattern) is sufficiently complicated to prevent an intuitive feel for the correctness of the failure numbers. This is particularly true for people working these functions only on an occasional basis. Due to this situation, invalid numbers survive without identification due to not expending the effort in the tedious tasks required for validation.

This book will not continue beyond this point into the semi-infinite field of product reliability functions. However, the great majority of reliability functions have been addressed in this appendix. The burden of how the distribution functions are generated rests with the person modeling the data. The path from raw failure data to mathematical model generation should be clearly available and explainable by the generating source. Be skeptical of conclusions that do not coincide with common sense.

APPENDIX C

References

David K. Lloyd and Myron Lipow, *Reliability: Management, Methods, and Mathematics* (Milwaukee, Wis.: ASQC Quality Press, 1984).

J. M. Juran, Frank M. Gryna Jr., and R. S. Bingham Jr., *Quality Control Handbook,* 3rd ed. (New York: McGraw-Hill, 1974).

Armand V. Feigenbaum, *Total Quality Control,* 3rd ed. (New York: McGraw-Hill, 1983).

J. M. Juran and Frank M. Gryna Jr., *Quality Control Handbook,* 2d ed. (New York: McGraw-Hill, 1962).

James Cortada and John Woods, *McGraw-Hill Encyclopedia of Quality Terms and Concepts* (New York: McGraw-Hill, 1995).

Design Standard for Rigid Printed Boards and Rigid Printed Board Assemblies, ANSI/IPC-D-275, Original Publication (IPC, 1991).

James K. Hollomon, *Surface-Mount Technology for PC Board Design* (New York: Macmillan, 1989).

Performance Specification for Rigid Multilayer Printed Boards, ANSI/IPC-ML-950C, revision C (IPC, 1986).

Performance Specification for Rigid Single- and Double-Sided Printed Boards, ANSI/IPC-SD-320B, revision B (IPC, 1986).

Proceedings of a Technical Program, Surface Mount International Conference and Exposition (Proceedings, 1992).

Qualification and Performance Specification for Rigid Printed Boards, IPC-RB-276 (IPC, 1991).

Sammy G. Shina, *Concurrent Engineering and Design for Manufacture of Electronics Products* (New York: Van Nostrand Reinhold, 1991).

Surface Mount Counsel, *Status of the Technology Industry Activities and Action Plan* (EIA and IPC, 1992).

Surface Mount Land Patterns (Configurations and Design Rules), ANSI-IPC-SM-782 (IPC, 1987).

APPENDIX D

Sampling Tables

Lot or Batch Size			Special Inspection Levels				General Inspection Levels		
			S-1	S-2	S-3	S-4	I	II	III
2	to	8	A	A	A	A	A	A	B
9	to	15	A	A	A	A	A	A	C
16	to	25	A	A	B	B	B	B	D
26	to	50	A	B	B	C	C	D	E
51	to	90	B	B	C	C	C	E	F
91	to	150	B	B	C	D	D	F	G
151	to	280	B	C	D	E	E	G	H
281	to	500	B	C	D	E	E	H	J
501	to	1,200	C	C	E	F	F	J	K
1,201	to	3,200	C	D	E	G	H	K	L
3,201	to	10,000	D	D	E	G	J	L	M
10,001	to	35,000	C	D	F	H	K	M	N
35,001	to	150,000	D	E	G	J	L	N	P
150,001	to	500,000	D	E	G	J	M	P	Q
500,001	and	over	D	E	H	K	N	Q	R

TABLE **D1.** Sample size code letters

Acceptable Quality Levels (Normal Inspection)

(Each AQL column gives the pair Ac He, where Ac = Acceptance number and He = Rejection number. ↓ = Use first sampling plan below arrow. ↑ = Use first sampling plan above arrow.)

Sample Size Code Letter	Sample Size	0.010	0.015	0.025	0.040	0.065	0.10	0.15	0.25	0.40	0.65	1.0	1.5	2.5	4.0	6.5
A	2	↓	↓	↓	↓	↓	↓	↓	↓	↓	↓	↓	↓	↓	↓	0 1
B	3	↓	↓	↓	↓	↓	↓	↓	↓	↓	↓	↓	↓	↓	0 1	1 2
C	5	↓	↓	↓	↓	↓	↓	↓	↓	↓	↓	↓	↓	0 1	1 2	2 3
D	8	↓	↓	↓	↓	↓	↓	↓	↓	↓	↓	↓	0 1	1 2	2 3	3 4
E	13	↓	↓	↓	↓	↓	↓	↓	↓	↓	↓	0 1	1 2	2 3	3 4	5 6
F	20	↓	↓	↓	↓	↓	↓	↓	↓	↓	0 1	1 2	2 3	3 4	5 6	7 8
G	32	↓	↓	↓	↓	↓	↓	↓	↓	0 1	1 2	2 3	3 4	5 6	7 8	10 11
H	50	↓	↓	↓	↓	↓	↓	↓	0 1	1 2	2 3	3 4	5 6	7 8	10 11	14 15
J	80	↓	↓	↓	↓	↓	↓	0 1	1 2	2 3	3 4	5 6	7 8	10 11	14 15	21 22
K	125	↓	↓	↓	↓	↓	0 1	1 2	2 3	3 4	5 6	7 8	10 11	14 15	21 22	↑
L	200	↓	↓	↓	↓	0 1	1 2	2 3	3 4	5 6	7 8	10 11	14 15	21 22	↑	↑
M	315	↓	↓	↓	0 1	1 2	2 3	3 4	5 6	7 8	10 11	14 15	21 22	↑	↑	↑
N	500	↓	↓	0 1	1 2	2 3	3 4	5 6	7 8	10 11	14 15	21 22	↑	↑	↑	↑
P	800	↓	0 1	1 2	2 3	3 4	5 6	7 8	10 11	14 15	21 22	↑	↑	↑	↑	↑
Q	1,250	0 1	1 2	2 3	3 4	5 6	7 8	10 11	14 15	21 22	↑	↑	↑	↑	↑	↑
H	2,000	↑	↑	↑	↑	↑	↑	↑	↑	↑	↑	↑	↑	↑	↑	↑

⇩ = Use first sample plan below arrow. If sample size equals or exceeds lot or batch size, do 100% inspection.

⇧ = Use first sampling plan above arrow.

Ac = Acceptance number.

He = Rejection number.

TABLE D2. Single sampling plans for normal inspection

Acceptable Quality Levels (Normal Inspection) Cont'd

Sample Size Code Letter	Sample Size	10		15		25		40		65		100		150		250		400		650		1000	
		Ac	He	Ac	He	Ac	He	Ac	He	Ac	He	Ac	He	Ac	He	Ac	He	Ac	He	Ac	He
A	2	↓		↓		1	2	2	3	3	4	5	6	7	8	10	11	14	15	21	22	30	31
B	3	↓		1	2	2	3	3	4	5	6	7	8	10	11	14	15	21	22	30	31	44	45
C	5	1	2	2	3	3	4	5	6	7	8	10	11	14	15	21	22	30	31	44	45	↑	
D	8	2	3	3	4	5	6	7	8	10	11	14	15	21	22	30	31	44	45	↑		↑	
E	13	3	4	5	6	7	8	10	11	14	15	21	22	30	31	44	45	↑		↑		↑	
F	20	5	6	7	8	10	11	14	15	21	22	30	31	44	45	↑		↑		↑		↑	
G	32	7	8	10	11	14	15	21	22	30	31	44	45	↑		↑		↑		↑		↑	
H	50	10	11	14	15	21	22	30	31	44	45	↑		↑		↑		↑		↑		↑	
J	80	14	15	21	22	30	31	44	45	↑		↑		↑		↑		↑		↑		↑	
K	125	21	22	30	31	44	45	↑		↑		↑		↑		↑		↑		↑		↑	
L	200	30	31	44	45	↑		↑		↑		↑		↑		↑		↑		↑		↑	
M	315	44	45	↑		↑		↑		↑		↑		↑		↑		↑		↑		↑	
N	500	↑		↑		↑		↑		↑		↑		↑		↑		↑		↑		↑	
P	800	↑		↑		↑		↑		↑		↑		↑		↑		↑		↑		↑	
Q	1250	↑		↑		↑		↑		↑		↑		↑		↑		↑		↑		↑	
R	2000	↑		↑		↑		↑		↑		↑		↑		↑		↑		↑		↑	

TABLE D2. (continued)

APPENDIX E

CRITICAL VALUES OF **t** (TWIN-TAILED DISTRIBUTION)

df	$t0.10$	$t0.05$	$t0.01$
1	6.314	12.706	63.657
2	2.920	4.303	9.925
3	2.353	3.182	5.841
4	2.132	2.776	4.604
5	2.015	2.571	4.032
6	1.943	2.447	3.707
7	1.895	2.365	3.499
8	1.860	2.306	3.355
9	1.833	2.262	3.250
10	1.812	2.228	3.169
15	1.753	2.131	2.947
20	1.725	2.086	2.845
25	1.708	2.060	2.787
29	1.699	2.045	2.756
Inf.	1.645	1.960	2.576

F

Reverse Engineering: Getting to Know Your Competition

One of the most effective ways to understand and to predict what your competition is going to do is by benchmarking your competitive products. This type of benchmarking is called *reverse engineering*. It is one of the best sources of competitive reliability and design data that is available.

Introduction

Most organizations are still willing to share information about their business processes. However, this is not normally the case when an organization tries to benchmark a competitor's hardware, software, customer performance, customer-related services, manufacturing methods, and product design approaches. Even some manufacturing processes and performance data are treated very confidentially by most organizations. Although a lot can be learned through a literature search, contact with appropriate consumer groups, and discussion with subject-matter experts, there is nothing more meaningful than firsthand observation, testing, and dissection. For this reason, items are often purchased for competitive product benchmarking.

Figure F-1 is a flow diagram of a revised engineering process, consisting of 11 tasks. These tasks are unique to the competitive product benchmarking analysis activities often referred to as "reverse engineering." Motorola, for example, used reverse engineering in developing its mobile phones and Bandit pager. When Ford Motor Co. began to design its Taurus model, it disassembled about 50 different midsize cars from around the world to define each

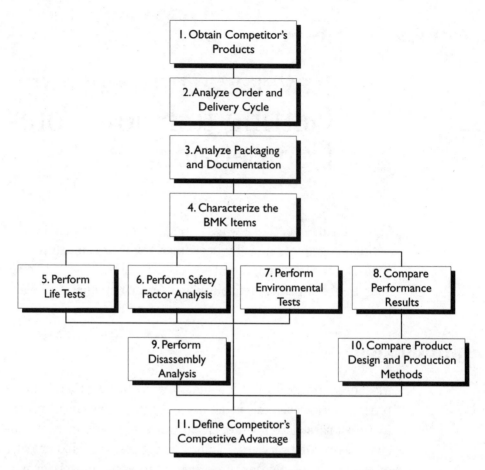

FIGURE 1.   **Expanded flow diagram of the reverse engineering process**

car's best features and assembly methods. There is a competitive evaluation laboratory in one corner of Xerox's Webster plant where, at almost any time, you will see between 20 and 30 competitors' products carefully disassembled, with each of their parts characterized.

There may seem to be something unethical about obtaining competitive products with the sole objective of comparing them with yours, but it is done all the time. In fact, if you are not doing competitive product benchmarking, you are not providing your organization with all the information it needs to make the very best product decisions. As long as the product is available to the general public, it is a candidate for competitive evaluation.

Apple Computer Inc. came out with its first portable computer, weighing 18 pounds, in 1990, only to have Compaq Computer Corp. come out with a notebook computer that weighed only 6 pounds. After disassembling Compaq's notebook computer, Apple engineers were surprised to find out that they could not make an equivalent product. This triggered a major catch-up project that resulted in Apple introducing in 1991 its own notebook computer, weighing 5.1 to 6.8 pounds depending on the configuration.

The ethical issue is not collecting the data, but how you use it. If you use the data to set performance goals, there is no problem. If you use it to copy the design, you may be infringing on patents, and your organization may run into legal problems. There is a fine line between using competitive product benchmarking data to improve your design and copying a competitor's design. In performing competitive product benchmarking, be careful not to infringe on patents when you are implementing your corrective action.

(Note: It is not the intent of this appendix to provide the reader with specific life, stress, and environmental test recommendations. The correct tests for each product must be adjusted to the individual product. This report only identifies typical tests that might be performed under specific conditions.)

Task 1. Obtain Competitive Products

There are two options for obtaining competitive products. Some organizations order products directly from their competitors. For example, many of IBM's new product's first month's production was delivered to direct competitors. The other option is to buy the item from a distributor. There are points in favor of both. If you buy directly from your competitor, everything is open and above board. It also allows the buyer to evaluate the competitor's order-processing and delivery activities. The disadvantage is that the competitor can select the sample that they send to you, providing you with biased results. The other option, buying from a distributor, ensures that the benchmarking organization receives a random sample of their competitor's product. This is acceptable as long as the distributor also provides the competitor's products to other organizations. Never hire a third party to buy a competitor's products with the objective of keeping the competitor from knowing you have the product. If you buy products from a distributor, you lose the ability to evaluate the competitor's order-processing activities.

Task 2. Analyze the Order and Delivery Cycle

As you prepare to place the order, consider all the evaluations you plan on conducting so that a large enough sample size is ordered. This sample size should already be specifically defined in the benchmarking plan. If the sample is large enough, give consideration to dividing the order up and submitting it at different times. This will help you obtain a more accurate picture of the competitor's product process capabilities. Often, products from different lots and setups perform very differently. When you place the order, keep detailed records related to key performance items (for example, how many times the phone rings before it is answered, the length of time required to input the order, etc.). Ask for a very short delivery date, one that the Benchmarking Improvement Team (BIT) believes is not possible to meet. This will allow the BIT to evaluate how special requests are handled and will also provide the BIT with the competitor's normal cycle time. Be sure to record the promised delivery date so that the target and actual order cycle can be calculated. When the product is delivered, ask questions such as

- ▶ How and by whom was the package delivered?
- ▶ Was the package damaged?
- ▶ Was there anything that showed how much the shipping charges were?

Task 3. Analyze the Packaging and Documentation

Be very careful when you unpack the item. Use a video camera to record the entire process. Record the type and weight of all the packing materials and how the package was organized. Ask yourself how well the item was protected. Evaluate the container to determine how easy it would be for the customer to remove the item from the container without damaging the item. Visually inspect the item to ensure that it is not damaged in any way. Count all the items that should be in the package to be sure they are there.

Often, the level of protection the packing material provides will also be measured. Units are repackaged using the original packing material and subjected to an eight-corner drop test, an incline plane shock test, and a vibration test. Following each test, the item is unpacked, functionally tested, and visually inspected for damage. Normally, this is an evaluation that is among the last tests done. Often the item has successfully completed one of the performance tests prior to this evaluation.

Review the accompanying documentation to determine if it is adequate, if the safety issues are well covered, how the warranty is handled, etc. Analyze the documentation to determine what educational grade level it is prepared for and if the grade level of the written documentation is in keeping with the potential customer education level. If the item has to be assembled by the customer, follow the assembly instructions exactly to assess how adequate they are and how easy the item is to assemble. Record how many different tools are required to complete the assembly. Ease of assembly is a very important consideration for most consumers.

Task 4. Characterize the Benchmark Items

Now is the time to characterize a control sample of your product and the competitor's product. We like to measure one of the competitor's items, then one of the BIT's items, to ensure the measurement processes are equivalent. Variables data should be recorded whenever possible, even if your normal practice is to use go-no-go measurement methods. It is well known that differences in distribution can make a big difference in both short- and long-term performance.

For example, when one of the big U.S. auto companies' shipping schedule called for too many gear boxes to be built at their U.S. facility, they turned to a supplier in Japan that provided them with gear boxes manufactured and assembled to the U.S. specifications. When the U.S. auto company compared the field performance of the parts manufactured in Japan with their own, they found that the Japanese product's reliability was much better. As a result, they decided to benchmark the Japanese supplier's product.

To accomplish this, they disassembled a group of the Japanese gear boxes and a control sample of their own, carefully checking the adjustments and measuring each component. Both the Japanese supplier and the U.S. manufactured parts all met specification. Further examination of the two sets of data revealed that, although the U.S. parts met specification, they varied from one extreme of the specification to the other. In fact, in most cases, it was obvious that parts had been screened, causing a truncated distribution. On the other hand, the Japanese parts were all closely grouped around the center of the specification, using up no more than 50% of the total tolerance.

The lesson they learned is that all parts within a specified tolerance are not equal. Parts that are close to the designed theoretical center point are best, and as they move farther away from the center point, they are more susceptible to failure.

To characterize the product, test the product to its acceptance specification. Put the data into the database and compare the initial quality of the competitor's product with the control sample. Any product that does not meet the engineering specification should be dropped from the evaluation at this point.

Task 5. Perform Life Tests

A sample of the competitor's product and the control sample should be put on a life and wear test. Exact tests performed differ based on the product. If it is a switch, it could be switched on and off at maximum voltage rating plus 10%, until a failure occurs. A motor could be tested at maximum load, cycling it up to maximum speed and then turning it off, allowing it to cool down before the next cycle starts.

Life tests vary widely from product to product and how the customer will be using the product. Often, stress tests are used to reduce the time to failure. Although this method does not give precise mean-time-to-failure data, frequently used stress tests can provide accurate estimates of mean time to failure and, with the use of the control sample, can provide effective comparisons.

When a failure occurs, it should be failure analyzed to identify the failure mechanism (the root cause of the failure). Throughout the test, means should be provided so that intermittent failures can be detected. For example, on electronic equipment, power should be continuously applied to the input circuitry, and the output circuitry should be monitored to detect intermittence.

When a failure occurs, accurate data need to be recorded on the circumstances related to the failure. It is not enough to know that the product failed. You need to determine when it failed and under what circumstances. In some cases, life testing could continue for an extended duration that provides little or no additional information. As a result, life testing is often limited to two times the projected life expectancy of the product under test.

Products that successfully pass the life test should be recharacterized and compared to their initial characterization readings to identify defects and to measure drifts in performance characteristics. Frequently, drifts in key measurements are warnings of potential failures and warrant additional study and failure analysis.

Task 6. Perform Safety Factor Analysis

In many cases, products will be tested at levels well above their projected customer usage requirements to measure the safety factor designed into the product. These tests typically push the product to failure. Example: raising the hi-pot voltage or electromagnetic interference noise level to the point that the unit malfunctions. These tests can provide you with excellent insight into your competitor's design strategy. The BIT should also examine the competitor's product to determine any and all unique features designed into the product to provide safety protection to the customer/consumer, even if the customer is misusing the product.

Hi-Pot Test—Used on an electronic unit to ensure that the unit is insulated correctly.

Task 7. Perform Environmental Tests

Environmental tests are designed to define how the product functions under extreme external conditions. Typically, these tests are performed at 10–20% higher stress levels than the actual external environment that the item is required to operate under. Typical environmental tests are temperature, vibration, shock, input voltage variation, humidity, static discharge, etc.

The environmental conditions can be applied one at a time or in combination. Maximum stress can be realized when they are applied in combination and rotated from one environmental extreme to another. For example, computers are often tested at maximum humidity while cycling them from high temperature to low temperature and subjecting them to random frequency and magnitude vibration. Glassware can be cycled from a tub of boiling water to a tub of ice water, while being shock tested at the same time.

It is always best to have voltage applied during the environmental testing of electronic components. Circuitry should be carefully monitored to ensure that intermittent failures do not occur. If failures do occur, information needs to be collected on the exact time of failure and the environmental conditions the product is being subjected to at the time of failure. All failures should undergo a thorough failure analysis to determine their failure mechanism. Often, life testing and environmental testing are combined to reduce sample size and to increase potential failure rates.

Products that successfully complete the environmental tests should be recharacterized and compared to their initial readings to identify drifts. Frequently, drifts in key measurements are warnings of potential failures. These products are excellent candidates for further evaluation and failure analysis.

Task 8. Compare Performance Results

As the three different types of tests are completed, the results of the tests and the failure analysis should be added to the database. The control sample performance should now be compared to the competitor's product's performance. All areas where the competitor's product outperforms your product should be considered improvement opportunities and be added to the root cause and corrective action database. The failure analysis activity should provide you with much of the root cause data needed to develop future corrective action plans. The product disassembly analysis will also help the BIT identify why the competitor's product outperforms the BIT's product.

Task 9. Perform a Product Disassembly Analysis (Reverse Engineering)

There is a great deal that an organization can learn from understanding how their competitors manufacture their products. One of the best ways to accomplish this is by disassembling competitors' products and comparing the product design, assembly methods, and each component part to your product. This type of analysis is often called *reverse engineering*. Typical things that reverse-engineering activities can reveal are

- ▶ Number of different parts required to accomplish a specific function
- ▶ Level of standardization of parts used by the competitor
- ▶ The suppliers used by the competitor
- ▶ Actual tolerance variations
- ▶ Assembly methods
- ▶ Lubrications used
- ▶ Materials used
- ▶ Ease of repair

I have seen rows of engines from each of the organization's competitors disassembled and laid out in a large design laboratory. The rows were laid out north to south, showing how the engine came apart down to the component level. If you viewed the area from east to west, each row would contain the equivalent part from each of the competitors. For example, one row would contain the organization's and its competitors' pistons, laid out for easy comparison.

Often, samples that have completed the life test are included in disassembly evaluation to measure how much wear the component parts have as a result of the life test. These measurements will often allow the organization to predict when the item will fail. These data also provide meaningful improvement opportunities.

A well-defined disassembly process needs to be developed and documented by the BIT. It is always best to train the personnel who will be doing the disassembly activities by having them disassemble and reassemble a number of your own products. It is important to realize that products are designed to be assembled, not for ease of disassembly. Disassembling a product without damaging it is a real art and requires highly skilled individuals. Great care must be used not to damage the item as a result of the disassembly process.

Products are designed today to facilitate easy, fast repair. Throw-away assemblies are often used because it costs too much and requires too much skill to repair the item at the component level. If a customer has to pay $25 an hour to a repair person who takes 2 hours to diagnose a defective resistor and replace it with an assembly that only costs $20, you are not providing good customer service.

The personnel used to disassemble the product need to be highly skilled technicians who have a great deal of creativity and understanding of the function of each component. In addition, part of the disassembly team has to have in-depth knowledge of the process you use to produce the product. Little things are critical here. The difference between using a flat washer and a lock washer can be critical.

A major part of the disassembly analysis is dedicated to defining the difference in the cost to correct similar problems in the competitors' products versus your products.

The disassembly sample should provide adequate parts for destructive testing of component products, for example, measuring plating thickness, hardness testing, materials analysis, etc.

Adequate space must be set aside for the disassembly. In most cases, this space must be kept very clean because the component parts often have oil and lubricants on them that attract dirt. We like to use at least a Class 1000 Cleanroom. One of the mistakes made by organizations that are just starting their product benchmarking activities is to underestimate the space required to lay out the disassembled parts and the length of time the space will be required.

Once you have trained personnel, set up a disassembly area, and characterized products, you can start the disassembly process. A key person on the disassembly team is an experienced video camera operator who has good video equipment and appropriate lighting. It is extremely important to carefully record the entire process so that no detail will be missed. It is also very valuable to have a disassembly record that will help the disassembly team reassemble the competitor's products.

It is advisable to disassemble two products in parallel with each other, one of your own products, and one of the competitor's products. The disassembly team should divide the work into small tasks (for example: pull the engine block). You should then perform the disassembly task on your own product first and repeat the task on the competitor's product, comparing the differences. Care should be exercised to keep excellent records. Typical things that should be recorded are

► Number and types of different tools used
► Ability to use standard tools

- ▶ All clearances and adjustment measurements (example: spring tension, timing, torque requirements to unloosen screws, etc.)
- ▶ Amount of lubricant
- ▶ Parts suppliers
- ▶ General workmanship comments

This process is repeated until the products are disassembled to the desired level. Once the product is disassembled, the key individual parts are characterized. Here again, variables data are extremely important. After the component parts have been characterized, the disassembly team should review its disassembly log and the disassembly video. The team will then prepare an assembly procedure for the competitor's item. This assembly procedure will be used to reassemble the competitor's item. The disassembly team will use the normal manufacturing procedures to reassemble its own product. The disassembly team should follow its version of the competitor's assembly process as close as possible. When it is necessary to deviate from the documented assembly procedures, the procedures should be changed so that they reflect exactly how the item was reassembled. It is important to note that it is not practical for fixturing to be made to support this assembly process. As a result, some differences can occur. When the products are reassembled, they should be recharacterized to ensure that the simulated assembly process provides compatible products.

Task 10. Compare Product Design and Production Methods

The disassembly team has collected a great deal of data and opinions during the preceding activities. These data need to be analyzed on an ongoing basis during the disassembly and assembly process. Key differences between the BIT's and the competitor's item need to be identified. Differences will exist, but that does not mean that the competitor's product is better. The competitor's drive gear may be made of a different material that is harder than yours, but is that good or bad? Disassembly analysis could reveal that this gear wore much less than the benchmarking organization's gear during its life cycle, but the other material costs significantly more. It is up to the disassembly team to define the differences between the products and list the pros and cons of these differences. This information should be entered into the database.

Task 11. Define Competitor's Competitive Advantage

The data collected during the characterization, life, safety factor, and environmental tests were used to define improvement opportunities based on a comparison of your competitor's product's and your product's performance. The disassembly analysis provides you with a good understanding of the product design and production methods. The disassembly analysis process can also provide you with additional improvement opportunities and insight into why the competitor's products perform better than your products during the test phase.

Now these two databases need to be analyzed to define where the competitor's competitive advantages are. The BIT then needs to review each improvement opportunity to determine if it provides the competitor with a true competitive advantage. Thus, the BIT needs to evaluate each opportunity to determine if making the change is truly value-added to the stakeholders. The BIT should ask itself: Would a potential change decrease cost and/or increase customer satisfaction? It is easy for the BIT to want to pursue changes that make your products perform better than your competitors' but that do not have a positive impact on the customer and/or the organization. These types of changes are a waste of time, effort, and money.

Positive-impact areas for the customer are reduced cost, increased features, improved quality, and ease of operation. Positive-impact areas to the organization are increased market share and/or a decrease in the resources required to produce the products, resulting in a bigger profit margin. Don't get carried away with improvements for improvement's sake. All improvements cost money. Adding performance that will never be used is wasteful.

Summary

Many people feel that reverse engineering is unlawful or, at least, unethical. Neither is true. If you are not doing reverse engineering, you are putting your organization at a severe competitive disadvantage because your competition is probably testing and disassembling your latest products as you read this paragraph. There is nothing unethical about understanding your competition's products, as long as you do not copy patented parts of their product.

Gaining knowledge about who your suppliers are, how their products are designed, and how well their products perform can be a very important part of helping the product engineering function make the best decisions related to your next-generation products.

Combining reverse engineering with a good research/data collection system is imperative. Information that is in the public domain provides an effective tool for projecting what performance breakthroughs are in the mill and approximately when they will be made available to the general public. These are essential inputs to the product's reliability specification and the product's engineering design considerations.

Index

ERNST & YOUNG LLP/SYSTEMCORP INC.

GUIDED TOUR

Included with this book is Ernst & Young LLP's/SystemCorp Inc.'s Multimedia Guided Tour CD-ROM called "No-Pain, No-Strain Reliability: Reliability = Profits" and other related information.

System Requirements:
- Windows 3.1 or higher
- Sound Blaster or comparable sound card
- CD-ROM Drive
- 8MB RAM
- 4MB free disk space

Installation Instructions:
1. Start Windows.
2. Load Guided Tour CD into CD-ROM drive.
3. Select Run from the File or Start menu.
4. Type in **<drive>:\setup** where **<drive>** is the drive letter of your CD-ROM drive.
5. Follow instructions given in setup program.

CONTENTS OF CD-ROM GUIDED TOUR

1. **Multimedia overview of this book**

2. **Author's biographies**

3. **Other books in this series**

4. **High Tech Enablers Examples**
   To compete, today's organizations need to make effective use of technologies. Included are examples that we find helpful.
   - **ISO 9000 STEP-BY-STEP**
     An interactive multimedia application designed to help small, medium, or large companies attain ISO 9000 registration much faster and at an affordable cost.

- **PMI's Managing Projects**
  An interactive multimedia application, based on PMI's latest version of A Guide to the PMBOK, that allows you to customize your organization's project management methodology and maximizes your ability to standardize, communicate, and control all aspects of your project through groupware task management.
- **OFFICE CONTROL WEB**
  It is a browser-based document management solution for single or multi-site organizations. Integrate existing electronic documents or design powerful forms processing capabilities in full compliance with ISO or QS-9000.

ANY QUESTIONS?

If you need any technical assistance or for more detailed product information on any of the programs demonstrated, contact **SystemCorp** at (514) 339-1067.
Fax in a copy of this page to get a 10% discount on any of our products.